ONE MILLION MERCENARIES

One Million Mercenaries

Swiss Soldiers in the Armies of the World

by
John McCormack

LEO COOPER

LONDON

First published in Great Britain in 1993 by
LEO COOPER
190 Shaftesbury Avenue, London WC2H 8JL
an imprint of
Pen & Sword Books Ltd,
47 Church Street, Barnsley, South Yorkshire S70 2AS

A CIP catalogue record for this book is available from the British Library.

ISBN 085052 312 5

Typeset by Yorkshire Web, Barnsley, S. Yorks
in Plantin 10 point

Printed by Redwood Books
Trowbridge, Wiltshire

FOR PHILIPPA

ACKNOWLEDGEMENTS

All the illustrations have been provided by the *Musée des Suisses à l'Etranger* at the *Château de Penthes, Pregny-Chambesy, Geneva*, whose assistance is gratefully acknowedged. The originals of illustrations 2, 3, 4 and 5 are in the *Musée des Beaux Arts, Basle* and of illustrations 8, 11, 12, 13, 14 and 25 in the Swiss National Museum, Zurich.

CONTENTS

INTRODUCTION

"We are well aware that God and nature have set you such skill and strength that you yourselves are in a position to defend yourselves against powerful enemies."
Oliver Cromwell — Writings III.159.

The modern mercenary suddenly arrived on the world's television screens in the Congo in 1960. Against the background of an African State experiencing a difficult transition from colonialism and riven by civil war appeared the disturbing but fascinating pictures of white guns for hire, described by the media as mercenaries. Who were these paid killers, and what exactly was a mercenary?

During the five years of the Congo troubles, from the Katanga secession in July, 1960, to the end of the Simba War in October, 1965, there were at any one time only about 2-300 mercenaries in the Congo, possibly rising to 500 on occasion. Their impact on public opinion, however, far outweighed their small numbers. The brutalities of war, spotlighted by the television camera for the first time instead of hidden away on some distant battlefield, and the racist overtones of white professional soldiers slaughtering black Africans, created a sinister and troubling image for these new soldiers of fortune.

Most of the mercenary officers were ex-officers or NCOs of the various European armies — Hoare, who fought with the Chindits in Burma, Peters and Wicks were all ex-British army; Denard ex-French marines; Faulques ex-French Foreign Legion; Moeller ex-German army. The Belgian, Schramme was the principal exception, having been drawn into the war through his position as a planter in Katanga. Although some of the rank and file came from similar backgrounds, the majority were young South Africans and Rhodesians without previous military experience.

A UN Official, Dr Mekki Abbas, found that the motives for the mercenaries enlistment ranged from the desire for financial gain, lust for adventure or domestic troubles to the wish to serve for a good cause. For young Afrikaaners enlistment was not too serious a step — the enlistment period was only six months, there was just enough danger to be glamorous without too high a chance of being killed, and if the going got too tough the border was nearby. As will be seen, this mixture of half-understood motivations were the same as those that had driven one million of their Swiss predecessors to join up during the previous five hundred years.

The mercenary phenomenon reappeared at this time because of the special nature of the conflict in the Congo. Guerrilla warfare without major engagements and the absence of a major force of trained regular troops. (The UN troops from Ireland, India, Sweden and Ethiopia were peculiarly ineffective.) The mercenaries developed tactics of highly mobile jeep patrols, that stuck to the highways, and quickly concentrated heavy machine-gun and mortar firepower to compensate for their small numbers. These circumstances were unique to the Congo and the mercenaries' brief reappearances in Yemen and Biafra were much less successful. Since the Congo, regular army troops serving as military advisers and unofficial combatants have appeared in several war zones, such as the Trucial Oman Scouts, the Cuban advisers in Angola or the American advisers in the early years of the Vietnam conflict.

The mercenary concept that suddenly reappeared in the 1960's was the antithesis of twentieth century thinking on the composition of armies. The system of universal short service conscription had been introduced by Napoleon, developed by the Prussian army and remained the standard method of recruiting in all Western armies for at least one hundred years. Conscripts were expected to understand and accept with greater or lesser enthusiasm their patriotic duty to defend their country. These new soldiers of fortune contradicted the whole basis on which armies were recruited and wars were fought.

During the sixteenth, seventeenth and eighteenth centuries, however, all the armies of Europe had hired foreign troops as a matter of course. Changes in the practice of warfare during this period had led to dramatic increases in the size of armies. When states could not cajole or coerce sufficient of their own citizens into the ranks, they recruited foreign mercenaries. Many of these were rapacious adventurers. Many others were culled from the dregs of society, swept into the army as cannon fodder. But, generally, the foreign regiments were composed of professional soldiers, offering their services for hire according to the terms of agreed contracts. Such mercenaries considered that they were earning their living from a respectable occupation in the largest industry of the time. The best mercenary regiments provided their employers with elite cadres of experienced combat troops.

Switzerland was at the forefront in providing mercenaries to the armies of Europe. Over one million Swiss are estimated to have served as mercenaries in foreign armies between the end of the fifteenth and the beginning of the nineteenth centuries.(1)

The largest recruiter of Swiss mercenaries throughout the period was France. Swiss troops formed around one fifth of the French army from the Italian wars of the early sixteenth century, through the Wars of Religion, the Thirty Years War, and the campaigns of Louis XIV and Louis XV up to the French Revolution. The Prince of Orange described the Swiss regiments as "the main nerve" of the French army.

In addition to the French army, significant numbers of Swiss mercenaries served in the armies of Holland, Spain, Austria, Sweden, Naples and Savoy, as well as most of the lesser German and Italian states. Smaller numbers served in the British army and in the American Civil War.

The Swiss military tradition was based on the social systems, weapons and tactics developed during the Confederation's struggle for independence in the fourteenth and fifteenth centuries. The Swiss pike square was perhaps the real Military Revolution of early modern times. Thousands of men on foot were massed together in a huge column armed with long pikes and halberds. This infantry phalanx proved able to defend itself against cavalry for the first time in a millenium and to steam-roller opposing infantry formations. For a period of about fifty years between 1470 and 1515 the Swiss were unbeatable, decisively defeating the Burgundian and Habsburg armies in open battle.

The short-lived Swiss military supremacy ended abruptly at the Battle of Marignano in 1515. Opponents had learned to stop the advance of the infantry square with obstructions and cavalry attacks so that the stationary formation could be destroyed by new gunpowder weapons in the form of artillery and the handheld arquebus. The single-arm Swiss heavy infantry was defeated at Marignano by the combined-arms tactics of the French army led by Francis I. This stunning military setback for the Swiss coincided with a period of political and religious dissension within the Confederation and led to the abandonment of any further territorial aspirations beyond the natural boundaries already established. After Marignano the Swiss army never again fought an offensive war outside the borders of Switzerland.

Although Swiss tactics became stereotyped and overtaken by the development of firearms, the Swiss infantry was still widely accepted as the best in Europe. The Great Powers competed to hire Swiss troops and there was a confused period at the beginning of the sixteenth century when official and unofficial contingents served in several armies. In 1516, however, Francis I negotiated a perpetual alliance with his previous adversaries that formed the basis of the nearly three-hundred-year special relationship between France and the Swiss Confederation.

Thousands of Swiss mercenaries served in the French armies during the rest of the Italian Wars, including the defeats at Bicocca and Pavia and the victory at Cerisoles. During the French Wars of Religion, the Swiss maintained a steadfast loyalty to the reigning king and formed the core of the royal army. Despite the turbulent politics of France and constant non-payment of wages, levies of ten and twenty thousand Swiss mercenaries regularly served in France throughout the sixteenth century. The introduction of Capitulations, a sort of military contract, formalized administrative arrangements and enabled the Swiss authorities to stamp out the unauthorized raising of troops by other powers. The royal bodyguard, the Cent Suisses, was formed in 1497 and the first permanent regiment in French service, the Swiss Guards, in 1616.

The special relationship with France continued under Louis XIII and Louis XIV. At the accession of the latter twenty-two thousand troops were serving in the French army. Military enterprisers recruited and supplied troops and considerable information is available about the methods of recruitment, the attractions of mercenary service for the Swiss and their conditions of service. The main role of the Swiss regiments was to anchor the centre of the French battle line, for example at Dreux, Ivry, Rocroy and Steinkerque. Brantôme commented, "When we have a body of Swiss in our armies we believe ourselves invincible."

In 1671, Louvois introduced a French standing army and by 1690 seven Swiss line regiments had been formed. Following this development, mercenary service became considerably less attractive, especially when set against new employment opportunities in industry. An increasing proportion of the Swiss regiments consisted of non-Swiss as well as Swiss recruits bribed or tricked into service. Nevertheless, a cadre of officer families that formed a social caste known as the Patriciat maintained the professionalism and discipline of the Swiss regiments. The climax of Swiss mercenary service came on 10 August, 1792, with the massacre of six hundred Swiss soldiers charged with defending the Tuileries against the Paris mob.

Whilst the majority fought with the French, Swiss mercenaries also served in most of the other armies of Europe. Holland in particular was able to recruit large numbers from the Protestant cantons, which were always suspicious of the Catholic kings of France.

In 1792 the Swiss regiments were all disbanded from the French army and in 1848 mercenary service was formally banned under the Swiss constitution. Declining numbers served in the nineteenth century under Napoleon, in the British army, in the Neapolitan army, and some four thousand in the American Civil War. Increasingly, however, these were individuals following their own inclinations rather than the organized exodus of thousands of Swiss mercenaries that had taken place in previous centuries.

The final remnant today of the Swiss as soldiers in the pay of foreign states is the Papal Guard. The slightly ludicrous picture presented by this largely ceremonial anachronism should not degrade the serious history of the Swiss mercenary. For two hundred years in the fourteenth and fifteenth centuries the Swiss were one of the strongest military powers in Europe. For another three hundred years, to the close of the eighteenth century, Swiss soldiers played a prominent role on the battlefields of Europe in the service of foreign states. The Swiss deserve to be recognized as an important strand in the rope of European military development throughout the early modern period.

The principal objective of this book is to provide a better appreciation of the Swiss mercenary for the English-speaking reader, who may not have access to all the German and French texts. While Oman and Delbrück, the doyens of military history, were clear that the triumph of infantry over cavalry for the first time since the Roman era represented a real military revolution, later English military historians have been more concerned with debating whether the tactical changes of the early seventeenth century represent a development of similar importance. Even authorities on early modern military history are not well informed about the Swiss. Hale(2) believes that Voltaire rather than Racine is the source of the famous quotation "No money, no Swiss". McNeil(3) thinks the Swiss managed to march in hedgehog formation, while Addington(4) writes that the Spanish won the Battle of Novara and lost the Battle of Marignano. Ropp(5) believes that *enfants perdus* were the dregs of society. There deserves to be a better understanding of why soldiers from the small country of Switzerland came to play such a prominent role in the armies of Europe for five hundred years.

As the bibliography shows, a large number of books and articles have been published on different aspects of Swiss military history. The emphasis of the different works is noticeably language-related. The French-speaking works from Zurlauben and May de Romainmotier through Vallière to Bory concentrate on the Swiss in the service of France. Early German-speaking authors such as von Rodt, Elgger and Häne, and more recently Schaufelberger, concentrate on the formative period of the Swiss military system. Later German-speaking authors such as Allemann, Suter and Bührer have intensively researched specific features of the mercenary business. None of the Swiss authors appears to have paid overdue attention to the broader investigations of early modern military history by English-speaking historians.

Curiously, not since Vallière's *Honneur et Fidélité* was published in its updated second edition of 1940 has there been a comprehensive study of the Swiss mercenary in any language. Even Vallière has limitations. While beautifully produced and a mine of information, Vallière's book tends to be effusive on the glorious exploits of the Swiss in general and individual officers in particular, but does not adequately discuss the social, economic and military reasons for the growth and decline of the Swiss mercenary system.

There seems to be room for a work that pulls together the published information that is spread through several languages and that draws on the latest research on the subject. As Duffy comments, the aim is not "to compile a history which will be complete or authoritative but merely one that will perhaps bring together things which have not been brought together before".(6) In particular the visibility of the Swiss mercenary to the English-speaking world should be dramatically improved.

It is with some trepidation that I tackle this objective. Firstly, a history spanning several centuries inevitably entails less depth of knowledge than that available to experts on particular periods. Secondly, I am conscious that the sources on which this history is based are largely the work of Swiss historians, many of whom have themselves been serving officers or are the scions of military families. There is an understandable Swiss tendency to consider that the role played by their own ancestors was decisive in securing victory in every engagement in which they participated. Hopefully, any Marlborough or Wellington buffs will allow some latitude on both points, and any Swiss readers will be supportive of this attempt to bring an illustrious history to the attention of a wider audience.

The Swiss fought in greater or lesser numbers in just about every campaign waged and battle fought in Europe for a period of more than three hundred years. The battles fought by the Confederation's own army are important to understanding how the Swiss military system developed and are described in some detail. Otherwise only selected actions are used to illustrate specific points. Swiss participation in famous battles such as Blenheim or Waterloo is briefly recorded for interest. This work does not intend to provide an encyclopaedic (and tedious) listing of all the battles of Western Europe during the period.

To the modern reader the phrase "Swiss mercenary" is an oxymoron. Twentieth-century Switzerland is renowned as a country of peace and serenity, a suitable home for the United Nations and the Red Cross. By contrast the term mercenary conjures images of bloodshed and atrocities, of shady deeds and sordid wars in the service of third world dictatorships. This book describes the history of the one million Swiss who followed an honourable military profession far removed from the vilification heaped on their twentieth-century successors.

SECTION ONE

THE MOST POWERFUL ARMY IN EUROPE
MORGARTEN TO MARIGNANO
1315-1516

I

The Vacuum in the Heart of Europe

"On other parts it is environed with a continual wall of steep and horrid mountains, covered all the year long with a crust of ice; not passable at all by armies, and not without much difficulty by single passengers; so that having but that one entrance to it, which before we spake of, no citadel can be made so strong by Art, as this whole country is by Nature."
Heylyn, *Cosmographie*, 1656.

In the twelfth century travellers from the rich northern plains of Flanders and Germany intent on reaching the southern centre of European prosperity in Italy were forced to swing either east into Austria to cross the Brenner and Simplon passes or west into France to cross the Mont Cenis or Great St Bernard. Routes directly southward led across the Swiss plateau into blind alleys rising up to the impenetrable barrier of the Central Alps. At the end of the cul-de-sacs leading into the mountains was an area of bare mountains, snowfields, heavy forest and alpine uplands. Rugged and menacing, dominated by the high mountains and the long winters, this was a hostile environment for human habitation. Along the valley bottoms small communities scratched a living from subsistence farming. Otherwise the population consisted of such individuals on the fringes of society as hunters, fugitives from justice and monks.(1)

Each isolated valley was inhabited by a closely knit, clan-like community, living largely free from outside interference. These valley communities had developed simple political organizations that facilitated their ability to work together to combat the rigours of the environment. The basic organization was the old German form of rural association(2), to which all the valley's inhabitants over 16 years of age belonged. The association administered its affairs through a general assembly where every man had a vote and decisions were taken by a majority. A leader or Allemann was elected by the assembly.

At first sight this was a community of freemen living in a classical democracy. Usually, however, prominent citizens had considerable influence on decisions by virtue of their persuasive powers or standing in the community, and the system was more oligarchic than democratic. It is also important to realize that these freemen were not defending the modern concept of personal liberty but their collective liberty to practice the customs and activities they needed in order to survive in their precarious balance with the environment.

The valley communities were loosely grouped together in cantonal structures, the three cantons Uri, Schwyz and Unterwalden being collectively known as the Waldstaette. This isolated enclave in the centre of Europe was largely ignored by the feudal lords to whom nominal allegiance was owed within the Holy Roman Empire, especially as the Zähringer and the Kyburg families, the most important dynasties in the region, died out leaving a political vacuum. Particularly difficult of access, Uri was regarded as the end of the world, its primitiveness symbolized by the wild bull, the aurochs, on its coat of arms.

Two changes took place during the thirteenth century that attracted renewed attention from the lowland princes who had largely forgotten this rural backwater. The first was the increased prosperity that resulted from the spread of pastoral farming. The transhumance system, utilizing the broad expanses of alpine meadows, enabled the widespread and profitable raising of cattle and horses. The spread of pastoralism brought both significant social changes and the need for stronger political organizations in response to additional contacts with the outside world. Disputes with neighbouring communities over cattle stealing and grazing rights on the previously unimportant high alps increased. Trade with the lowlands to export cattle and dairy products in exchange for grain and salt became a way of life and the mountain cantons became interdependent with the market towns at the valley entrances, particularly Lucerne.

The second change that transformed the Waldstaette from a rural backwater to an important strategic location on the political map of Europe, was the opening of the Gotthard Pass in the early thirteenth century. The col itself at 2112 metres had always been passable, the technical difficulty being to bridge the gorge of the Schoellenen in order to provide access to the col from the north. The Devil's Bridge and a path along the sidewall of the gorge were constructed sometime in the first quarter of the thirteenth century(3). The Gotthard allowed access to new markets in Italy for the pastoral products of the Waldstaette and brought new and profitable economic activity into the region in the form of taxes on travellers, as well as transport-related occupations such as guides, muleteers and innkeepers. The cul-de-sac was opened up to through traffic and not long afterwards two-thirds of the total traffic between the Low Countries and Italy was using the Gotthard.

Long ignored, the Waldstaette in the first half of the thirteenth century attracted renewed attention from the lowland princes, anxious both to share in the growing prosperity of the region and to secure strategic control of the new route linking the two halves of the Holy Roman Empire.

The House of Habsburg had become the dominant feudal power in Central Europe and three centuries of conflict followed as the mountain cantons struggled for their independence.

During the political vacuum between the dying out of the Zähringer and the Kyburg dynasties and the expansion of the Habsburgs, the Waldstaette had taken advantage of their growing prosperity and the political uncertainty to change their constitutional position within the Empire. In 1231 the people of Uri were granted a charter confirming that they had purchased the valley from the Habsburgs. This was followed in 1240 by the Charter of Faenza which similarly took Schwyz under the direct protection of the Empire.(4) During the second half of the century, however, Habsburg influence in the region increased significantly, especially when the aggressive Rudolf became the Emperor. In 1291 the Habsburgs purchased the vital market town of Lucerne and started a blockade of the mountain cantons.

On 1 August, 1291, the representatives of Uri, Schwyz and Unterwalden concluded a defensive pact promising each other assistance in case of outside aggression. Modern historians have demonstrated that this was one of many such pacts, and that its wording indeed refers to the previous existence of a similar contract. Nevertheless, the pact of 1291 is the oldest surviving example and is officially recognized as the foundation date of the Swiss Confederation.

The hunters and herders of the mountain cantons had certain unique advantages to help them in their struggle for independence from the Habsburgs. Unlike the lowland farmers, the carrying of arms remained common practice in the mountains. The herders needed to defend their charges against attacks by wild animals and hunting was both a specialized occupation and a regular way of filling the cooking pot. The inhabitants of the mountains were used to a rugged and violent way of life and the widespread practice of family feuds and vendettas further developed their personal belligerence. Their political organization also favoured a strong military tradition in the mountains. Whereas the feudal system increasingly separated the weapon-carrying class from the peasants, free men by definition had the right to bear arms and were expected to do so. Finally, the main military strength of their opponents, the armoured horseman, was much less effective in mountain terrain, as would shortly be demonstrated at Morgarten. The hunters and herders of the mountains, banded together in their political organizations, were the spearhead of the fight for independence.(5)

<h1 style="text-align:center">II</h1>

The Battles for Independence

"The nature of the country may be such as to contribute to the facility of a national defence. In mountainous countries the people are always most formidable... the inhabitants of mountainous regions have always resisted for a longer time than those of the plains — which is due as much to the difference in the natural features of the countries."
Baron de Jomini, *The Art of War*
(Napoleon's Swiss-born General)

The two decades after 1291 saw an uneasy coexistence between the mountain cantons and the increasingly powerful House of Habsburg. Internal dissensions and political developments elsewhere in the Empire distracted the Habsburgs, as otherwise the constant border skirmishes would have escalated into a major confrontation much earlier. In 1314, however, Schwyz attacked the monastery of Einsiedeln, with which it had long been in dispute over certain border pastures. Einsiedeln came under the direct protection of the Habsburgs, who could no longer ignore the provocations of their turbulent neighbours. The following year, 1315, the Habsburgs prepared a punitive expedition against Schwyz with the intention of at last suppressing what they saw as rebellious mountain peasants.

Duke Leopold of Habsburg, the younger brother of King Friedrich and the power behind the throne, called out the Feudal Levy, collecting a glittering array of knights from the whole of southern Germany, and supported by contingents from the Habsburg towns of Lucerne, Zug, Winterthur and Zurich. Around 9000 men, 2000 of them mounted knights, gathered on 14 November, 1315 at Zug, three hours march from the border with Schwyz.

Preparations on the Swiss side had been underway for several months with the building of defensive walls(1) at strategic points in the valleys leading into the mountains. One route along Lake Ägeri and over the saddle of Morgarten was deliberately left unblocked. In effect, the supposedly primitive mountain peasants had laid a careful ambush into which the unsuspecting feudal knights carelessly rode.

As soon as their intelligence confirmed that the Habsburgs were headed in the planned direction, the Swiss left only a small contingency guard on the barricades, while the main force assembled in the hills above Lake Ägeri. Around 1300 men (900 from Schwyz, 300 from Uri, and a few from Unterwalden) were probably under the command of Werner Stauffacher, the Landamman of Schwyz.(2)

The Habsburg army, not suspecting serious opposition from mere farmers, neglected even the precaution of reconnaissance ahead. The column, with the mounted knights in the lead, was several kilometres long as it straggled up the narrow paths towards the Morgarten saddle above the lake. A short distance before the saddle, the Swiss had constructed a barrier across the path, resolutely defended by a small troop of crossbowmen. The head of the advancing column was forced to halt by this unexpected opposition. The rear continued to advance, however, until the whole Austrian cavalry was jammed into a milling unmanoeuvrable mass between the valley walls. At this point the Swiss sprung the trap. From their concealment on the hillsides above, tree trunks and boulders were hurled into the mêlée of horses and riders below, followed by a charge of the main force of the Swiss armed with axes and halberds.

The mounted knights, encumbered by their armour and lances and unable to turn their horses, were helpless against the more mobile men on foot and were butchered en masse. The vanguard was hacked down and the rear ranks of the column were forced back into the lake and drowned. Although Duke Leopold escaped along a sidepath, 2000 men of the Habsburg army perished, while the chronicles relate only 12 deaths on the Confederate side. In the words of Johannes von Winterthur: "It was not a battle... it was a slaughter."

The Swiss tactics demonstrated a relatively sophisticated planning capability on the part of their leaders, probably acquired during mercenary service in Italy. But, although Morgarten was a major victory for footsoldiers over mounted knights, it was considerably facilitated by the mountainous terrain, and the full triumph of footsoldiers over the cavalry on even ground was to come at Laupen and Sempach. The Swiss either ignored or were not aware of the chivalric codes that had been developed to govern battles between feudal knights. The raw mountain peasants were simply intent on annihilating their enemy. The battle of Morgarten caused a sensation at the time and was widely reported, being the decisive defeat of an army of feudal knights by infantry (from a military viewpoint) and peasants (from a social viewpoint).

The political consequences followed immediately. Within four weeks the three cantons met to sign the Pact of Brunnen, which expanded the original defensive alliance into a closer political union. The following year, 1316, Emperor Ludwig of Bavaria reconfirmed the liberties of the Waldstaette within the Empire, and seven years later serfdom was formally abolished, all the inhabitants of the valleys becoming free men.

The mountain cantons also built on their military success by signing a series of alliances with their trading partners of the Swiss plateau. The important market of Lucerne concluded a formal alliance in 1332, followed by Zurich in 1351, Glarus and Zug in 1352, and the eighth confederate, Berne, in 1353. Although it is convenient to refer to these eight cantons as the Confederation,(3) they were more a network of alliances around the central core of the Waldstaette than a formal political entity. Each canton jealously guarded its independence and quarrels were fierce and frequent. Only the threat of the Habsburgs provided a unifying bond to hold the alliances together.

A particular tension was caused within the Confederation by the alliance with Berne, which introduced both a large and aggressive new partner and a more westward orientation. The Waldstaette had previously supported Berne at the Battle of Laupen in 1339. Berne's aggressive territorial expansion had brought conflict with the feudal lords of southern Germany and with Berne's neighbour and rival, the town of Fribourg. These joined together and assembled an army of 12000 men, led by 1000 knights, against which Berne opposed an army of 6500 infantry including a contingent of 900 men supplied by the Waldstaette. The Battle of Laupen was fought in two phases. In the first the Bernese infantry attacked and put to flight the infantry of the opposing alliance. Simultaneously the infantry of the Waldstaette defended themselves against the allied cavalry, using the tactical formation known as the hedgehog. The defenders were hard pressed to hold the cavalry at bay, however, their relatively short halberds not offering the same defensive capability as was later provided by the long pikes. In the second phase of the battle the Bernese turned and came to the assistance of the Waldstaette contingent. Once the confederates gained the upper hand, the murderous halberds again inflicted heavy casualties, and the allied cavalry was routed with 1500 dead.

The military significance of Laupen was that this was the first occasion on which the Swiss infantry was able to defeat cavalry in the open field without major advantage from favourable terrain.(4) The political significance was that the relationship forged between Berne and the Waldstaette on the battlefield led to Berne becoming the eighth member of the Confederation in 1353.

The conflict between the confederates and the Habsburgs rumbled on, not flaring up into a major battle again until 1386, when the immediate casus belli was the annexation of the town of Sempach by Lucerne. Duke Leopold III of Austria was once more provoked to assemble an army of knights with the intention of destroying the hated Swiss peasants. More circumspect than at Morgarten and learning from Laupen, the knights planned the new tactic of dismounting and using their armour and longer lances on foot against the lightly protected Swiss armed only with their shorter halberds.

At first the tactic succeeded and the confederates suffered many casualties as they were unable to break through the wall of lances. The legend of Arnold Winkelried, who supposedly clutched enough lances to his dying body to create a gap for his comrades to exploit, first appears in the *Sempacherlied* of the sixteenth century and is now part of the folklore learned by all Swiss schoolchildren. In fact, the more mobile Swiss were able to introduce fresh troops in a flank attack against the knights, who were by then wilting physically in their heavy armour under the summer sun. Once past the lances, the Swiss halberds again showed no mercy and 700 knights, including Duke Leopold, were among the 1800 Austrian casualties.(5)

Sempach was a crushing defeat for the Austrian knights and was followed by another Swiss victory at Näfels in 1388. It would be wrong, however, to give the impression that the Swiss fought only three or four major battles in the seventy years after Morgarten, with long intervening periods of peace. Nothing could be further from the truth. Feuds, conflicts and skirmishes between individuals, communities and cantons were virtually continuous in this turbulent and warlike society.

Two important agreements followed on the heels of Sempach. The first was a peace treaty with the Habsburgs, which was signed in 1389. The second in 1393 was a charter known as the Sempacher Brief, which included a series of regulations intended to govern the conduct of the confederates at war, the more important being:

— No confederate or community within the Confederation should start a war or feud without the approval of the Confederation as a whole.(6)

— All soldiers should be personally responsible to their captains.

— There should be no looting until the captains judged the battle to be finished (too hasty looting in the Battle of Sempach having hampered the full exploitation of the victory), and all booty should be handed to the captains for fair division.

— Deserters in the face of the enemy should be punished with death.

Although initially the provisions of the Sempacher Brief were rarely totally respected this covenant formed the basis for all the later rules of war that gradually came to govern the conduct of the Swiss troops both at home and abroad.

The early history of the Confederation is a major subject of scholarship in its own right. The brief summary that has been provided in these two chapters is intended only as a background for the more detailed description in the next chapter of the military organizations that developed in this society during the fourteenth and fifteenth centuries. Although adequate accounts of Morgarten, Laupen and Sempach are available in English from Delbrück and Oman, some mention of the early battles for independence has been necessary, firstly to position the emerging Confederation in the Europe of the thirteenth and fourteenth centuries, and secondly to set the scene for the military advances in the fifteenth century that would, for a time, make the Swiss unbeatable on the battlefield.

III

A Bellicose Society

"Nature and necessity have framed them to the warre, for a mountainous region, and woody ... breedes a rude people, patient of hardnesse, and of warlike disposition, and as taller trees and larger cattle, so stronger bodies of man, so as they seem to be borne souldiers."
Fynes Moryson, *An Itinerary*, 1617, III.266

Swiss historians have coined the phrase hirtenland (literally herder country) to describe the region of alpine and prealpine valleys and uplands stretching from Appenzell in the east through the Waldstaette and the Bernese Oberland into the Valais, in which the predominant economic activity was the rearing of cattle and the processing of dairy products. Whereas the cultivation of crops on the lowlands and the development of trade and industry in the towns favoured political stability, the regular movements of cattle under the half-nomadic transhumance system encouraged social as well as economic ferment in the mountains. "They are a tough strong people, insensitive to the climate or their physical surroundings, unacquainted with the pleasures of life, without interest in agriculture; they set little store by nice houses or clothing and are only really interested in raising cattle. They live mainly from hunting and stealing. They seek eagerly for every opportunity to pursue the warfare for which they are born."(1)

It was the practice in the eight Cantons of the Confederation that all menfolk reaching the age of sixteen entered both the citizen and military organizations of their communities and remained in the latter until they were sixty. Each citizen was expected to assist in defence against any enemy aggression. The chronicler Albert von Bonstetten estimated in 1479 that 54,500 inhabitants of the eight cantons had the duty to carry weapons out of a total population of 200,000. In case of emergency the Landsturm was let loose with bells ringing, fires and smoke signals lit, and messengers scurrying through the countryside. All citizens without exception were expected to respond and present themselves armed at predetermined assembly points to defend the community's territory. They were responsible for providing their own weapons, which were regularly inspected by the authorities.

As well as its overriding responsibility to defend its citizens, a land or town council would also frequently conduct offensive operations, either to further its own policies or in support of commitments to allies. Such expeditions were publicized by announcements read in the churches and by unfurling of the community's flags and banners. If a major campaign were planned the large square Landespanner would be erected on the village fountain or hung from the windows of the town hall. In the early part of the period all eligible men were expected to present themselves armed at the assembly place for the participants to be selected.

Towards the beginning of the fifteenth century a roll(2) was introduced which specified the number of armed men a village or town quarter was expected to provide for an expedition, calculated according to the number of households or fireplaces. A limited number of hired substitutes or *söldner* were allowed for households occupied by widows or where the householder was sick.

For small expeditions, a smaller triangular flag, the Vennli, was broken out, and it became customary to call for volunteers. These were usually the young unmarried men eager for adventure and booty. To ensure that the supply of volunteers exceeded the demand, a relatively high wage of four guilders per month was paid, at least one third more than the average day labourer's wage. Many of the surplus volunteers would march alongside the official expedition in free companies, unofficial and undisciplined bands of freebooters.(3) The use of volunteers had the immediate advantage that the married men could stay as much as possible with their families and their work, especially for wars of longer duration. The creation of these bands of young men used to roaming the countryside away from the authority of their political leaders would, however, cause serious problems for the Confederacy when it became necessary to control and administer the competing demands for Swiss mercenaries later in the fifteenth and sixteenth centuries.

As well as the official expeditions, a whole range of private wars also took place. These tended to be pursued by bands of youths, and usually started as a result of a feud. The duty to pursue a feud fell on the blood relatives of anyone considering himself victimized, and by extension on the community as a whole. Minor wrongs could be settled by retaliation against the property of the aggressor by such measures as home visiting(4), where a number of the complainant's friends and relatives would force themselves into the home of the other party and boisterously help themselves to food and drink, or by ripping his roof off.(5) More serious wrongs could only be exonerated by blood revenge(6), however, and such blood debts could quickly escalate from a family vendetta into a full scale war between villages or whole valleys. War was little more than an extension of a feud and as much part of everyday life as hunting.

One of the most striking characteristics of the Swiss herder-warriors was their youth. Boys ten years old were already expected to help with the herds on the summer pastures and by the age of fourteen or fifteen were fully fledged herdsmen. At this age, these youths or *knaben* would join a band of youngsters of similar age, in which they would remain until marriage.(7) Under names such as the foxes or the bucks these bands were the military training ground for the elite troops of the Confederation. The young herder would learn to use weapons on communal hunting expeditions for wolves and bears; would learn elementary tactics on cattle-thieving expeditions, skirmishes over pastures, and minor campaigns with his comrades to pursue a feud; would develop physically in sports and trials of strength; and would develop the pride and loyalty to the group that turned the elite into a cadre.

There were various events where these bands came into contact with similar groups from other villages, particularly religious festivals such as Shrovetide, parish fairs, or sporting competitions. The *hirtenknaben* would not let pass any disparaging reference to their physical prowess or taunts about cowdung, cowtails or even cowsodomy. The combination of tribal pride, heightened emotions and the presence of weapons meant that these events rarely ended without several broken heads, often initiated new feuds, and occasionally were the starting point for full scale military campaigns. The *Saubannerzug* involving 1800 young *knaben* in 1477 started as a Shrovetide celebration, and the *Plappartkrieg* of 1458 had its origins in a brawl at a shooting competition at Constance. The borderlines between a competition and a feud, a feud and private war, or a private war and an official war became increasingly blurred.

Similarly militaristic alpine herder communities have been identified among the clans of the Scottish highlands, in the Balkans and the Caucasus, and in Nepal where the Ghurkas also formed a military elite. The geographical contiguity of the herder culture with the Swiss Confederation goes a long way towards explaining the latter's emergence as the dominant military power in Central Europe at this time.

As well as embodying invaluable military qualities such as aggression, adventurousness, bravery and loyalty to comrades, the young *knaben* also excelled in the raw physical strength needed to wield the weapons and to lead the tactical formations employed by the Swiss. Feats of strength were much prized among them. As well as formal wrestling and stone throwing competitions, impromptu challenges such as carrying a boulder up a mountain often took place. One practical joke was to place an enormous rock outside a neighbour's door in the night and then watch him struggle to move it in the morning.

The principal weapon used in the early Confederation was the halberd. This was a heavy, pointed axe mounted on an eight-foot ash stave and weighing up to eight pounds. It was wielded two-handed, was used for both slashing and stabbing and could chop through limbs, armour, harnesses and even cleave skulls in two. To quote Oman, this "most ponderous" but "most murderous" weapon needed to be swung by "strong arms". The earlier primitive halberd was gradually superseded by the Bernese halberd which incorporated a hook on the reverse side to help unseat horsemen. Other short range weapons included the Lucerne hammer, various battle axes, and the six or seven-foot-long two-handed sword.(8) In addition, each soldier usually carried the Swiss dagger, a short sword hung from the belt as a back-up weapon.

A crucial change to the Swiss weaponry occurred in the early fifteenth century with the introduction of the long pike. The halberd, while murderously effective as a close-quarter offensive weapon, was too short to be equally effective for defence against cavalry. As already experienced at the near disaster of Sempach the twelve to fourteen-foot lance of the heavy cavalry outreached the eight-foot-long halberd. This lesson was driven home at Arbedo in 1422 where an unofficial expedition of 2500 *knaben* was carelessly caught in the open by 16000 Italian troops. Although the Swiss troop managed a fighting retreat, 500 men were lost, partly as a result of being vastly outnumbered but also because of the defensive difficulties of the halberdiers against the lances of the dismounted Italian knights. As the Confederation expanded from the narrow valleys of the Waldstaette, where the halberd was an ideal weapon, into less mountainous regions where cavalry could operate, a change in weaponry was required.

Probably introduced from Italy, the long pike spread quickly through the Swiss armies and only three years after Arbedo, nearly forty per cent of a Lucerne expedition to Italy were already armed with pikes. The pike was eighteen foot long, consisting of an ashwood shaft tipped with a six-inch iron point. For attack the pike was held at shoulder height which, with the centre of gravity towards the back, facilitated a downward thrust, thereby decreasing the likelihood of the point being knocked away or of the recoil hitting the pikemen behind. Wherever possible the Swiss aimed to fight on the offensive, but, if forced to defend, the base of the first pike was anchored to the ground with the foot and the following three pikes levelled against the oncoming enemy at waist and shoulder height. The attacker was faced with a bristling array of four pike points for each row of infantry, hence the name of the hedgehog for this defensive formation. Where there were more than four ranks of pikes, the next ranks of pikemen held their weapons upright, ready to step into any gap. The forest of pikes overhead acted as an umbrella against any incoming arrows or crossbow bolts. Determined pikemen holding their ranks could fend off the charge of even heavily armoured cavalry provided they received the charge on the points of the pikes and left no gaps for the horsemen to drive through.(9) By the time of the Swabian war 600 Zurich pikemen intercepted in the open by 1000 Austrian cavalry could confidently form their hedgehog and taunt the knights to attack them. Guicciardini described the tactic: "They would face the enemy like a wall without ever breaking ranks, stable and almost invincible."

The pike was a collective weapon, useless on its own, but unchallengeably effective when wielded by brave troops working together and trusting their comrades. The pikemen therefore tended to be the elite troops, both because they stood the shock at the point of contact with the enemy and because manipulation of the unwieldy pike required considerable strength and skill. Despite the prestige of the position, however, service with the long pikes was not unreservedly popular and the captains were always complaining about the shortage of pikemen. Transport of the pike on the march was tiresome, the equipment the individual had to provide was more expensive, and the pikeman was less mobile than the halberdier for looting once victory was assured. Nevertheless, from the middle of the fifteenth century about one quarter of the troops were armed with pikes.

The Swiss infantry carried little defensive weaponry. As both the halberd and the pike were two-handed weapons, it was not possible to handle shields. Neither was armour generally worn, both because its cost was prohibitive for the citizen soldier and because it was incompatible with the speed and mobility that were vital elements of Swiss tactics. Most soldiers wore a simple iron helmet and a leather tunic with iron reinforcements. In the late fifteenth and early sixteenth century the pikemen also protected themselves with a more substantial breastplate. Starting with the Battle of Laupen, the Confederates adopted the practice of sewing a white cross onto their clothes to distinguish themselves from the enemy. Captains were usually dressed the same as the troops except that they often sported plumes on their helmets.

While the halberd and the pike were the principal weapons of the Swiss infantry, around ten percent of a Swiss army generally carried long-distance weapons, initially crossbows and later arquebuses. The crossbow, in daily use as a hunting weapon, was effective up to three hundred paces, and a good crossbowman could fire off two to three bolts a minute. The crossbowmen, under the command of a designated officer,(10) had the task of forming a skirmishing line to occupy and distract the enemy while the infantry were forming up and closing with the opposing forces. They could retire behind the protection of the pikes if themselves attacked. Although the first firearms made their appearance at the end of the fourteenth century, they had not become reliable enough to replace the crossbow during the period of Swiss military preeminence. On the other hand, the Swiss occasionally made effective use of the most primitive distance weapon—throwing rocks. As well as the boulders rolled downhill at Morgarten, the Swiss at Näfels met the enemy with a barrage of rocks, and a French emissary at St Jakob an der Birs was killed by a rock thrown from the ranks.

Before considering the tactics adopted by the Swiss in the use of these various weapons, two other important tools of a Swiss army must be mentioned − musical instruments and flags. Every company included one or two drummers and a piper, whose role was to keep the troops in step when in formation and to signal orders. In addition, for full scale battles the cantonal warhorns were brought out, the most famous being the bull of Uri and the cow of Unterwalden.(11) Their bloodcurdling blasts, together with the battle cries of the advancing Swiss, were deliberately used to create a psychological advantage over more fainthearted opponents. The Swiss troops took to the field under the flags and banners that had been broken out to summon the troops to the assembly points, either the main cantonal banners or small vennli being carried, depending on the size of the expedition. In addition, individual villages, town guilds and troops of volunteers carried their own flags, which caused many disputes about order on the march and proximity to the main banner in the battle. The protection of the flags was regarded as the paramount duty of the army and each banner had not only a flag bearer but also a designated banner guard, all expected to defend the flags with their lives. At Morat, for example, more than thirty flags were guarded by fully one thousand men.

Two elements present in all other armies of the period were generally missing from the Swiss armies − cavalry and artillery. Although officers were usually mounted on the march, and allies occasionally provided some cavalry (as the Lorrainers at Morat), the Swiss army was a homogeneous infantry force. Horses were neither compatible with the mountain terrain nor the non-feudal society, and the Swiss developed tactics that could for a long time be successful without cavalry support. According to Machiavelli in *The Art of War*: "The superiority of the Swiss is a result of their ancient institutions and the lack of cavalry."(12) Similarly artillery was difficult to transport in the mountains and was a hindrance to speed and mobility. Even though by the year 1500 the Swiss probably possessed more than one thousand pieces of artillery, four hundred alone captured from Burgundy after Grandson, they were emplaced solely for defensive purposes. Eventually, cavalry and artillery were part of the combined arms that defeated the Swiss, but through the fifteenth century the Swiss were successful with no more than occasional use of either.

A despatch from one of the Duke of Milan's ambassadors, Bernadinus

Imperialis, dated 5 February, 1490, describes the departure of a Zurich army to fight in a dispute with St Gallen. This report provides a most colourful description of a Swiss fifteenth-century army and is worth reproducing at length:

"Then they all set off in order of march. First came twelve well-dressed noblemen on horses, armed with crossbows, then two knights and some pioneers with axes, and some drummers. A company of 500 long pikes followed, well armed, led by the sons of knights and marching three abreast in orderly ranks. These were followed on foot by 200 arquebuses and 200 halberdiers, a drum major and the pipers, followed by the Banner carried on foot by a striking looking man. With the flag bearer were two court ushers, carrying their staffs of office, and each with the authority to commit an offender to prison without argument. Then followed the executioner with three helpers, and six prostitutes chosen and paid by the town. 400 more halberdiers followed next, the strongest and best armed, for these had the task of guarding the flags; their weapons looked like a thick forest. 400 crossbowmen, including the sons of gentlemen drawn from all classes of the people, stepped proudly past next. They in turn were followed by many pikemen. All in all, the force numbered 4000 men and included participants from many surrounding districts, as well as more than twenty drummers. Following the main force came three trumpeters on horseback dressed in the colours of Zurich. Immediately behind was the Captain and Knight, Konrad Schwend, on horseback, well equipped with arms decorated with gold insignia, carrying the ceremonial staff of office and with a garland of flowers on his head. Following him, all on horseback, were a valet, whose lance and shield carried the captain's gold coat of arms, six bodyguards with lances on their thighs and twelve crossbowmen. The whole army displayed white crosses on either their armour, hats or stockings. After the captain came another Knight on horseback, whose function was to keep order in the field, accompanied by more mounted lances and crossbowmen, all with the same uniform. Then followed about 30 ammunition carts and four large cannons of 50 to 60 or 70 pounds. Behind the Zurich contingent marched the rest of the Confederate troops. It was a large and battleready army."(13)

Each soldier was expected to muster with provisions sufficient to last several days. Extensive supply arrangements were made only exceptionally and a Swiss army tended to march on the enemy and immediately fight the battle. They would, however, follow ancient superstitions and remain the customary three days on the field among the bodies to claim the victory before dispersing. Swiss offensive tactics were largely generated by the impatience of the young *knaben* but lack of arrangements to support the army in the field also played a role.(14)

A Swiss army marching in groups three abreast reckoned to cover about

4.5 kilometres per hour but could also move amazingly quickly under forced marches when necessary, the best known example being the Zurich contingent that covered the 220 kilometres to Morat in three days despite bad weather. The unwieldy pikes were usually ported on the shoulder, but were also trailed along the ground and occasionally bundled into carts. On arrival at the battleground, the Swiss would lay off several kilometres, usually behind a wood or hill to provide the time and freedom from interference to build their carefully constructed tactical formations.

The original Swiss tactical formation was in the shape of a wedge. This was used until Sempach, after which it was replaced by a square formation developed to exploit the offensive and defensive capabilities of the long pikes. Although the formations were often more rectangular than square, the use of the term square translating the Swiss *Gevierthaufen* seems more appropriate than the classical term phalanx.

Documents dating from the Alte Zurichkrieg of 1442-4 describe the detailed composition of a typical square.(15) The Zurich force in question consisted of 2760 men, one fifth crossbowmen, one quarter armed with long pikes, and the rest armed with short weapons, chiefly halberds. The force was divided into three units; vanguard (*vorhut*), main battle (*gewalt* − or *schlachthaufen*) and rearguard (*nachhut*) − in the proportions 30:50:20. The *schlachthaufen* consisted of 56 files, each 20 men deep. As each man was estimated to require three foot across the front and seven foot depth, this configuration resulted in a square 168 feet across and 140 feet deep. This was most likely a defensive formation, as an offensive formation would have been deeper. Calculating from the size of the square and the proportion of pikemen, three rows of long pikes would have surrounded the whole unit. Within the square, contingents from the same locality were kept together but carefully arranged so that potentially fainthearted troops were sandwiched between groups of proven courage. No soldier was alone − all were part of a group from their village or district or guild. The vanguard and rearguard were similarly constructed. The banners with their guards and the drummers were located in the centre of the main square. The crossbowmen operated outside the squares as a skirmishing line but were able to fall back into or behind the square for protection if necessary. The build-up of the whole formation was organized by a designated senior officer(16) and, when time allowed, much care was taken in the knowledge that the whole balance between victory and defeat hung on the performance of these units. Even the largest armies, including the 16,000-man *Schlachthaufen* deployed at Morat, were arranged according to similar principles.

A much debated question has been the amount of training needed by the troops participating in such a formation. One school of thought holds that intensive training would have been needed to avoid the closely packed troops disintegrating into a rabble. Another school holds that even new recruits had merely to follow-my-leader without prior training or experience. As usual the truth probably lies between these extremes. The cadre of experienced troops would have provided the example for new recruits to follow, especially as the elite troops were largely located among the pikemen at the head and on the outer fringes of the formation. Also, all the *hirtenknaben* were used to practising wargames from an early age. Certainly the published regulations all refer to matters of discipline rather than training, with the implicit assumption that the troops knew how to perform in battle.

Having formed up, the Swiss would aim to remain concealed from the enemy for as long as possible while moving to within attacking range. The approach would be covered by crossbowmen and other groups of volunteers skirmishing ahead of the main squares.(17) Once within sight, however, they would maximise the psychological impact of their appearance by closing the remaining gap with intimidating speed, horns blaring, drums beating and insults screamed. Holding their attack formations and able to cover the ground unencumbered by armour in *sturmlauf* almost as quickly as heavy cavalry, the massed pikes would be on their opponents before they realized what had hit them. The first objective of the attack was any enemy artillery, with the intention of preventing them firing off more than one round.(18)

The Swiss normally divided their forces into three squares to provide a balance between the need for offensive mass on the one hand and for manoeuvrability on the other. Machiavelli's writings have created the impression that the Swiss squares normally deployed in echelon, with the *vorhut* leading, the *schlachthaufen* alongside and slightly to the rear, and the *nachhut* yet further back awaiting developments. This neat arrangement was, however, by no means sacrosanct as the Swiss were much more concerned to take advantage of the local terrain, especially if a surprise flank attack could be prepared. At Morat the *vorhut* engaged the enemy while the *schlachthaufen* and *nachhut* went on a broad encircling movement to cut off the enemy's retreat, while at Nancy the *vorhut* and *nachhut* engaged the enemy while the *schlachthaufen* made a two-hour detour through the woods. By the time of the Schwabenkrieg the usual disposition was a main *schlachthaufen* accompanied by a small *vorhut* which marched ahead but then deployed as a tactical flanking unit according to the terrain.

Tactics were also varied according the enemy's composition and defensive precautions, although the complete, and sometimes excessive, self-confidence of the Swiss often led them to underestimate the importance of the enemy's strength.(19) During most of the fifteenth century the opposing forces consisted of heavy cavalry supported by inferior infantry. By the end of the century, however, the enemy included forces of *landsknechts* organized on the same lines as the Swiss. Defensive positions varied from battle in the open field as at Grandson, to lightly fortified as the Grünhag at Morat, to heavily fortified as at Nancy, Frastanz and Calven. In response to all these varying conditions, the Swiss always fought in their squares but deployed their squares as appropriate for the situation rather than exclusively in the neat but theoretical echelon format.

A battle with other heavy infantry such as the *landsknechts* was generally decided at the point of contact between the square and the enemy. The leading ranks were filled with the largest and strongest fighters, the "*Heerochsen*" or bulls of the army. These were usually arranged in the form of a point(20) in order to concentrate the maximum force on one part of the enemy line. If the square arrived with sufficient speed and force, the leading pikes would crash through the enemy line and then open their ranks for the halberdiers to swarm through and create havoc. Generally, however, the pikes from both sides would mesh and come under heavy pressure from the advancing ranks behind until one side gave way and let the opposition's halberdiers stream through to inflict heavy casualties on the unprotected backs of retreating opponents. The "push of pike" actually reduced the freedom of the front ranks to fight and wider formations were eventually introduced to reduce the pressure from the rear. The side that gained the initiative from the original pressure generally held the upper hand and won the battle. If the original impact was not clear-cut the battle would disintegrate into a mêlée where the ferocious fighting style of the Swiss would still usually win the day.(21)

In victory, the Swiss tactics showed a major weakness, in that the enemy was rarely pursued in order to turn the battle into a strategic gain. This was partly because of the Swiss lack of cavalry, and partly because the Swiss troops were more interested in searching for booty as soon as (or even before) the battle was won.(22)

In addition to the lack of cavalry and search for booty, another reason for the failure of the Swiss to take advantage of their victories was the absence of strategic leadership. For an official expedition, the troops of each canton or town were led by a captain who was usually selected in advance by the cantonal or town council or, exceptionally, elected by the troops themselves. In either case, the choice almost invariably fell on the *Landammann* or Mayor, as in this bellicose society, the important political positions tended to be filled by military leaders of proven ability and renown. The traditional criteria for the selection of captains were their experience, their financial means and political standing, their personal physical strength, and above all their military reputation. Unofficial expeditions elected their own captains, some of the more experienced later becoming established political figures.(23) The captains themselves met before a battle in a war council to decide tactics and elect commanders for the individual tactical units.(24) The captains generally fought in the first ranks where the battle was decided, while the flagbearers acted as seconds-in-command overseeing the performance of the square from the centre. The flagbearers in turn were supported by experienced soldiers drawn from such influential social groups as innkeepers, butchers and tanners. For the first time since the Romans, all social classes lined up alongside each other in the ranks.

An overall leader for an official Swiss army was only once appointed in the whole of the fourteenth and fifteenth centuries, namely Rudolph von Erlach at Laupen.(25) The democracies of the confederation preferred to leave the military leadership of their armies safe in the hands of seasoned proven captains rather than risk the potential military and political disruption that could be caused by the emergence of a generalissimo. Only in the sixteenth century when the armies were more distant and away for longer periods did the election of an *obersten feldhauptmann* become usual. The Swiss way of generalship by committee was cumbersome and conservative which partly explained the eventual decline of Swiss military supremacy. Nevertheless, it would not be appropriate to be too disparaging about the Swiss leadership. The captains were able to control and direct young undisciplined mountain herders, initiate tactical innovations, lead by example in the heat of battle, and above all use accumulated experience to win victory after victory.

Many of the military and political leaders were members of families whose names appear and reappear not only in these centuries but also in the history of the Swiss through to the French Revolution. As will be seen, dynasties of soldiers such as Diesbach, Reding, Hallwyl, Salis and Erlach played a leading role in the creation and maintenance of the Swiss military tradition.

Disciplinary rules for the army were specified in a number of orders, all based on the Sempacher Brief. Administration of discipline was the responsibility of the captains, and the troops of each contingent swore loyalty to the captain in person, usually during an oath-taking ceremony at the mustering point. The oath covered such matters as obedience, suspension of feuds, ban on gambling, cowardice and the disposal of booty. Maintenance of discipline among the fiery, prickly, young soldiers was a difficult task. On a major expedition the captains were assisted in the administration of justice by the presence of judges and an executioner, with punishments ranging from fines and repatriation to death by beheading or drowning.

The issue of booty became increasingly important towards the end of the fifteenth century. Whereas earlier Swiss armies had been driven by the need to defend their homeland and by the thirst of the young *knaben* for adventure and glory, the search for booty gradually became the main motivation of the troops. Stripping the bodies of the defeated foe and looting enemy territory of everything that could be transported home had always been accepted practice, and an army was usually accompanied by empty carts to transport the plunder. After Grandson, however, where the confederates seized the treasures of the richest court in Europe, the Swiss were insatiable in their lust for booty. Recent research depicts the *knaben* more as selfish roughneck looters rather than the nineteenth century view of disciplined heroes fighting for the freedom of their country.(26) Enforcing the prohibition on troops starting the search for booty before the battle had been won was a serious problem and a *beutemeister* was often appointed to ensure fair distribution of the spoils.

The final element in the Swiss military system was the esprit-de-corps and morale of the soldiers themselves. The Swiss fought with a brutality and cruelty that terrified their enemies. Callousness in battle and readiness to slaughter their enemies was a natural consequence of a way of life that involved butchery of animals as a daily routine. Opponents previously accustomed to negotiating a ransom if captured or to the gentlemanly manoeuvrings of the Italian style of war were faced with an enemy who took no prisoners and was intent on mass slaughter. A Zurich war regulation of 1444 found it necessary to forbid the troops from cutting the heart out of a dead enemy. As well as taking no prisoners, the *knaben* also regarded their own capture as the height of dishonour and would get themselves killed rather than be taken prisoner. An offer by Emperor Maximilian in the Swabian Wars of one hundred ducats for a Swiss prisoner found no takers. Even in that cruel age the ferocity of the Swiss was legendary.

Equally famous was their bravery. The *knaben* fought with, and could not hide from, their peers, and fear of injury or death meant less than fear for their reputation. While feats of courage were remembered in songs and renowned in the taverns of the alpine villages for generations, the hundred Bernese soldiers who slunk off into the woods during the first attack at the Battle of Laupen were taunted as foresters for the rest of their lives. Each man was expected to kill any coward on the spot. Häne has described their morale as follows: "The secret of their extraordinary composure in battle lay without doubt in their great awareness of their own strength and in a sort of military honour that all accounts confirm as strongly developed and specially nurtured. The Swiss of all periods were well aware that they were considered the best soldiers in the world, and they wanted to preserve this reputation at all costs."(27)

Such peer group pressure when not controlled could push the behaviour of the *knaben* from confidence and courage to overconfidence and foolhardiness. The overadvancement of the *vorhut* at Dornach and Novara, the attacks against overwhelming odds at St Jakob an der Birs and Bicocca were occasions when impatience and impetuosity took bravery beyond sensible limits. At the extreme the *knaben* could be overtaken by an uncontrollable bloodlust similar to that ascribed to the Scandinavian *berserkers*. Despite these occasional excesses, however, the reckless behaviour of the Swiss *knaben* in battle provided the main difference between them and their opponents. While their arms and tactics could be and were copied, the ferocity and wildness of the alpine herdsmen were unique.

At the end of the fourteenth century the Swiss had fought as a pack of barely controllable individual warriors. During the fifteenth century, experienced captains managed to preserve the wildness and ferocity of the soldiers while instilling enough discipline for them to operate in cohesive military formations. With the introduction of the long pikes and the tactical development of the square, the armies of the Confederation were the first infantry that could be confident of defeating heavy cavalry since the Roman Era. Although the simple robust tactics of the Swiss squares were eventually overtaken by the more sophisticated combined-arms tactics, pike-carrying infantry were thenceforth employed by all European armies until the introduction of the musket with bayonet at the beginning of the eighteenth century. The supremacy established by the Swiss infantry over the medieval heavy cavalry, in this author's opinion, deserves to be called a "Military Revolution" rather more than the realignment of infantry formations in the early seventeenth century that has attracted so much recent attention from British military historians.

IV

The Burgundian and Swabian Wars

"These men are cruel and rough people and fight all their neighbours if they ask for anything, and in the plains as well as the mountains 40,000 or 50,000 men can be found to fight."
Berry Herald, *Le Livre de la description des pays*.

The triumph of Swiss arms and tactics came in the brief period from 1475 to 1515 when firstly the Burgundian army (at that time recognized as the most powerful in Europe) was destroyed, then Swiss independence was finally assured by the defeat of the House of Habsburg in the Swabian War, and finally when Swiss troops played a major role in the wars in Italy. It is necessary to look at this period in some detail to understand the strengths and weaknesses of both the military and political systems of the Swiss, and therefore the reasons why Swiss troops subsequently entered into mercenary service for other European nations rather than following the more usual course of military strength underpinning the development of Switzerland itself into a Great Power. It is also worth looking at the battles of Grandson and Morat in detail from a Swiss perspective as examples of the Swiss military system at its height.

During the last quarter of the fifteenth century, the fundamental interests of four powers — France, Austria, Burgundy and the Swiss Confederation — came into conflict in the region of the Upper Rhine. In particular, the Swiss struggle for independence and territorial definition collided with the expansion of Burgundy, driven since 1467 by the ambitions of Charles the Bold. Just as the turbulent warlike cantons of the Swiss Confederation in the fifteenth century should not be confused with the serene orderly Switzerland of today, so fifteenth-century Burgundy should not be thought of as a small wine-growing province in Central France. Charles had inherited from his father Philip the Good the Low Countries, Flanders, Artois, Burgundy and the Franche Comté; had hopes of inheriting Milan and Provence; and planned to annexe Alsace and Lorraine with the dream of recreating the Carolingian Middle Kingdom of Lotharingia, stretching from the North Sea to the Mediterranean. By 1473 Charles was at the height of his power.

During much of the fifteenth century the eight cantons of the Swiss Confederation had been following separate and often conflicting policies. The Waldstaette and Lucerne were attracted southward, aiming to secure the trade route across the Gotthard into the prosperous valley of the Po. Zurich was more interested in securing the northern frontier of the Confederation against the Habsburgs, while Berne was pursuing an aggressive policy of expansion northward and westward. Conflicts among the cantons were increased by the economic and social tensions between the new towns of the plateau and the agrarian and mountainous areas, tensions which had led to open war between Zurich and Schwyz in 1439-42. Although the cantons met regularly in a Diet to discuss matters of mutual interest, the Diet had no formal authority and was powerless to impose decisions on the Cantons. This lack of balance between the cantonal autonomy and central authority was to stifle the development of the Confederation for the next three centuries.

The turbulent Swiss were difficult neighbours. Groups of marauding *knaben*, often numbered in hundreds, would suddenly invade Southern Germany, Northern Italy or the Vaud. These expeditions generally erupted spontaneously during meetings of heightened emotions such as fairs or sporting competitions, but were also nudged in the right direction by influential political figures. The Saubannerzug in 1468, for example, which led to an attack on the town of Waldshut, more than coincidentally supported Berne's ambitions to expand northward. This Bernese initiative was blocked, however, by the peace of Waldshut with Austria paying an indemnity of 10,000 florins in return for Berne withdrawing from the territory north of the Rhine. Berne was pressured into accepting these terms by the other cantons led by Zurich, which viewed with strong mistrust both Berne's expansionist policies and its increasing influence within the Confederation. The peace of Waldshut committed the provinces of Southern Germany to a destiny outside the Swiss Confederation, and reoriented Berne's ambitions in a westerly direction and therefore into direct conflict with Burgundy.

By the Treaty of St Omer in 1469 Sigismund of Austria mortgaged Alsace and several strategically important possessions on the Upper Rhine to Burgundy for 50,000 florins, as well as agreeing a secret joint aggression pact against the Swiss. With the Burgundian occupation of Alsace, the territories of Berne and Charles the Bold had a common border for the first time, and a zone of friction was created in the area that is now French-speaking western Switzerland. In this area Berne had already established alliances with Bienne, Solothurn, Fribourg and Neufchâtel, and coveted the Vaud, possession of which would ensure communications with the Valais and extend Bernese territory up to the natural defensive barrier of the Jura.(1)

The first conflict between Berne and Burgundy came in 1474. By this time, disappointed with lack of action from Burgundy, Sigismund of Austria had decided to secure his position with the Swiss by reconciliation. In March, 1474, a treaty of "perpetual peace" was signed, by which Austria formally recognized the existence of the Confederation for the first time. This was received with widespread celebrations in all the Cantons.(2) During the summer of 1474 a revolt broke out in Alsace against the Burgundian occupation and Charles's unpopular governor Peter von Hagenbach was captured and executed at Breisach. Sigismund came to the assistance of the Alsatians, and in response to his appeal under the Treaty of Perpetual Peace, the Swiss also declared war on Burgundy. The Confederation sent 8,000 troops into the Franche Comté and together with the Austrians laid siege to Héricourt. Charles, still bogged down in a siege outside Neuss, despatched a relieving army under the Count of Neuenburg-Blamont, which was decisively beaten by the Swiss-Austrian army near Héricourt in November. Although not led by Charles in person, this was the first defeat suffered by his army and a humiliation he could not overlook.

Tensions between Burgundy and the Swiss were further increased by the activities of Louis XI of France, the "universal spider" as he was called by the Burgundian chronicler Molinet. How far Louis was a *deus ex machina* carefully orchestrating events and how far taking advantage of opportunities as they arose is open to debate. It is probably reasonable to suppose that he was following a general policy aimed at impaling the Burgundian army on Swiss pikes.

On 26 October, 1474, Louis signed an alliance with the Confederation that would form the basis of all subsequent agreements between the French throne and the Confederation into the eighteenth century. The first three clauses of this alliance specified that the King would "help, support and protect" the Confederates in case of a war with Burgundy, would pay 20,000 francs a year during the king's lifetime, and that in return the Swiss would provide 6000 armed troops for the service of the King (3). In the short term, while the financial support promised by the French was provided (and used by the Swiss to stock up with artillery and gunpowder), the further protection promised by Louis never materialized. Nevertheless the alliance of 1474 marked the beginning of the three-hundred-year special relationship between the Swiss and the kings of France, and for the first time directly linked annual payments from the French with supply of troops by the Swiss.

In June, 1475, Charles humiliatingly lifted the siege of Neuss where he had been bogged down for twelve months, leaving himself free to turn his attention to other matters. In November he invaded Lorraine. Meanwhile

Burgundian relations with the Swiss had deteriorated even further. Bernese troops invaded Vaud on three separate occasions during 1475.(4) Although originally reluctant to fight the Swiss, there being neither honour nor material gain in defeating mere peasants, Charles could not ignore the attacks on Vaud, the possession of his ally Duchess Yolande of Savoy and ruled by one of his senior captains, the Count of Romont. Moreover, the Swiss attack on Vaud threatened his flank and the vital strategic supply route for bringing his Italian troops north.(5)

That November, Louis XI, despite the pact of 1474 with the Confederation, suddenly executed a volteface and agreed a nine-year peace with Burgundy. Two days later the Emperor agreed to provide active support to Charles, and the way lay open for Charles to clear the Swiss from Vaud and revenge the defeat of Héricourt.

In January, 1476, Charles the Bold crossed the Jura with an army of around 20,000 men, and on 19 February lay at the western end of Lake Neufchâtel outside the Castle of Grandson. This was occupied by the only detachment of troops the Bernese had left in Vaud, following their invasion the previous autumn. On the 28th Charles persuaded the garrison to surrender, presumably in exchange for a guarantee of safe conduct. In fact all 412 members of the garrison were either hanged from trees surrounding the castle or drowned in the lake. Charles's intention was to intimidate the Swiss into submission, but the result was the opposite, to stiffen Swiss resistance and create a bloodfeud. The 7000-man Bernese army under Nicholas von Scharnachtal and Hans von Hallwyl assembled on the Bernese border and Berne sent daily messengers to the other cantons demanding support. On 23 February the Diet, meeting at Lucerne, finally agreed and on 1 March, a full Confederate army of 18,000 men had massed at Neuenburg on the eastern end of Lake Neufchâtel.

The Burgundian army was camped a few kilometres east of Grandson on the plain that stretches along the north side of the lake. Charles had also established an advance post in the castle of Vaumarcus, a further three kilometres to the east. On 1 March the Swiss held their Council of War. The Swiss leaders recognized the strong defensive position of the Burgundian camp, especially as it contained the largest artillery park in Europe. It was therefore decided to try to tempt Charles out of his defences by an attack on the Burgundian forward position at Vaumarcus, which was held by Charles's personal guards whom he could be expected to support.(6) Meanwhile an exploratory reconnaissance in strength would be despatched towards the main Burgundian camp along the old Roman pathway leading through the woods about one kilometre from the lake and above the plain.

An initial attack on Vaumarcus that night was enough to bring Charles out of his prepared defensive position, and on the morning of 2 March he broke camp and moved his forces eastward across the plain. Early that same morning the 2500-man Swiss Vorhut (including contingents from Schwyz, Zurich, Lucerne and St Gallen), too impatient to await the end of Mass, set off westwards along the lightly snow-covered high path. This force easily overran a Burgundian guardpost but news of the skirmish was reported back on the Swiss side in terms of the *vorhut* having engaged the main enemy forces. Accordingly the main *schlachthaufen* with contingents from Berne, Solothurn and Fribourg promptly set out after the *vorhut* along the high path, and the *nachhut* followed behind along both the high road and the lower road next to the lake, leaving only a small force to tie down the garrison of Vaumarcus.

The *vorhut* showed more discipline than in previous battles such as Arbedo and St Jakob an der Birs by waiting in the woods for the support of the main Swiss force. With the arrival of the *schlachthaufen*, however, the captains were unable to restrain any longer the impatience of the *knaben* to attack, especially with the arrival of the Bernese contingent lusting to revenge the murdered Grandson garrison. Shortly before midday the *vorhut* and *schlachthaufen* knelt for the customary prayers, descended on to the plain, and quickly formed up into one huge square of ten thousand men, with pikes at the front and protecting the flanks, halberdiers surrounding the flags in the centre, a few cavalry on the right flank and preceded by a skirmish line of 300 *enfants perdus*.

Charles launched the full force of the Burgundian heavy cavalry in several charges against the flank of the Swiss square. This was the first time in a major battle that the Swiss had deliberately set out to oppose a defensive pike square against the full force of a heavy cavalry charge. The heavy horses and armoured riders, each weighing half a ton, advancing 250 metres a minute at the trot or double that at the gallop would have been an intimidating sight. When the cavalry reached the pikes three alternatives could occur, possibly in combination – the cavalry shied from the impact, or they charged into the pikes which held firm and caused heavy casualties among horses and riders, or if the pikes wavered the cavalrymen could drive through the gaps into the square creating havoc. At Grandson the pikemen held, encouraging each other "to stick a pike in the nose" of the Burgundian horsemen. Although the cavalry were able to break into the wall they were thrown back, and one Bernese pikeman, a Hans von der Grub, is credited in the chronicles with unseating the Burgundian cavalry leader, the Count of Chateauguyon. Then occurred the turning point of the battle. Believing the entire Swiss army to be facing him, Charles decided to redeploy his forces in order to bring more artillery (which was having some success against the Swiss square) into line of fire and to allow his cavalry to attack both flanks. To permit these changes, the infantry in the Burgundian centre were ordered to retire. In the middle of this sensitive manoeuvre the two remaining Swiss battle groups appeared from the high and low paths and hurled themselves against the enemy from two additional directions. Their great warhorns blaring, the troops screaming for revenge and rushing headlong into the attack at "stormpace", the Swiss well knew how to exploit the psychological benefits of their reputation for ferocity and bloodthirstiness and the knowledge that they took no prisoners. The brittle morale of the diverse and disunited Burgundian troops broke. With the cry of *"sauve qui peut"* the tactical withdrawal of the infantry in the centre disintegrated into a panic-stricken flight.

The battle was over almost before it started, and the Burgundian flight took place so quickly that they lost only 1000 men. As usual the lack of cavalry to hack down a defeated enemy prevented the Swiss from fully exploiting their victory. Additionally in this case, the Swiss pursuit came to a virtual halt when they overran the Burgundian camp with its fabulous treasures. The Swiss captured over 400 cannon, 800 arquebuses, 300 barrels of gunpowder, 10,000 horses, jewels (including the 133 carat Florentine diamond), gold and silver plate, carpets, and tapestries; with an estimated worth of 3 million florins.(7)

There were only 100 casualties on the Swiss side, but Grandson, while a stupefying victory, was by no means decisive. The Swiss failed militarily to annihilate the Burgundian army and, by demobilizing immediately after the battle, leaving the Vaud unoccupied for Charles to reassemble his army for a second attack, failed to capitalize politically. Another battle would be necessary to resolve the conflict between Burgundy and the Confederation, and this duly took place four months later at Morat.

Despite Berne's protestations that the Burgundian army had been dispersed rather than defeated, suspicions by the other cantons of Berne's expansionist policies again took over. The troops not only returned home with their spoils, but the Diet also forbade Berne to garrison any towns in the Vaud beyond its frontiers. Berne deliberately ignored this instruction in the case of Morat, a town strategically positioned on the main route along which any invader intent on attacking Berne would pass. In March, Morat was garrisoned by 1500 men under the renowned Captain Adrian von Bubenberg, who urgently started buying in stores and improving the town's defences.(8) The Diet did recognize, however, the failure to exploit the victory at Grandson and issued a new ordinance tightening up discipline and expressly forbidding the taking of prisoners. Nevertheless, Charles was left unhindered to reassemble his army outside Lausanne with the clear intention of revenging his recent defeat.

Charles broke camp outside Lausanne and on 9 June arrived before Morat. Three Burgundian corps laid siege to the town from west, south and east, but they were unable to seal off access to the lake. Bubenberg inspired an aggressive defence of the town, even leaving the main gates open day and night to signal the confidence of the defenders. In any case, the recent fate of the Grandson garrison made surrender unthinkable. Bubenberg's thirteen-day defence of the town bought the Swiss invaluable time for the usual disputes and prevarications in the Diet to work their way through to a decision. Berne had been urgently requesting assistance since 5 June, but only on the 12th, when an advance force of Burgundian troops crossed the Saane river onto Bernese home territory, could Berne demand unequivocal support from the other cantons according to the established defensive pacts on which the Confederation was based. On the 13th the Grand Banner of Berne was paraded out of the town and all the cantons started to mobilize. The neighbouring Fribourg contingent arrived first, followed by troops from the Waldstaette, Solothurn, and the other cantons. More support arrived from Alsace and South Germany, and a strong force of cavalry under Duke Réné of Lorraine. Last of all, on the morning of the 22nd, 2000 troops arrived from Zurich after marching 220 kilometres in three days. The detachments from the furthest cantons, St Gallen and Appenzell, did not arrive in time for the battle. On 22 June, the anniversary of the victory of Laupen, the Swiss army totalled 25,000 men, including 1800 cavalry, a much higher proportion than usual.(9) The speed of the Swiss mobilization had made up for the delay in its authorization.

Charles, with a slightly smaller force of around 23,000 men, was naturally expecting the Swiss to mount a relief operation and had prepared a strong defensive position around his camp on the plateau south of Morat. This position was fortified with a palisade known as the Grünhag, well supported with artillery but situated rather far from the main Burgundian camp. Nervous of again being surprised by the Swiss, Charles had had his troops standing to arms on several occasions since the 15th and by the 21st his army was tired and rebellious. As it rained all day on the 21st, and a personal reconnaissance had convinced him that only a small Swiss force was in the neighbourhood, Charles ignored all advice and stood down the majority of his forces, leaving a watch of 2000 infantry and 300 lances of cavalry to guard the Grünhag. This was still the Burgundian position at midday on 22 June, again after a morning of heavy rain.

The Swiss army passed the night of 21 June about six kilometres from the Burgundians, hidden by thick woods and the bad weather. The leaders of the different contingents held the Council of War that night. There has been much debate as to whether the Swiss appointed a Commander-in-Chief for this battle alone in the person of Wilhelm Herter, but it is now generally agreed that they retained their normal procedure of electing several leaders and that Herter was the *ordnungsmacher* who organized the battle formations. The captains at the War Council recognized that this time the Burgundian army must be annihilated, to which end the line of flight must be cut off. As well as a limited attack on the Burgundian camp, therefore, a strong force sweeping around the Burgundian army was planned to pen in the enemy so he could be driven into the lake. While Grandson had been an improvised Encounter Battle, Morat was to be a planned Battle of Annihilation, with the relief of Morat a secondary objective.

The *vorhut*, consisting of 5000 troops from Berne and Fribourg under the command of Hans von Hallwyl of Berne, was directed to a frontal assault on the Grünhag. The cavalry under Réné of Lorraine lined up to the left of the *vorhut* with the task of engaging the Burgundian cavalry and protecting the flank of the *vorhut*. This task would normally have been the responsibility of the main Swiss square, but at Morat the 16,000-man *schlachthaufen* under Hans Waldmann of Zurich was directed on a broad circling movement around the left with the objective of cutting off the Burgundian line of retreat. The small *nachhut* under Kaspar von Hertenstein of Lucerne probably held back before circling round to the right to meet up with Bubenberg's forces from the town.

The Swiss attack began at midday on 22 June when the *vorhut*, having stolen quietly through the woods, suddenly appeared in front of the Grünhag and immediately stormed the palisade. The Burgundian defence put up a strong resistance and stopped the advance of the Swiss with several hundred casualties. A detachment from Schwyz under Dietrich in der Halden was able to find a small path round the Grünhag on the right and attack the Burgundian defenders from the flank, allowing the Swiss advance to restart. Having crashed through the palisade the *vorhut* headed at storm pace for the Burgundian camp. Here Charles's main forces were still looking for arms and horses in complete disarray while Charles himself seemed paralysed with shock. The *schlachthaufen* also descended on Charles's camp and the demoralized, disorganized Burgundian army was unable to mount any serious defence against the power and fury of the Swiss assault. Only isolated pockets of resistance, including some English archers under the Duke of Somerset, put up even temporary opposition to the Swiss steamroller. In the words of the Italian observer Panigarola, the whole Burgundian army was put to flight during the time it took to say a Miserere.

As planned, the Burgundians were driven back on the lake and either cut down or drowned. Knights offering handsome ransoms, disarmed soldiers cowering on the ground and hiding in trees were all deliberately and cold-bloodedly slaughtered. The Burgundian army lost 10,000 dead, Charles himself being one of the few who escaped. Swiss losses totalled only 410, most of these falling in the attack on the Grünhag. The plunder captured in the Burgundian camp, while considerable, was not as spectacular as that captured at Grandson. Following their ancient custom, the Swiss remained on the battlefield three days before dispersing.

At Morat, the Swiss demonstrated most of the strengths of their military system, particularly the experience of battle-hardened captains in tactical planning, the use of surprise and speed in the attack, and the power and ferocity of the Swiss troops with their ruthlessness and total confidence. Because of the terrain, however, Morat was not a *bataille rangée* where the tactic of infantry squares needed to be exploited to full effect. The Swiss were aided by Charles's mistakes in generalship, especially by dividing his forces around the town and between the Grünhag and his camp, selecting a defensive position with the lake blocking his line of retreat, allowing himself again to be surprised and then not providing forceful leadership at the critical moment. These errors did not detract from the widespread recognition by contemporaries of Morat as a famous Swiss victory. The Confederate forces had shattered the most powerful army in Europe and established their heavy infantry as the model for all other armies to imitate.

Despite the annihilation of the Burgundian army, Charles's escape left the need for one further battle before the Swiss triumph would be complete. This took place six months later, in January, 1477, at Nancy. Réné of Lorraine, besieged in his capital by Charles, requested assistance from the Confederation. Although prevaricating about providing a formal expedition, the Diet authorized Réné to advertise in the cantons for mercenaries, offering four and a half guilders salary per month. 8400 volunteers answered the call and in December assembled in Basle, where they elected Hans Waldmann of Zurich as overall leader of the expedition before marching north. The pillaging by this group in the supposedly friendly Alsatian territory they crossed, including a pogrom in Mulhouse, demonstrated the negative side of the wildness and cruelty of the Swiss *knaben* that were such positive attributes on the battlefield. Together with contingents from Lorraine, Alsace and South Germany, Réné's army of 20,000 men was far larger than the 12,000-man Burgundian force.

Charles had again drawn his troops up in a strong defensive position, behind 30 guns protected by a stream in a narrow river valley outside Nancy. Again, however, the Swiss subordinated their classic tactic of three squares in echelon to the demands of the terrain. The *schlachthaufen* circled wide through woods and frozen marshes to launch a surprise attack on the Burgundian defences from the flank. Another 7000 Burgundian troops fell in the mêlée, including Charles himself, whose body was only discovered in a ditch by his squire two days after the battle.

Nancy finally ended the Burgundian war. From such an outright victory the Swiss achieved relatively little. The threat of Charles's expansionist ambitions was removed, considerable spoils and booty were obtained, and a formidable military reputation was established. Because of the jealousies and dissensions between the cantons and a lack of overriding strategic vision, however, no territorial gains were made, despite the whole of the Vaud being there for the taking. Fribourg and Solothurn formally joined the Confederation as the ninth and tenth cantons but the opportunity for a major expansion was passed by.

The second of the major wars which the Swiss fought at the end of the fifteenth century was the Swabian War (known to German historians as the Swiss War). While the immediate cause of the war was a dispute over whether the Confederation would pay a new tax(10) passed by the Imperial Diet of Worms in 1495, the issue at stake was really the final assertion of Swiss independence from the Empire and the Habsburgs. The bitterness in what was essentially a civil war between the German-speaking peoples north and south of the Rhine was exacerbated by the professional military rivalry between the Swiss and Maximilian's detested new *landsknechts*. The war took the form of a series of battles (the most important being Schwaderloh, Frastanz, Calven and Dornach) along the semicircle of the Confederation's northern and eastern borders during the first half of the year 1499. Neither side managed to concentrate its forces for a single decisive engagement, and there was little strategic direction on either side, the war almost being fought for the pleasure of its fighting. Swiss plans recognized their inability to keep an army long in the field, both because of the lack of an administrative capability to handle supply logistics and because of the unwillingness of the *knaben* to participate in a drawn-out campaign. In so far as the Swiss had a strategy, it was to wait on the defensive with light fortifications and garrisons located at critical border points, and to mobilize quickly using the advantage of interior lines to repel any assault on home territory. In each village one or two reserves stood constantly at the ready to be at the front within hours. The only offensive moves were impromptu plundering expeditions into Austria and southern Germany.

A significant military development took place in the Swabian War when the Swiss were opposed for the first time by similar forces of heavy infantry, the *Landsknechts*, as well as by cavalry. In response to this new development there was a progressive change in the composition of the infantry square with the proportion of pikemen increasing from one-third to two-thirds. Instead of two or three rows of surrounding pikes in stationary defensive positions to fend off cavalry attacks, the square now needed a preponderance of pikemen who could storm forward in the attack as a mobile battering ram intending to smash through the opposing forces. If the attack stalled, the battle became a "push of pike" against the opposing force of similarly armed infantry. The "push" entailed both ferocious hand-to-hand-combat between the first ranks and the forward drive of the whole square striving to advance by using its strength and weight. At Dornach the fight to win the push lasted several hours before the arrival of fresh troops allowed the Swiss to break through. Whichever side won the push was usually victorious in the battle, as the supporting troops with the short weapons had a considerable advantage from fighting going forward. There was generally a huge difference in casualties between winners and losers, as the latter had to turn their backs on the enemy to disengage from the battle. At Frastanz, for example, the Swiss claimed 3000 enemy casualties against eleven of their own. The war was fought in mountainous country and throughout the Swiss adapted their tactics to the terrain to take maximum advantage from any possibility of surprise rather than relying solely on the fury and impetus of the attack. At Frastanz and Calven large forces of 2-3000 men crossed 1600-metre and 2300-metre mountain ranges respectively in order to attack from the rear strong Letzi in the valleys below. At Dornach the *vorhut* was able to creep up on the unsuspecting enemy camp before attacking with such speed that the opposing artillery was put out of action without a shot being fired.

The contemporary German chronicler Pirckheimer commented that: "It was the greatest and most destructive war in living memory not only because of the scale of mobilizations and the number of troops, but also because of the wildness of the battles and the numbers of defeats." The Basle peace treaty finally severed all formal links between the Confederation and the Empire, and three new cantons (Basle, Schaffhausen and Appenzell) brought the Confederation up to the 13-canton configuration that would remain until the eighteenth century. Yet again, however, the Swiss chose not to capitalize on their military dominance by making extensive territorial gains. A Greater Switzerland including Alsace and much of southern Germany could have been created if the political will had existed within the Confederation. But, for two centuries, Swiss foreign policy had been directed at independence from the Habsburgs. With the final achievement of this goal and the arrival of several natural physical frontiers, no clear further objective was recognized by all the cantons. There was on the contrary a considerable divergence of views — between towns and countryside, between Protestants and Catholics; between Berne with its westward orientation, Zurich looking north and the Waldstaette southward. No strong political organization existed to override these dissensions. The Diet, hampered by its consensus politics, unbalanced by the diplomatic manoeuvrings of the Great Powers, and weakened by bribery and corruption, was reduced to impotent bickering rather than providing forceful leadership. Frustrated by the vacillations of the politicians, the Swiss *knaben* increasingly chose to search for wealth and glory by offering their skills to foreign powers in mercenary service.

V

Early Mercenaries

"Swiss mercenary troops who were notorious for their ferocity and brutality."
Samuel Butler, *Hudibras*

The last two chapters have described the new infantry arms and tactics developed by the Swiss during the fourteenth and fifteenth centuries and the final achievement of the Confederation's independence by using these arms and tactics as the basis for Swiss military supremacy in the Burgundy and Swabian Wars. As we have seen, the Swiss army was deeply rooted in its homeland. Each town, village and valley as a political entity provided troops for the canton, and the cantonal contingents joined together to become the Confederate army. Troops from neighbouring allies such as Alsace, the Swabian towns or the Valais could be folded into the Confederate army but it was inconceivable that soldiers from further afield would be hired. The Swiss army was a homogeneous selfstanding unit, tightly linked to the political structures of the Confederation.

The armies of other European powers had developed differently, however, and in particular the hiring of outside troops as mercenaries had become standard practice. This provided the opportunity for the Swiss, at the height of their reputation and frustrated by the disinclination of the Confederation to follow a policy of territorial conquest, to hire themselves out to foreign armies. The Swiss became the mercenary soldier par excellence.

Before looking in detail at the Swiss as mercenaries, it will be helpful firstly to venture a definition of the term mercenary, and secondly to trace how the profession of the mercenary soldier had emerged in the armies of Europe while the Swiss had been fighting for their independence.

Basically, a mercenary soldier is no more than a hired soldier. In his study of warfare in thirteenth-century Italy, however, Mallet has pointed out that, in using the term mercenary, we mean primarily foreign mercenary.(1) As most soldiers were being paid by this time, the key differentiation was not so much between those serving for pay compared with those serving from some sense of obligation or patriotism, as between those serving their own state and foreigners serving another state. Taking this point, the following adaptation of a definition proposed by Contamine may be advanced:

> The mercenary is a professional soldier whose conduct is dictated not by membership of his own political community but by the desire to gain from providing his services to another political community.(2)

More simply, Kiernan has offered a similar definition:

> A foreign soldier enlisting for pay.(3)

Looking back to the beginning of the twelfth century, all the armies of Europe at that time were feudal armies, consisting of a lord's vassals who provided military service as payment for their fiefs. Facilitated by the growing use of money in the economy, however, the practice of scutage gradually became widespread. According to this system, vassals could either make a monetary payment to their lord in lieu of personal service or hire professional soldiers as direct substitutes. By the end of the thirteenth century the composition of European armies had changed from a purely feudal relationship, through a transitional period when soldiers raised under the feudal system were paid some sort of campaign fee, to an essentially free mercenary system whereby a prince would raise an army of professional soldiers for agreed rates of pay. The core of such an army was often the prince's bodyguard or household troops, which gradually expanded from being a few personal retainers to the beginnings of a permanent army.

From the prince's point of view, the hiring of mercenaries offered several advantages. He could find larger numbers of experienced knights than his own nobility alone could provide in order to carry out some of his more ambitious schemes. Professional soldiers were more motivated than reluctant vassals and more skilled in the practice of war. Specialists, such as English longbowmen, Genoese crossbowmen or Swiss heavy infantry, could be imported. Finally, he avoided the risk of spreading arms among his own potentially rebellious subjects.

Once started, the process gained momentum. The technical gap widened between professional soldiers, trained from their youth for a career in arms, and the remaining nobility, who became less and less conscientious about practising their military skills. The administrative system for raising taxes to finance the hiring of professional soldiers was an instrument that could be used time after time to generate more revenue to hire more soldiers, limited only by the extent to which the prince was able to impose on his subjects. As only the richest princes could afford to hire large numbers of mercenaries, their position was strengthened against their nobles and against the people.

The first mercenaries were usually armed adventurers hired to serve in the feudal heavy cavalry. Rootless knights were readily available to meet this demand, particularly younger and illegitimate sons of the ruling caste who had no inheritance on which to fall back and no skills other than the practice of war.

A particular problem arose when the wars which were the sole occupation of these adventurers dried up. With no demand for their services and no other means of support, the redundant knights often formed themselves into outlaw bands that terrorized the civilian population and plundered the countryside for their pleasure and needs. Such bands included the routiers who appeared in France on several occasions during lulls in the Hundred Years War, the Great Companies of knights left behind in Italy from the Crusades and from the invasions of the German emperors, and the *Ecorcheurs*. The Swiss twice repelled incursions by such bands, defeating a horde of English and Welsh free-booters known as the Guglers at Fraubrunnen in 1375, and the *Ecorcheurs* at St Jakob an der Birs in 1444.

During the thirteenth and fourteenth centuries the Great Companies were periodically hired by the Italian States for service in their never-ending disputes and wars. The Companies progressively developed from their origins as bands of brigands to become permanent military organizations available for hire. By the 1380s the situation in Italy had become formalized, with the city-states entering into formal contracts with captains who arranged to hire and command troops in exchange for agreed payments. From their contract of hire or Condota these soldiers became known as Condottiere. The initial contracts were of short duration such as a single campaign, but by the mid-fifteenth century had extended into semi-permanent and even lifetime arrangements. In effect the Italian states started employing standing armies.

As well as the knights, there was also a regular need for footsoldiers. Medieval warfare was made up of a succession of sieges of castles and fortified towns, with a few major battles interspersed. Infantry were needed for the essential if less glamorous tasks of siege warfare, both in attack and defence, as well as for manning garrisons. The main sources of lowgrade footsoldiers were the poorer classes, who could not afford the upkeep of warhorses or the time needed to practice cavalry skills, and who were generally enrolled in the communal militia. Higher quality footsoldiers could be hired from hilly regions where infantry expertise had strongly developed as the advantages normally available to the mounted soldier were largely offset by the terrain. Switzerland of course was just such a region.

The first references to Swiss mercenaries appear in the thirteenth and fourteenth centuries. Contingents from Schwyz served with the Emperor Frederick in Italy in 1240 and Rudolf von Habsburg in 1289. Bernese troops are recorded on several occasions working for Savoy, and as covering the French retreat at Crecy in 1346. As well as these official troops there were numerous Swiss *knaben* wandering Europe individually or in small groups spoiling for a fight and eager for the opportunity to take some loot. In 1373 Bernardo Visconti, having been given permission to raise troops in the Confederation, was able to attract 3000 volunteers to cross the Gotthard. To put the importance of mercenary service for the Swiss in perspective even at this early date, Visconti's force was twice the size of the Confederate army that won the crucial victory at Sempach a few years later. These early mercenaries brought back skills, experience and the crucial weapon (the long pike) that formed the basis for the new Swiss infantry tactics.

During the fifteenth century the demand for Swiss troops accelerated, reflecting both their growing reputation and the increasing demand for infantry as the pike squares established their place on the battlefield. In 1453 a force of Swiss served with the French against the English at Bordeaux. In 1465 Swiss mercenaries served with both Louis XI and the rebels of the Ligue du Bien Public (including Adrian von Bubenberg, the later defender of Morat, who on this occasion fought on the same side as Charles the Bold). These were described by Commines as: "The first one saw in the Kingdom and who set the tone for those that came afterwards." A particularly interesting expedition from this period was the troop of 800 volunteers that was hired by the town of Nuremburg in 1450, as one of the earliest surviving Swiss mercenary contracts dates from this expedition. The terms of this agreement are typical of the period and it is therefore worth summarizing the main conditions.(4)

The pay for each soldier was agreed as five guilders of the Rhine per month, with one month payable in advance at the mustering point of St Gallen. Any month once started would count as a full month. If the contract were cancelled the soldiers would receive a payment for their homeward journey, fourteen days' pay if Nuremburg cancelled or eight days' pay if the Swiss cancelled. The troop would not be split up, would participate in a share out of any loot, and wounded would be cared for and paid. The soldiers had to swear an oath that they would not rob or mistreat women, priests or friends; would not take women with them or gamble; would not burn or plunder churches; would not pursue old enmities or grudges, and would bring any disputes before their captains. Anyone not acting according to the oath would be sent home.

The prohibitions contained in the oath clearly reflect the appalling behaviour that might be expected of the *knaben*. A group of fifteenth century Swiss mercenaries was more a turbulent band of marauders than an organized military formation. To quote Redlich's description, they were "pugnacious, quarrelsome, courageous, faithless, vying for military glory, living an unfettered yet dangerous life with a chance for easy and big gains."(5)

The difficulty of controlling the troops was a serious problem for the authorities, in terms of both operational control in the field by the captains and political control over which foreign requests for troops should be accepted and which denied. After the triumphs of the Burgundy War, with their reputation at its highest, the Swiss were inundated from all directions with official and unofficial requests for troops. France, Austria, Savoy, Pope Sixtus IV, Hungary, and all the Italian and South German city states were jostling to hire the Swiss pikemen that had defeated the most powerful army in Europe. The *knaben* themselves, apart from some emotional prejudices against the Habsburgs, were basically unconcerned by the niceties of the Confederation's political relationships and were ready to follow the lure of pay and the possibility of loot and glory in the service of whichever paymaster offered the best opportunity.

The accepted custom was for a foreign power to apply to the Diet to hire troops. If the Diet accepted the request, it would negotiate terms, appoint captains and share out the authorized levy among the cantons for them to request volunteers. However, this procedure was largely ignored both by other powers and within the Confederation. Foreign powers turned down by the Diet would nevertheless send their recruiting agents into the cantons to hire troops. Mayors and other influential personages could be bribed to turn a blind eye to the recruiters and local meeting places such as inns and butchers shops were turned into recruiting offices. Antoine de Bessey, for example, the Bailli of Dijon, operated from just across the border recruiting for France with or without the permission of the Diet. Similarly, inside the Confederation, Swiss captains of renown would gather around them a troop of personally known *knaben* which they would lead into foreign service.(6)

Mercenary service was an important national asset that the Swiss authorities felt it their duty to control. There were also some very practical concerns. The Diet feared that the uncontrolled emigration of too many young men would have serious political and economic consequences, leaving too few to defend the country and to maintain the economy, or to fill the places in the official contracts accepted by the Diet. Furthermore, the Swiss leaders lived with the nightmare of hired Swiss turning up on both sides of a battle and killing each other in a fratricidal bloodbath. This possibility first occurred in Flanders between 1489 and 1492 when both Maximilian's and the French army included Swiss troops, which luckily never met on the battlefield. The central administration of the Confederation was, however, at this stage so modest, not to say primitive, that the control of the mercenary bands was simply beyond its capability.

The regulation of unofficial recruitment remained a major headache for the Confederation until the system of capitulations was made to work in the sixteenth century. In the meantime, as the demand for Swiss mercenaries accelerated after the Burgundy War, the temptations mounted for the *knaben* to ignore the strictures of the authorities. The young men flocked across the borders to answer the recruiters' calls. New legislation such as the Pensionen brief of 1503 was passed, threatening penalties of imprisonment and confiscation of property. The penalties were not strictly applied, however. In 1494 for example an October law threatening the death penalty on transgressors had already been diluted by that December into a sentence of five weeks' imprisonment on bread and water. The *knaben* were well aware that, whatever their official posturing, many members of the Diet were accepting bribes and undercover payments to turn a blind eye to unofficial recruitment. Impatient with the vacillations and hypocrisy of their leaders, the *knaben* streamed out of the alps individually or in groups into the service of the surrounding powers.

The unauthorized recruitment of Swiss mercenaries reached its height with Charles VIII's expedition to Italy in 1494-5. Intent on pursuing a dynastic claim for the Kingdom of Naples, the young Charles started the campaign that would involve the French in half a century of war in Italy. In the autumn of 1494 the largest army seen for a hundred years was assembled at Lyons. Despite a strict ban by the Swiss authorities, the *knaben* swarmed out of the valleys to join the French army. 8000 Swiss joined the King, while a further 2000 recruited by the Bailli of Dijon joined the King's uncle, Louis of Orleans, at Genoa. Ambassadors sent by the Diet instructing them to return home were completely ignored.(7)

Leaving Louis to hold Turin, Charles set off down the leg of Italy towards Naples. The French army met practically no resistance, especially after French and Swiss troops massacred the inhabitants of Mordano, one of the few fortresses to resist the French advance. On New Year's Eve Charles entered Rome with the 10,000 Swiss at the head of the army. The Swiss were described by Jovius in a famous passage: "They carried short swords and long spears made of ashwood tipped with an iron point. A quarter were armed with huge four-pointed axes. These could be used for hacking as well as stabbing, needed two hands and were called 'alabardes'. For every thousand men there were a hundred arquebuses that shoot small lead balls at the enemy. The Swiss give little worth in the battle to armour, helmets or shields, and these are only used by the leaders and front ranks. After the Swiss came 5000 bowmen from Gascony and the rest of the infantry, but they looked unimpressive compared with the powerful stature and proud bearing of the Swiss."(8)

Although by February Charles had completed the conquest of Naples, the foolhardiness of the venture was already becoming apparent. With the Italian states finally submerging their differences to provide a united opposition that cut the French army from its base in Piedmont, and with no fleet or hope of relief, Charles was in a critical position. He therefore decided to return north with 10,000 men, including 3000 Swiss. The rest of the army was left in Naples to occupy the newly conquered territory. This occupying force was decimated by sickness and disease and only 200 Swiss eventually found their way home, bringing back their flags, but little else other than venereal disease.

Charles's route northward was threatened by the alliance of Italian states which had moved to block the passes across the Apennines. It seemed that the French would have to abandon their artillery. Earlier on the march north, however, the Swiss had run amok and looted the small town of Pontremoli, massacring every man, woman and child in a drunken orgy of bloodlust. To make up for their shameful behaviour the Swiss offered to carry the artillery across the mountains. Led by the French General Le Tremouille they manhandled fourteen guns each eight foot long and weighing nine hundred pounds across pathways unpassable by draught animals during five days at the height of summer. As Commines wrote, the Swiss carried not just the guns but the whole French army across the mountains.

The Italian alliance brought the French to battle at the crossing point of the Taro River near the town of Fornovo, on a plain wide enough for the Italians to deploy their cavalry. The French army was forced to march across the Italian front in order to continue its northerly advance. The 3000 Swiss formed a square and took position as the French vanguard, ready to clear the road. Fornovo was a cavalry battle, however, and the Swiss played little part in the French victory other than beating off with scornful laughter a half-hearted cavalry attack on their square.

In late July Charles finally regained the safety of Piedmont with the remains of his army. In the meantime, however, Louis of Orleans had attacked Milan and was besieged in Novara when Charles arrived back in Turin. Antoine de Bessey was urgently dispatched to raise another 5000 Swiss to join a French relieving force. Lured by the prospect of plundering the rich Italian plain, the Swiss again poured out of the mountains in answer to the French call. Ignoring the entreaties of the Swiss authorities, 20,000 men descended on Novara. 8000 of these were taken into the French army to join the 2000 remaining Swiss that had accompanied Charles from Naples. A truce was negotiated between France and Milan before this new army saw action.

To put in perspective the size of the problem this uncontrolled exodus gave the Diet, around one-fifth of the total adult male population of the Confederation had crossed the Alps looking to enrol as mercenaries in the

French army. The cantons were left denuded of the labour needed to maintain normal economic activities and defenceless against any aggression from another quarter. The problem of controlling the numbers of mercenaries and directing which armies they should serve remained throughout the Italian wars until the Capitulation system eventually brought some semblance of order.

As well as hiring the Swiss themselves, several of the European powers sought to copy the new long pike tactics by producing their own home-grown army of pikemen. The Swiss were contracted to train some of these new infantry forces.

Following the French defeat by Maximilian at Guinegatte, Louis XI resolved to overhaul the French army, in particular by introducing Swiss-style heavy infantry. In 1480 a training camp was set up at Pont-de-l'Arche near Rouen for 10,000 French footsoldiers. 6000 Swiss were hired to spend one month at the camp training the French before the King himself in the drill and weapons-handling techniques used in the pike squares. These French pikemen were immediately involved in the war with Maximilian and became the Bande and eventually the Regiment de Picardie, the first French regiment after the Guards.

In 1483 Ferdinand of Spain also hired a group of Swiss mercenaries to serve as an example for his new infantry. Little is known of their activities and in fact Spanish tactics developed in a different direction to emerge as the *tercios*.

The third army to adopt Swiss tactics was that of Maximilian. During the decade after Morat, Maximilian built up his own force of infantry, directly copying the arms and tactics of the Swiss. These troops became famous as the *landsknechts*. As they were initially recruited in Bavaria and Swabia, the parts of South Germany closest to Switzerland, many of the *landsknechts* were well aware of Swiss tactics and had even fought in the Confederate armies. Indeed, one of the captains charged by Maximilian with establishing the *landsknechts* was Wilhelm Herter, who despite originating from the German town of Tübingen had been the *ordnungsmacher* for the Swiss at Morat. For half a century, as we will see, the *landsknechts* were bitter enemies of the Swiss and professional rivals for any mercenary contracts on offer. About the only technical difference between the *landsknechts* and the Swiss was that the former held their pikes slanting upward while the Swiss held theirs nearer the middle slanting down.(9)

Charles VIII had one further lasting impact on the history of the Swiss in foreign service. In 1497 he formed the first permanent corps of Swiss in the French army as his personal bodyguard. Originally called the "*Compagnie des Cent Guards de Corps du Roi Suisses*" this guard became known as the

"*Compagnie des Cent Suisses*". The *Cent Suisses* were charged with the personal protection of the king. The soldiers themselves had to be a minimum of six feet tall and of the Catholic religion. They served under Swiss laws and enjoyed a variety of special privileges. On the other hand they were expected to protect the King to the death, a fate which befell them to a man at Pavia thirty years later. The *Cent Suisses* were commanded by a French Captain-Colonel, a highly prestigious position held by only sixteen nobles between the first, Louis de Menthon, and the disbanding of the company in 1791. (See Appendix VII.) Their colours carried the Swiss cross and the motto "*Es est fiducia gentis*" (such is the fidelity of this nation). The colourful costume of the *Cent Suisses* was initially yellow and red, then black and silver, before settling in the seventeenth century on the royal colours of red, white and blue.

VI

The Italian Wars

"The unity and glory of their armies have made this savage uncultured people famous."
Guicciardini, *History of Italy*.

"They go forth of their country in great companies together, and whosoever lacketh soldiers, there they proffer their service for small wages. This is the only craft they have to get their living by. They maintain their life by seeking their death."
Sir Thomas More, *Utopia*, 1506

The wars that took place in Italy in the first quarter of the sixteenth century involved a constant shifting in the alliances between the participants that makes their understanding quite complicated. The Swiss involvement is, however, more straightforward and can be divided into three phases. In the first, which lasted from 1499 to 1509, the Swiss supplied mercenaries to serve in the armies of Louis XII of France. In the second, from 1510-1515, Swiss armies took to the field in their own right against the French. This period ended with the Battle of Marignano in 1515. In the third, from 1516 onwards the Swiss again served as mercenaries in the French army, under Francis I. Throughout the period, unofficial Swiss contingents served in other and occasionally opposing forces, but the main thrusts of the Swiss activities were the three with or against the French.

This was a pivotal period in Swiss military history from both a political and a military point of view. Politically, the Confederation entered the sixteenth century having assured its independence and tentatively willing to experiment with a role as a major European power. After the defeat at Marignano, however, the Swiss drew back within their borders and developed the policy of armed neutrality that is still followed by modern day

Switzerland. Militarily, the Swiss heavy infantry entered the Italian wars having recently defeated the Burgundians and Austrians, and as the most feared army in Europe. But at Marignano the Swiss were defeated by new combined arms tactics that would thenceforth relegate the Swiss infantry to being one arm of a multi-arm force.

Only seventeen years earlier, however, when Charles VIII died unexpectedly in April, 1498, and Louis of Orleans took the throne as Louis XII, none of these changes could have been foreseen. Louis promptly renewed the alliance with the cantons for a period of ten years, promising annual payments of 20,000 florins in exchange for the right to recruit mercenaries. Six months later, in October, 1499, he invaded northern Italy with the aim of reconquering Milan from Ludovic Sforza. The French army included 12,000 Swiss mercenaries, recruited once more by the invaluable Antoine de Bessey and his agents. Having taken Milan, Louis dismissed most of the Swiss without pay. Aggrieved by this treatment, 6000 Swiss crossed to Sforza's side to assist him in retaking Milan, causing the long dreaded confrontation of Swiss against Swiss to take place early the following year at Novara. The Swiss supporting Sforza were besieged in the town by a French army containing the main official contingent of Swiss troops. To avoid a conflict the Swiss captains on the two sides met and agreed that the troops besieged in Novara could leave the city unmolested provided they surrendered Sforza to the French. Despite the agreement some of the Swiss tried to smuggle Sforza out of the city disguised and hidden in their ranks. For 200 livres, a Hans Turmann of Uri betrayed the plan, however, and Sforza was arrested by the French.(1) Turmann was executed when he returned home, but the "treason of Novara" was instrumental in gaining the Swiss the reputation for duplicity and disloyalty that became enshrined in the dictum "No money, no Swiss."

While in the case of the wretched Turmann this reputation was richly deserved, the issue of Swiss loyalty is more complicated. Only rarely did the Swiss change sides or refuse to fight in order to obtain an increase in their wages. Problems generally arose with the Swiss because the king who had hired them could not or would not pay them as promised. Louis XII was particularly negligent in this respect and it was his refusal to pay his mercenaries that caused 6000 Swiss to change sides and eventually led to the confrontation at Novara.

Apart from personal meanness, Louis was an early example of the temptation for rulers to hire more troops than they could pay. During the Italian wars, armies increased substantially in size. Charles VIII invaded Naples with 20,000 men, while twenty years later Francis I fielded over 30,000 men at Marignano. The new infantry tactics developed by the Swiss, and the enhanced ability of towns protected by the sophisticated defensive works of the *trace italienne* to resist sieges, both led to the need for more troops, especially footsoldiers. Mercenaries were available for hire to meet this demand, but the need to hire large numbers of expensive mercenaries placed increasing financial strains on the resources of the princes who hired them. Arrears of pay was a constant bone of contention in the armies of the sixteenth and seventeenth centuries.

Although the reaction of all the mercenaries (not just Swiss but also *landsknechts*, *tercios* and others) to arrears of pay was the same — grumbling and discontent, leading in the last resort to either mutiny or mass desertion — the Swiss have often been singled out as the most cynical and turncoat of the lot. Certainly, even without difficulties over pay, the Swiss troops were at this time notoriously difficult to control. The quarrelsomeness and rapacity of the *knaben* led to constant problems of discipline. These were compounded by the lack of decisive leadership. The Swiss captains took major decisions by consensus after lengthy democratic discussion, and frustrated French generals had to wait helplessly while the Swiss debated their cause with "the kind of cantankerous democracy one finds in a successful trades union".(2) It is hardly surprising that the Swiss did indeed become adept at downing tools or threatening to return home at critical moments in order to obtain arrears of pay. In Italy the Swiss were close to home and it was relatively easy for them to decamp and recross the Alps when all other recourses failed.

The French General Monluc summed up the difficulty of working with the Swiss. "It is true that they are veritable soldiers and form the backbone of an army, but you must never be short of money if you want them, and they will never take promises in lieu of cash."(3) Nevertheless, whatever the difficulties, there were never enough of them, and the Great Powers were falling over themselves to obtain the services of these awkward but formidable soldiers.

The uneasy relationship between Louis and the Swiss continued throughout the first decade of the century. In 1503 Bessey was again caught recruiting illegally and this time was imprisoned. The same year an unofficial expedition of 400 men under the leadership of Ulrich von Hohensax seized and occupied Bellinzona. Despite these frictions, the French officially raised 4000 troops in the cantons. In 1507 a further army of 4000 was raised, but later that year the Diet formally withdrew all troops from French service in protest at the continued lack of payments.(4)

During these years the Swiss troops served principally in the 'small war'(5) that was being waged in Italy. In another well known passage, Monluc described such a war as a matter of "fights, encounters, skirmishes, ambushes, an occasional battle, minor sieges, assaults, escalades, captures and surprises of towns".(6) Although the reputation of the Swiss was based on the success of the pike square in the *bataille rangée*, the hardy independent mountaineers were also ideally suited to this sporadic guerrilla warfare.

The sketches of Niklaus Manuel and Urs Graf vividly portray the Swiss soldiers of this period. Their pictures show mature bearded men of proud bearing, always carrying either halberd or pike. Their usual dress was a short collarless tunic, reaching to the waist and with billowing sleeves. The lower body from waist to knees was clothed in tight-fitting culottes. The fashion was to sew multicoloured bands on the trousers as decoration, and many of the troops affected a jutting codpiece. The white cross was prominently displayed on tunics and trousers. Although eschewing body armour, many pikemen wore a breastplate and most halberdiers a padded leather jerkin as protection against both the weather and glancing blows in battle. Usual headgear was an iron helm or a leather cap, which the captains decorated with ostrich feathers.

Three larger battles of the first phase of the Italian wars are worth commenting on from a Swiss viewpoint. The storming of Genoa in 1507 was a typical example of the exasperating contradictions involved in employing the Swiss at this time. Of the 8000 Swiss serving in the French army, 6000 from the main cantons refused to take part in an assault on the city on the grounds that their contract did not require them to participate in sieges. However, 1700 volunteers from the small Swiss allies(7) under the command of an experienced captain called Oswald Rotz accomplished a notable feat of arms in twice scaling the promontory of Genoa and taking the citadel. Prevented from sacking the captured city, the Swiss pillaged the town of Alessandria instead on their homeward journey as recompense.

At Cerignola in 1503 the great Spanish General Gonsalvo de Cordova first used one of the tactics that would eventually neutralize the pike square as an offensive force. Gonsalvo placed his arquebusiers in a position on the lower slopes of a hill behind a ditch and bank. The advancing Swiss square was unable to cross the ditch under fire and was forced to retreat in disorder.

The most important French victory during this first phase of the Italian wars was against Venice at Agnadello in 1509. The French forces consisted of 13,000 cavalry and 12,000 infantry, two-thirds of the latter being Swiss. The Venetians had about 30,000 men, including a core of Romagnol pike infantry trained in the Swiss style, but were thoroughly defeated in open field by the French army.

In 1509 the ten-year alliance between Louis XII and the Swiss expired and was not renewed by the Diet. Louis' cavalier attitude to the arrears of pay owing to the Swiss troops was the main cause of the rupture, but there were also a number of political considerations. Anti-French feeling had been increasing in the cantons for several years. The people were more and more resentful of French recruiting methods and there was a popular backlash against the methods of Bessey and the other French recruiters with their liberal dispensation of bribes and disregard for Swiss laws. The reaction against the open French corruption of Swiss politicians created fertile ground for Zwingli and the Reformation.

Distrust of France was particularly widespread in the Waldstaette. The occupation of Bellinzona in 1503 had realized a longstanding ambition in the mountain cantons to control the southern access to the Gotthard.(8) They saw the consolidation of the French position in Milan as a threat to their new possessions south of the Alps.

The feelings against France found their expression in the politics of a forceful leader who emerged at this time. In 1499, at the age of thirty-four, Mathew Schiner became Archbishop of Sion in the Valais and the papal delegate to the Confederation. Like the Waldstaette, the Valais was the direct neighbour of Milan and was fearful that the French would try to annexe Savoy and the Valais in order to guarantee access to the Po Valley. Schiner was strongly anti-French, both as a Valaisan and in keeping with the papal policy to see the French out of Italy. Schiner's personal asceticism and his oratorical skills enabled him to reach the people with his anti-French message. In 1510 he succeeded in negotiating an alliance between the Pope and the Swiss Confederation. This included a provision for the Holy See to hire 6000 Swiss mercenaries in its defence. But in the main the Swiss troops fought in Italy for the next five years not as mercenaries but as the army of the Confederation. The Swiss policy was overtly to support Maximilian Sforza's claim to the Duchy of Milan and to protect the Papal States, but their real aim was to force the French out of Italy. The rupture with France was widened further by Louis' decision to replace the Swiss with their bitter professional rivals the *Landsknechts*. In 1511 Schiner became a Cardinal and the Swiss joined the Holy See, Venice, Spain and England in the Holy League against France.

Swiss troops descended on Italy with their new Papal ally in the inconclusive "Chiasso Expedition" of 1510. In November of the following year 10,000 men took part in the "Cold Winter Expedition" which was again inconclusive as the French avoided being brought to battle. In May, 1512, however, 24,000 men assembled at Chur for the decisive campaign that became known as the "Pavia Expedition". Unusually for the Swiss an overall Commander-in-Chief was appointed in the person of Ulrich von Hohensax, who had been one of the leaders at Frastanz in the Swabian War, and in the capture of Bellinzona, as well as many other campaigns.(9) Descending on to the Swiss plains Hohensax divided his forces into three columns each of around 8000 men(10), all preceded by the violent aggressive *enfants perdus* led by Ludwig von Erlach of Berne. The Swiss advanced rapidly westwards taking one after another of the Italian towns, including the key stronghold of

Pavia. Under constant pressure the French were unable to consolidate their forces and stand in a good defensive position. The harassment of the *enfants perdus* was so vigorous that at one point several hundred stripped naked and swam a river, halberds in hand, in their eagerness to get at the enemy. In only six weeks the demoralized French army was forced out of Italy and back across the Mont Cenis passes into France. Leaving 6000 Swiss troops to protect the reinstalled Sforza in Milan, the remainder of the expedition returned home, laden with booty and fêted as the liberators of Italy. The only permanent gain made by the Confederation from this campaign, however, was the annexation of the territory around Locarno and Lugano.

The following June, 1513, Louis recrossed the Alps at the head of an army of 20,000 men intent on recovering the Milanais. The Swiss troops left to defend Sforza retreated to the town of Novara. The French laid siege and opened a hundred-metre breach. Although attack after attack was repulsed the Swiss position looked increasingly desperate. At midnight on the 5th, however, the French commander Le Tremouille became aware of the imminent arrival of a Swiss relieving force. 6000 men under the banners of Berne, Solothurn, Fribourg and Basle reached Novara after a forced march over the Gotthard, and a further 4000 from the eastern cantons under Ulrich von Hohensax were another day's march behind.

The French force consisted of 3500 cavalry and 10,000 infantry, the latter including 6000 *landsknechts*, and with some 26 pieces of artillery. In order to avoid being attacked by the relieving force with the still active garrison at his rear, Tremouille withdrew to a position about four kilometres south-east of Novara. Not unreasonably expecting the Swiss to rest after marching three hundred kilometres in ten days and await their second relief column, Tremouille took no urgent defensive measures that night to fortify his position. The Swiss held their council of war, however, and decided that rather than wait for Hohensax they would attack immediately at dawn. The opportunity for a surprise attack was irresistible and it would probably have been impossible anyway to hold the adrenalized *knaben* from hurling themselves on the hated *landsknechts*. To conceal their intentions the Swiss ostentatiously celebrated the relief of Novara throughout the night.

Including the defenders of the town, the Swiss numbered about 9000, nearly all infantry as usual but with a relatively small proportion of pikemen. The plan was for the *vorhut* to maximise the advantage of surprise by rushing the French artillery, while the main squares would circle the enemy and fall on his rear. In practice, however, much of the advantage of surprise was lost by the impetuosity of the *enfants perdus*, who advanced too far ahead of the main force.(11) While they were able to hold down a large portion of the French forces, including most of the cavalry, the French were able to move their artillery to face the main Swiss encircling movement. A small force of about a thousand Swiss circled to the left and sacked the French baggage train. The main force, 6 to 7000 strong, having circled to the right but lost the advantage of surprise, had no alternative than to try a frontal charge on the *landsknechts* lined up behind their artillery.

The Swiss formed a tight square and attacked at storm pace. Despite heavy casualties from the French artillery (700 men fell in three minutes including the captain, Benedict von Weingarten) the square held its ranks and kept up its momentum. Four hundred *enfants perdus* were sent off in a wider circling movement to clear the artillery and the Swiss were finally able to fall on the *landsknechts* where a bitter hand-to-hand fight to the death took place. At the end of the slaughter all 6000 *landsknechts* lay dead as well as 2000 Swiss. The remains of the French army fled and again straggled westward across the Alps out of Italy.

The Swiss victory at Novara was achieved by blind courage and bloodlust rather than the application of superior arms and tactics. It was the last triumph by the Swiss-style homogeneous infantry force. The Swiss had become far too complacent about not adapting their tactics to changing developments in the art of war. Blinded by their string of successes since Grandson, proud of their individual courage and strength, lacking a military leader of vision, they stagnated technically while their opponents developed new methods for defeating a purely infantry force. Gonsalvo had already shown at Cerignola how the use of a physical obstruction could halt the advance of a pike square. Then at Novara the French started to implement the combined arms tactics of artillery, cavalry and infantry that would win the day at Marignano, with the artillery playing a much enhanced role. The Swiss had never suffered such heavy losses, at least half of which came from artillery fire during their advance. Although the French cavalry played little part at Novara, these also were already starting to operate as a cohesive force rather than a group of individual knights. Finally, in the *landsknechts* the French had found an alternative infantry, which was defeated by the Swiss, but at least stood its ground and offered a serious resistance. The Swiss won the Battle of Novara, but only just, and the signs were there of the developments that would lead to the decline of the Swiss military system.

At the same time cracks were appearing in the political and social structure of the Confederation. One of the principal causes of dissension was the issue of mercenary service. Even while the Swiss army had been winning spectacular victories over the armies of Louis XII, French recruiters had continued to be active in the cantons. A whole network of agents permeated the Confederation, directed from across the border as well as clandestinely by French diplomatic representatives to the Diet. Many of the political leaders of the cantons were open recipients of French presents and pensions, and the largesse found its way to all levels of Swiss society. Several thousand

1. Le Pont du Diable, the bridge across the Schoellenen Gorge that opened up the Gotthard Pass into Italy during the first quarter of the thirteenth century (from Baron Zurlauben's *Tableaux Topographiques de la Suisse*, 1780).

2. The Battle of Morat, 1476, in which the Swiss Army annihilated the forces of Charles the Bold. The Burgundian Army, then considered the best in Europe, lost 10,000 dead (from the *Schwytzer Chronica* of Johannes Stumpf, 1548).

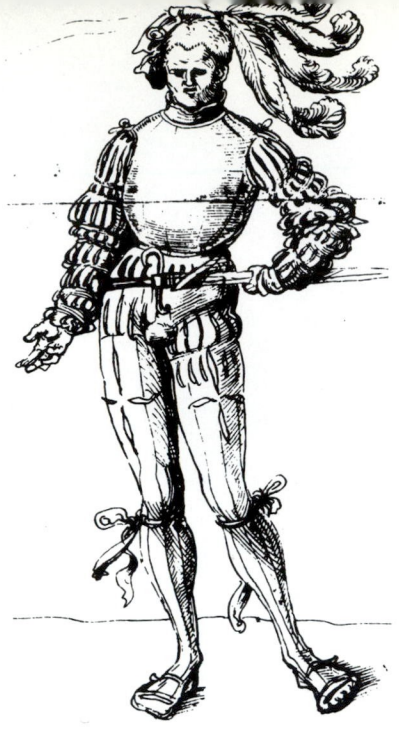

3. Swiss pikeman armed with sword and wearing typical billowing tunic and tight fitting culottes (drawn around the year 1500 by Niklaus Manuel of Berne).

4. Swiss captain from the Italian wars of the early sixteenth century, armed with halberd. (contemporary drawing by Niklaus Manuel of Berne).

5. Battle scene from the Italian wars (contemporary drawing by Urs Graf of Solothurn, who like Manuel was a soldier as well as an artist).

6. Swiss captains drawn at about the time of the Battle of Marignano in 1515 by Urs Graf.

7. An executioner carries out the sentence passed by a tribunal (from the *Schwytzer Chronica* of Johannes Stumpf, 1548).

8. Wilhelm Fröhlich (1505-1562), the victor of Cerisoles and the most important of the Swiss colonels in French service as regimental formations were introduced in the middle of the sixteenth century (from *Vie des Hommes Illustres* by André de Thévet).

9. Cardinal Schiner accompanying the troops into battle at Marignano in 1515, having tricked the Swiss into giving battle under unfavourable circumstances. After Marignano the Swiss never again fought outside Switzerland except as mercenaries (by Hans-Melchior Füssli in 1713).

mercenaries, largely from the western cantons, drifted secretly across the borders and served with the French army in Picardy, not directly confronting the official Swiss army in Italy but nevertheless releasing additional French troops from the north to do so. The revulsion against French influence and the bribery and corruption it entailed spilled over some weeks after Novara into popular uprisings against the authorities in Lucerne, Berne and Solothurn.

Partly to distract attention from this issue, the Diet decided in August, 1513, to support its allies in the Holy League with an invasion of France. An army of 30,000 men was assembled at Besançon under Hans von Watteville. Unusually this army included both three thousand cavalry and a strong park of artillery(12), both provided by the Swiss ally, Maximilian of Austria. The Swiss laid siege to Dijon, which was defended by Le Tremouille in his capacity as Governor of Burgundy. Within days Tremouille capitulated and negotiated a Treaty that included payment of a war indemnity of 400,000 crowns and a promise to cease recruiting on Swiss soil. 20,000 ecus were paid on the spot to a dozen of the Swiss captains. Content with these terms, the Swiss immediately decamped and returned home, upon which Louis announced that Tremouille had no authority to negotiate such terms and refused to ratify the Treaty.

The Treaty of Dijon was seen both within and outside the Confederation as another proof of Swiss venality and shortsightedness. The opportunity to secure major strategic gains in the Franche Comté was sacrificed for cash in hand, while the Confederation's allies in the north, the Emperor Maximilian and Henry VIII of England, were left exposed in their invasion of Picardy by the Swiss withdrawal. The 400,000 crowns which Louis refused to pay were added to the list of Swiss grievances, assisting Schiner and the anti-French party in retaining control of Swiss policy for a while longer. There was uproar in the cantons that their representatives could so easily be bought off and the probity of the Swiss leadership again came into question. The sudden death of Louis XII on the first of January, 1515, and the accession of Francis I changed nothing, as Francis was equally intent on pushing his claim to the Duchy of Milan. Although one of Francis' first actions, on 2 January, was to request a safe conduct to the Diet for ambassadors charged with negotiating peace, negotiations foundered and in the early summer of 1515 the French started to assemble a new army for another invasion of Italy.

The Diet acted forcefully to news of the French mobilization and despatched a further 14,000 men to reinforce Milan, bringing the Swiss force up to 23,000 men. Following the plan of the Bernese captain, Albrecht vom Stein, the Swiss took up positions in the Alpine foothills with the intention of preventing the French from crossing into Italy. The mountain cantons were against this strategy, preferring to remain in Milan where there were better opportunities to plunder. Bitter quarrels came close to open mutiny and vom Stein himself was manhandled by some troops from Schwyz before order could be restored.

While the Swiss bickered, Francis achieved a notable coup. Avoiding the regular passes of the Mont Cenis and the Genevre, the French brought their army secretly across the mule paths of the little-used Colle Madalena and formed a bridgehead on the Italian side before the Swiss could respond. Although the Bernese troops remained anxious to defend the foothills, the troops of the mountain cantons fell back on Milan, dragging the whole Swiss army with them.(13) Despite a further reinforcement of 15,000 men sent by the Diet, the French had achieved their first objective by establishing themselves on the Italian plain.

Francis again initiated discussions with the Confederation and a tentative peace was negotiated at Gallarate in early September. In return for abandoning the Duke of Milan and leaving the Swiss possessions south of the Alps to the French, the cantons would obtain the 400,000 ecus owing from the Treaty of Dijon, plus a further 300,000 compensation for their Italian possessions and a further 300,000 ecus to reimburse their expenses for the present expedition. Francis dredged his resources in Italy to make an immediate downpayment of 150,000 ecus to seal the Treaty.

Again there was violent disagreement among the Swiss. The troops from the central and eastern cantons, encouraged by Cardinal Schiner, saw the terms of Gallerate as a betrayal of the aims for which they had fought at Novara. On the other hand, Albrecht vom Stein promptly accepted the terms and on 12 September led 10,000 men from the western cantons back across the Gotthard.(14) Unrest and indecision spread through the remaining troops, further contingents preparing to head for home.

Meanwhile, the French army had arrived outside Milan and set up a fortified camp at Marignano, using the deep canals that covered the area as defensive features. The numbers involved on both sides are subject to a wide spread of estimates, but it is probable that the French forces totalled something over 30,000 men. The army was positioned in three consecutive lines facing Milan. A very strong vanguard of some 15,000 men was drawn up behind 72 large artillery pieces and 6000 arquebusiers. Francis himself commanded the main battle, drawn up about a kilometre further back, and including the gendarmerie and 6000 *landsknechts* known as the Black Bands of Guelders. A further 8000 men were held in reserve in the rearguard, while the Venetians, at that time allied to the French, had not yet arrived.

During the afternoon of 13 September Cardinal Schiner used a ruse to trick the wavering Swiss into battle. The general alarm was given after no more than a minor skirmish between a French cavalry detachment and a Swiss guard post and the whole Swiss army poured out of Milan to answer the call.

Although realizing they had been tricked, the troops' fighting spirits had been aroused and they could not be restrained from marching immediately on the French camp despite the lateness of the hour. They probably totalled about 20,000 men, but at any event substantially less than the French.

Approaching Marignano the Swiss formed into three squares in echelon. The *gewalthaufen* was formed by the mountain cantons led by Imhof and Püntiner of Uri, Kätzi of Schwyz, Würch of Unterwalden, Tschudi of Glarus and Schwarzmaurer of Zug. Cardinal Schiner and the later leader of the Reformation, Zwingli, were in the ranks. The *vorhut* on the right was formed by the eastern cantons and the Grey Leagues under Roüst of Zurich and the *nachhut* on the left from Lucerne and Basle under Hertenstein and Offenburg. The *enfants perdus* preceded the main squares led by Werner Steiner of Zug. With no more than six cannon and 200 horsemen, the artillery and cavalry arms were as usual practically non-existent on the Swiss side.

The Swiss reached the battlefield at about five in the afternoon and had worked themselves into such a frenzy that they could not be held back from immediately attacking the enemy. A commanding general would never have fought the battle. Apart from the lateness of the hour, the inferiority in numbers, the lack of artillery and cavalry, the terrain with its irrigation ditches and orchards was entirely unsuited to manoeuvring a large body of infantry in close formations. There was also no possibility of surprise and the only tactic was a full frontal assault. Despite all these disadvantages the squares advanced on the French vanguard.

As heavy artillery and arquebus fire took their toll on the Swiss squares, the *enfants perdus* succeeded in fording the ditches and, closely followed by the *gewalthaufen*, attacked the French vanguard. After an hour of mounting Swiss pressure the French wavered and Francis committed the main French force to the battle. The Black Bands reinforced the French centre against the Swiss push while the Gendarmerie launched more than thirty attacks on the flank of the Swiss squares, forcing them to turn to defend against the cavalry which took impetus away from the advance. Nevertheless, slowly but inexorably the Swiss advance continued, pushing the French back nearly a kilometre. The bitter fighting went on until midnight when the moon disappeared and darkness covered the battlefield.

The troops on both sides rested as best they could where they stood. Even the King was reduced to drinking water from a body-filled ditch. On the Swiss side a Council of War was held to decide whether to break off or continue the battle. Messengers were sent back to the cantons claiming the victory, but it was decided to press on for a more decisive result.

At dawn the blasts of the warhorns(15) called the Swiss to reassemble and three new squares were formed. The French also reformed their lines with the Black Bands holding the centre and the artillery and cavalry threatening the flanks. The Swiss again advanced straight on the enemy despite the murderous artillery fire and the harassment of the French cavalry. Closing with the *landsknechts* the French centre was again pushed back one hundred metres, but then the Swiss advance ran out of steam. Weakened by cold and hunger after the long night, their originally inferior numbers reduced by the French artillery, the strength of the Swiss had been sapped. Several times they built a wedge to try to restart the advance but the force was no longer there to push on. One gigantic Swiss fought through alone to touch the French cannons before being cut down.

At this point, about ten in the morning, the fresh force of Venetians arrived on the field and the Swiss had finally to accept the reality that the battle was lost. The trumpets blared to reassemble and one huge open square was formed with the wounded and flags in the centre. Slowly and deliberately the Swiss fought their way off the battlefield more like victors than vanquished in a retreat that was the marvel of their contemporaries. Repeated cavalry attacks could not break through the pike square, even when it had to cross a last deep ditch, and the Swiss withdrew defeated but not routed. In adversity the Swiss showed the iron discipline that often failed them off the battlefield.

Despite the legendary retreat and the heroic endeavours, Marignano was a bloody and stunning defeat for the Swiss. 12,000 dead lay on the battlefield, about half of them from the Swiss side. Within two days the Swiss had left Milan and returned home. The invincible pike squares had been defeated by new military tactics and the Swiss never again fought outside Switzerland except as mercenaries.

The significance of Marignano has been succinctly described by the English historian F. L. Taylor: "Marignano proved to the world that an army of infantry only, however bravely it may fight, is bound to fail before a skilful combination of infantry, cavalry and artillery."(16)

The previous string of resounding successes had allowed the Swiss leaders to become complacent in the belief that the pike square could continue to steamroller all opposition into the ground. While Swiss tactics had become stereotyped, however, alternative tactics were being developed to counteract the pike square.

The first response had been to face the Swiss with a similarly armed and deployed force of pikemen. The *landsknechts* were the main Swiss rivals in this role and meetings between the two were always bitter and bloody.

At the same time improvements were being made to firearms. The sheer size of the pike square had always made it relatively easy to hit and a cannonball ploughing through the ranks did enormous damage. A primary objective of the Swiss was always to overrun the enemy guns, an objective in which they succeeded at Novara, though with bloody losses, and failed at Marignano. The French had greatly improved the mobility and therefore tactical effectiveness of the artillery by mounting light bronze cannon on two-wheeled carriages pulled by horses. The manoeuvrability of their artillery was one reason for the French success at Marignano. Technical improvements that made the arquebus more reliable were also increasing the value of handheld firearms. At Marignano for the first time the arquebuses were able to keep up a more or less continuous fire rather than just getting off one or two shots at the beginning of the battle. Portable firearms were by this time sufficiently well developed to hold a well defended position against frontal assaults by the pikes.

Arquebuses and cannon still had a desperately slow rate of fire, however, and the immediate tactical challenge was to find ways to hold up the implacable advance of the pike square long enough for repeated volleys of firearms to be trained on it. The objective was to turn back the square or at least to draw off its strength so that its effectiveness in the push of pike was severely reduced. The use or creation of a physical obstacle was the best solution. At Cerignola a ditch and parapet had halted the Swiss advance; at Marignano the irrigation trenches running across the battlefield hindered the Swiss manoeuvres, and at Bicocca a few years later the defence of a parapet behind a sunken road allowed the *landsknechts* to destroy the Swiss square.

The second method of slowing the advance of the pike square was the use of repeated cavalry attacks on the flanks. Cavalry were still unable to break through the pike wall but they could force the square to halt and face about to protect its flanks, giving time for the artillery to take effect. At Marignano the French launched more than thirty cavalry attacks for this purpose.

Combined arms tactics, consolidating cavalry, infantry and firearms, would become much more sophisticated during the sixteenth century, especially with the Spanish *tercios*. 1515 was, however, the specific date when a homogeneous force of infantry was no longer able to hold its own on the battlefield. During fifty years the pike square had come full circle. Originally developed as a defensive formation against cavalry attack, the squares then became attacking units able to advance and crush any less compact body of men. Now that ways had been found to hinder the advance of the square, they returned to their original purpose as a defensive unit. On an open battlefield the square became the defensive shelter for arquebusiers against cavalry. Pike squares would continue to play an important role for another 200 years, but their control passed from the Swiss to the generals of other nations able to raise and direct a multi-armed force.

Only such a massive defeat as Marignano could demonstrate unequivocally to the Swiss how sterile their tactics had become. The courage and recklessness of the troops in the face of the enemy had previously covered the tactical failings. A competent general in control of his troops would never have attacked the superior French position at Marignano, especially with a numerical disadvantage of three to two. Even then the result was a "close run thing." The participation of vom Stein's 10,000 men or the late arrival of the Venetians could have postponed the Swiss decline. As it was, even pride in the legendary retreat could not cancel the fact nor the manner of the defeat.

Marignano was the last battle the Swiss Confederation ever fought on foreign soil. After this stunning defeat, a policy of deliberate neutrality replaced any aspirations towards external expansion. A number of political considerations explain the change in Swiss policy, as well as the military reverse.

In the half-century up to 1515 the geopolitical situation in Europe had crystallized. During the two centuries that the Confederation had been fighting for independence, it had been surrounded by weak neighbours — a France racked in a struggle for supremacy between the king and his barons, an overextended Burgundy, the fragmented states of south Germany and northern Italy, and an ineffectual Austria. In 1516, however, with the death of Ferdinand and the addition of Spain to the Habsburg Empire, all the Confederation's neighbours were either Habsburg or Valois. It would have been infinitely more difficult for an expansionist Swiss state to emerge between these two power blocs.

In any case, by this time the Swiss no longer had the will. The long effort in Italy was simply beyond the Confederation's economic capability. Local agriculture and industry had suffered from shortage of manpower. A large proportion of the labour force was serving in the armies, killed in action, or indirectly supporting the army as transporters, armourers, recruiters and so on. After Marignano there was a noticeable physical and moral fatigue, as though the small nation was exhausted by its efforts.

The third important consideration was the constitutional structure of the Confederation. The thirteen cantons were actually sovereign states bound together by a network of alliances in a loose federal structure. Even vaguer arrangements tied the cantons to surrounding states such as the Valais and the Grey Leagues that would eventually become cantons but at this stage were just allies. The cantons followed a whole range of different and sometimes contradictory policies. The long-standing tensions were further aggravated in the sixteenth century by the spread of the Reformation. The only central organization, the Diet, reached its decisions by the painstaking process of consensus, and even then the cantons jealously guarded the right to accept or reject the decisions of the Diet. Lacking a central direction and with the refusal of the cantons to give up any power in favour of a superior organization, the policies of the Confederation were capricious and inconsistent. Often paralysed in its decision-making capability, the

Confederation allowed the opportunity to become a major player on the European stage to pass by default. Vettori, a Florentine contemporary of Machiavelli, writing after the Battle of Novara, described the Swiss as follows: "I can scarcely imagine what army could oppose them...(but) a republic as fragmented cannot make progress; it is not possible for them and they do not wish to rule a large number of subject states or to organize a costly administration; they prefer instead to arrange a more convenient method of financial exploitation through the system of pensions."

Machiavelli himself agreed in a letter to Vettori: "Republicans such as the Swiss will never make great conquests. A striking proof for this is the fact that they could have held Lombardy but did not."(17)

SECTION TWO

THE DEVELOPMENT OF THE
MERCENARY SYSTEM
BICOCCA TO ARQUES
1521-1590

VII

The Special Relationship With France

'A body of Swiss in the French army is like the bones in the human body'
  Marechal Schomberg

'The French have come to believe that without (the Swiss) they cannot win a battle. Because of this, the French are no match for the Swiss, and without Swiss help feel no match for anyone else'
  Machiavelli, *The Prince*

In the days after Marignano Francis redoubled his efforts to win the Swiss back over to the French side. On 7 November, 1515, less than two months after the battle, a provisional peace was signed at Geneva with similar terms to the agreement negotiated at Gallarate. Zurich, by this time heavily influenced by Zwingli and the Reformation, opposed the peace and another year of negotiations was needed before all the cantons signed the Perpetual Peace with France at Fribourg on 21 November, 1516. Two of the leading members of the Diet(1) travelled to Paris to seal the peace and returned laden with presents. On 21 May, 1521, the Perpetual Peace was formally recognized in a Treaty of Alliance, and once more a Swiss delegation under Sebastian von Diesbach of Berne was cordially received at the French court. Zurich again refused to sign the Treaty. Despite continuing representations to the Diet by Henry VIII of England and the Austrian Emperor(2), the Confederation was committed to the special relationship with France that would endure nearly three centuries.

As well as the terms of the political alliance, the Treaty of 1521 also included a number of clauses that would thenceforth govern the supply of Swiss mercenaries to France. The King of France was given the right to raise levies in the cantons, provided he had been attacked in any of his possessions(3). The King would pay all recruiting costs. The levies could be of not less than 6000 and not more than 16,000 men, although this maximum could be exceeded if the King personally took to the field with his army. The Swiss troops could not be split up during the period of war and could only be used on land. Captains and officers would be nominated by the King and confirmed by the cantons, which had to allow the departure of the troops within ten days of being requested. The King could retain the troops as long as he needed them and they could only be refused or recalled if the Confederation were itself at war. Each soldier would receive a monthly wage of four and a half florins, payable from the time he left home. Once the troops had crossed the frontier, the King was committed to pay a minimum of three months' wages even if he no longer needed the men. Other clauses repeated previous agreements such as the payment of two thousand livres to each canton and preferential rates for Swiss merchants and on imports of salt. In these clauses, the Treaty of 1521 established the basic principles under which Swiss mercenaries would serve the Kings of France during the next two hundred and seventy-one years.

Until this time, diplomatic relationships between France and the Confederation had been in the hands of occasional ambassadors, despatched by the French Court to negotiate specific issues with the Diet. Because of the closer relationship envisaged by the alliance, however, Francis decided to establish a permanent embassy in the Confederation. In November, 1522, Louis de Boisrigaut arrived in Solothurn, which became the home of the French Embassy for the duration of the Alliance. Boisrigaut, an experienced diplomat, was the longest serving as well as the first ambassador to the Confederation, remaining at Solothurn until 1544. His role has been described by Edouard Rott as 'almost exclusively occupied with procuring Swiss mercenaries for his masters, with or without the consent of their superiors, and inventing a variety of excuses to pacify the creditors of the crown, whether cantons, captains or individuals.'(4) As a symbol of the new relationship Francis invited his new allies to become the godparents of his third son, Charles, Duke of Angoulême, a flattering gesture that was emulated by many later French kings.

The mechanism for the raising of troops was the Capitulation, a term which may be defined in this context as 'a convention by which one State authorizes another State to raise troops on its territory.' When the King decided that he needed a levy, his ambassador would send a formal request to the Diet. The request would normally be accepted and a capitulation would be agreed that would specify the number of men and the terms of their employment. A typical capitulation would also detail any requirement for special arms such as the percentage of arquebusiers, the pay of the officers and men, lay out regulations on discipline, and specify the duration of the agreement, which in these early capitulations was generally for one campaign.

The French recruiters would then be free to enrol troops according to the terms of the capitulation. Often a canton would commit to raise a complete company,(5) even though the French agents might still be left with the responsibility for the recruiting process on behalf of the canton. Gradually it became customary for experienced local leaders to be entrusted with raising the whole company instead of French agents recruiting each soldier individually. These leaders would then take up the position of captain in the companies they had raised.

To grease the wheels of the system, the French representatives paid out a whole range of 'pensions' and 'gratifications.' These were ostensibly no more than presents or marks of esteem, implying no obligations on the part of the recipient. Opponents of the French would accept them as readily as the French supporters. In practice, however, as the distribution of pensions crept insidiously into the fabric of the society, the whole system gained a justified reputation for bribery and corruption. Opponents of the system, particularly the clergy of the Reformation, thundered against it, and those outside the system increasingly regarded it with suspicion and jealousy. Anne de Montmorency, later one of the most prestigious French nobles of the mid-sixteenth century, commented after his embassy to the Diet in 1522: 'It is so expensive that it costs a remarkable amount of money; because these people demand so many payments and are so unreasonable, that it is almost impossible to please them, so avaricious are they.'(6)

A detailed study made of pensions in the canton of Solothurn, although applying to a period a hundred years later in 1632, demonstrates the scale and variety of the payments made by the French. Firstly, the annual payment of 2000 livres allocated to the canton by the Treaty of 1521 was paid directly into the Cantonal Treasury. A further 3000 livres were openly distributed to prominent citizens according to an officially published pensions list. Highest paid were the major and three other cantonal officials, but a clear indication of the sort of citizens that could be most influential in the recruitment process was the inclusion of thirteen innkeepers, seventeen blacksmiths, thirteen butchers, fourteen tanners on a total list of 157 local personages. An additional official pension of 4000 livres was allocated to provide free places at the University of Paris for two sons of the Cantonal Assembly, who naturally grew up to be prominent francophile citizens in their own right.

Then came the unofficial pensions. That same year a further 5000 livres were secretly distributed in Solothurn to 183 individuals, some on the official list and some not, as 'individual pensions.' An additional group of 'voluntary pensions' totalling 2650 livres was concentrated among only twenty-three of the most prominent citizens, eight of whom came from three families. Most secret of all were the 'gratifications' much larger amounts of thousands of livres at a time, paid for specific services such as the signing of a treaty or turning down a capitulation from an opponent of France. Unfortunately no details of the gratifications are available. Even without knowing of any gratification, however, Mayor von Roll of Solothurn collected that year 192½ livres official pension, 100 livres individual pension and 300 livres voluntary pension, the tidy sum of nearly 600 livres. By comparison the mercenary wage stood at 4½ livres per month. Needless to say, Mayor von Roll could have been counted an avid supporter of the French cause.

Francis took immediate advantage of the Treaty and recruited 20,000 Swiss mercenaries to serve in Italy against the Habsburgs. Prosper Colonna, the general in charge of Charles V's forces, spent the winter of 1521-2 avoiding battle with the French. By April, with pay badly in arrears, the Swiss troops were discontented and near mutinous. When the opportunity arose to attack Colonna in the grounds of the Bicocca, a country house four miles north of Milan, the Swiss captains presented the French General Lautrec with an ultimatum. Either he gave battle next day, giving them the chance to take some spoils in lieu of their arrears of pay, or they would return home.

Colonna had occupied a very strong defensive position. He had thrown up a rampart about six hundred metres long behind a sunken road. The rampart was lined with arquebusiers. His forces included a strong contingent of *landsknechts* under Georg von Frundsberg. Lautrec made the Swiss captain, Albrecht vom Stein, review Colonna's position expecting that this would dissuade the Swiss from forcing a battle. Vom Stein, however, still smarting from the public criticism of his decision to leave Marignano before that battle, and seeing this as an opportunity to re-establish his reputation, insisted that an attack on Colonna's position was feasible.

At dawn on Sunday, 27 April, the Swiss formed up in two squares each about 4000 strong and rushed headlong against the enemy in a frontal assault. One column under Arnold Winkelried of Unterwalden (a descendant of the hero of Sempach) consisted of troops from the Waldstaette, the other under vom Stein was mainly troops from Berne. Despite the efforts of the French generals to hold back the advance so that their artillery could be brought into play, the Swiss had worked themselves into such a frenzy that there was no holding them. In open rivalry to be the first to reach the *landsknechts*, the two squares took more than a thousand casualties before coming to a grinding halt at the sunken road. The crack troops (called double pay men for obvious reasons) were called forward in one desperate assault after another against the face of the rampart, as the German arquebusiers shot them down like fish in a barrel. Even scrambling on the growing pile of bodies, a stretched-out pike could not reach the *landsknechts* above the rampart. By the time the Swiss retreated, 3000 dead were left in the ditch, including Winkelried, vom Stein, twenty other captains, and many French nobles who had sought glory fighting on foot with the Swiss.

Bicocca was the last occasion on which the Swiss attempted a direct assault on a well defended position occupied by opponents armed with improved types of firearms. The lesson of Novara and Marignano was finally learned, at the cost of 3000 dead. Next day the survivors went home. As the contemporary Italian historian Guicciardini commented: 'They went back to their mountains diminished in numbers but much more in audacity, for it is certain that the loss they received humbled them to the degree that for several years afterwards they did not show their accustomed vigour.'(7)

It was discovered after Bicocca that the failure to pay the Swiss, thereby causing their impetuous rush into a battle they had no chance of winning, was because the Queen Mother Louise of Savoy had appropriated the money collected to pay the mercenaries. As a result of the ensuing scandal the French treasurer Semblancay was executed. The strains imposed on French finances by the need for payments to the Swiss were again demonstrated the following year, when Francis had to offer to deposit the crown jewels in Berne as a guarantee that he could pay the troops he needed.

In 1523 Francis again resolved to campaign in Italy and recruited 12,000 Swiss for his army. Remaining in France to ensure stability in the wake of the treason of Constable Bourbon, Francis entrusted the campaign that year to Admiral Bonnivet. The season was entirely undistinguished and marked by constant bickering between Bonnivet and his Swiss mercenaries over pay. The next year Bourbon himself descended into Italy with a force of 10,000 *landsknechts* and routed Bonnivet on the Sesia, where the Swiss rearguard suffered heavy losses and the famous chevalier Bayard died in the arms of the Swiss captain von Diesbach. The long campaign of 1523-4 culminated in Francis, who had taken personal command of the army, laying siege to the town of Pavia in a long winter siege that lasted from October to February. A relieving army of imperialists under the Duke of Bourbon forced the decisive Battle of Pavia on 24 February, 1525.

Up to and including Bicocca, the details of the major battles have been important to an understanding of the rise and decline of the Swiss military system. From Pavia onwards, however, the Swiss occupied a subsidiary, if still important, position among the forces involved. For this history of the Swiss Mercenary, it will be sufficient to provide only enough details of later engagements to assist in understanding the role and activities of the Swiss rather than a detailed blow-by-blow account more appropriate to a full scale military history of the period.

The Battle of Pavia turned out to be a decisive defeat for the French, including the capture of Francis himself. The Swiss were involved with very mixed degrees of success. Four days before the battle even took place, 5000 troops from the Grey Leagues returned home, decisively weakening the French forces. For once the departure of the Swiss was not the result of a quarrel over arrears of pay, but on the orders of their Council to defend against a possible attack by the Milanese.

The remaining 5000 Swiss did not acquit themselves well during the battle itself. Forming Francis's right flank, the Swiss square was badly exposed to the opposing artillery, suffering 3000 casualties before reaching the enemy lines. The Swiss wavered and retreated. Several captains, including Hans von Diesbach, kept to the field to face certain death rather than accept the dishonour of retreat but for the first time in their military history the remaining Swiss either surrendered or fled the field.

Ironically, the Swiss presence in the French army was, as we have seen, largely due to the proven effectiveness of combined arms tactics over their single-arm pike squares. At Pavia, however, the failure of Francis to use his forces supportively had left the Swiss square totally exposed on the right flank to the enemy artillery and without cavalry support, so that it fought and lost as a single arms unit. Further massive casualties, in addition to those of Bicocca and Marignano, must have contributed to the Swiss temporary loss of will. On the other hand, the King's bodyguard of the *Cent Suisses* fought and died to the last man in an unsuccessful attempt to prevent the capture of their master, prompting the comment from Francis that: 'If all my troops had fulfilled their duty like these brave men, I would not now be your prisoner, but you mine.'

After Pavia the French made one further levy of Swiss mercenaries before uneasy peace was established between Francis and Charles Quint. With that levy, in 1527, an important innovation was introduced at the request of the Swiss authorities. General disorder during the recruiting process had led to constant disputes as to the number of men reporting for duty and eligible for pay. That year the recruits were instructed to assemble with all their equipment at the eastern end of Lake Geneva near Aigle, and a count was made that formed the basis for the payroll throughout the campaign. From this date it became standard procedure to hold such a signing-on review, the area around Chalon-sur-Saône becoming the usual location.

Throughout his reign, Francis seized any opportunity presented by the distraction of Charles Quint's attention by troubles elsewhere in his Empire to renew the offensive in Italy and Picardy. Each time hostilities broke out, Francis called for Swiss mercenaries. The Diet, attempting to follow a delicate policy of neutrality, varied between officially approving French requests for troops and turning a blind eye to their unofficial recruitment. In 1537, for example, more than 30,000 men joined the French army — a formal but unofficial force of 10,000 men, some 15,000 men clandestinely enrolled by the French recruiters, and 8000 low grade vagabonds and near criminals recruited by two French adventurers. Similarly in 1542, the Diet approved a levy of 6000 men and closed its eyes to the simultaneous unofficial recruitment of another 8000. In 1543 it was an official force of 14,000 men that served in Picardy.

In 1544 the Battle of Cerisoles took place, in which the Swiss both gained revenge on the *landsknechts* for the defeats at Bicocca and Pavia and made a significant change to their infantry tactics. The French army in Italy at this time was commanded by the Duke of Enghien and included two groups of Swiss infantry, 4500 battle-hardened troops under Wilhelm Fröhlich that formed the 'core of the army' and 3500 inexperienced men raised by the Count of Gruyères. In April they joined in pitched battle with an Imperial army containing 7000 *landsknechts* near the village of Cerisoles south of Turin.

The land contours of the battlefield were such that the left and right flanks were out of sight of each other and two separate battles effectively took place. On the left flank the new Gruyère infantry panicked and threw down its arms. Despite the efforts of the captains to rally their men and three desperate charges by the French cavalry under Enghien himself, the Gruyère and French infantry on the left were overrun and Enghien believed the battle lost.

On the right, however, the Swiss under Fröhlich, supported by a force of Gascon infantry, decisively won a classic pike battle against the *landsknechts*. Under the iron hand of Fröhlich, the Swiss adopted much more disciplined tactics, for once holding a defensive position instead of rushing headlong into the attack as usual. The Swiss were positioned at the crest of a gentle slope and held their ground while the *landsknechts* advanced up the hill, blocking most of their own artillery lines of fire, and losing their formation on the marshy ground of the valley bottom. While awaiting the attack, the Swiss lay flat on the ground as artillery and arquebus fire passed harmlessly overhead. As the *landsknechts* approached the Swiss formed up but still held their ground. Only when the *landsknechts* were within thirty paces did the Swiss spring into the attack, their concentrated force and downhill impetus smashing through the somewhat disorderly opposition. The *landsknechts* broke, to be cut down or captured by the Swiss and Gascons. To complete the day's triumph, the Swiss reformed, marched to Enghien's assistance and won the day on the left as well.

Although Cerisoles turned out not to be an important victory in terms of strategic gain for the French, it marked a significant change in Swiss tactics and organization. The Swiss infantry had won its reputation as an attacking force that would steamroller through all opposition while able to defend itself against cavalry attack. The combination of improved firearms and improved tactics to delay the advance of the pike squares while they were destroyed by artillery and arquebus fire had led to the eclipse of Swiss infantry domination during the first quarter of the sixteenth century. At Cerisoles the Swiss demonstrated the defensive capability that would give their infantry a new battlefield role for the rest of the sixteenth century. Rather than an attacking arm, the function of the Swiss became to shelter the slow-loading arquebusiers and to protect the artillery, in both cases against attack by either cavalry or an opposing force of heavy infantry. Throughout the sixteenth century, forces of Swiss infantry continued to be hired en bloc to fulfil this function.

During the campaign of 1542-4 the Swiss, also for the first time, began to divide their battle formations into regiments, each consisting of around ten companies and commanded by a colonel. Each company was about 300 strong and commanded by a captain, supported by a flagbearer, lieutenant, sergeants and corporals. The official companies marched with the cantonal flags, while the flags of unofficial companies generally showed the arms of the colonel, in both cases overmounted with a white cross. The men continued to wear their own clothing with a white cross sewn onto their sleeves and chest, and by this time almost all wore the metal helmet known as a morion. One of the first of the new colonels was Wilhelm Fröhlich, originally of Zurich and later of Solothurn. Born in 1505, he had taken part in the Battle of Bicocca at the age of seventeen and commanded the Swiss at Cerisoles, and died in 1562.

The colonels and captains had become used to covering any temporary hiatus in pay from their own financial resources in order to preserve discipline and combat desertion. Delays in payment by the French remained a constant problem, and after each campaign the troops were disbanded as quickly as possible, relieving the strain on the French treasury but leaving arrears and much acrimony. After Cerisoles, for example, the Swiss troops that had won the victory had still not been paid ten months later. When Fröhlich personally travelled to Fontainebleau to argue their case, he received many honours including a lieutenancy in the *Cent Suisses* but still no arrears of pay. One improvement, however, was the introduction in 1534 of a tribunal consisting of two French and two Swiss judges to arbitrate the case of a Fribourg captain for costs he claimed to have incurred in raising a company for the Crown. At least the mechanism for agreeing the amount was improved even if the money itself was still slow in coming.

Francis I died on 31 March, 1547. His tomb in the Cathedral of St Denis is decorated with bas-relief of the Swiss who fought against him at Marignano and with him at Pavia and Cerisoles.

VIII

The Organization of the Mercenary System

'To make good infantry, it requireth men bred not in a servile or indigent fashion, but in some free and plentiful manner.... And this is to be seen in France and Italy (and some other parts abroad) where in effect all is noblesse and peasantry (I speak of people out of towns) and no middle people; and therefore no good forces of foot: insomuch as they are forced to employ mercenary bands of Switzers for their battalions of foot.'
Francis Bacon, *Works*, VI.95

During the sixteenth century armies progressively increased in size. In 1494 Charles VIII had invaded Italy with 28,000 men. By 1610 Henry IV had nearly 70,000 men under arms and his chief minister Sully was planning an army of nearly 200,000 men. The proportion of infantry within these enlarging forces also increased. Taking the same examples, Charles VIII's invasion force contained about as many cavalry as infantry, while by 1610 the ratio was down to one cavalryman to nine infantrymen.

The new development behind both the increasing size of armies and the proportion of infantry was the steady improvement in firearms during this period, and the impact of these improved firearms on the method of conducting warfare. The introduction of portable firearms to the battlefield had already been seen in the later battles of the Italian wars, largely causing the eclipse of the Swiss pike phalanx as an offensive unit. These early firearms were still relatively primitive weapons, but had the decisive advantage over long- and cross-bows that the user could be taught to fire them without a lifetime of training and experience.

The arquebus weighed about 5-8 kilos. With its primitive construction and the imperfection of early gunpowder, it had an effective range of only 100-200 metres. The matchlock musket that started to replace the arquebus during the second half of the sixteenth century had a longer range and greater penetration, but was some two metres long, much heavier, and could only be fired from a forked rest. A firing rate of two shots in three minutes was considered good for either arquebus or musket. Earlier tactics that had relied on the concentrated weight of the heavy cavalry charge or of pressure from an attacking pike phalanx were replaced by new tactics based on increasing numbers of vulnerable slow-loading arquebusiers and musketeers, protected by defensive pike squares. As firearms gradually improved, the ratio of shot to pike changed from one to three to three to one, and battlefield tactics concentrated on how best to combine pike with shot for maximum efficiency. Whatever the ratio, the spread of firearms required more infantrymen than before.

The sixteenth century also saw sieges replace pitched battles as the main method of conducting war. Artillery had improved as dramatically as handheld firearms, which in turn provoked the development of new designs of fortification. In particular the *trace italienne* in all its variations spread throughout Europe, and the defences of every major city and many smaller towns were rebuilt to withstand a lengthy siege. Parker has calculated that between 1529 and 1572 some 43 kilometres of modern defences were built in the Netherlands alone.(1) As no advancing general dared leave strong enemy forces in his rear to threaten his supply lines, warfare became a succession of sieges of fortified towns. The main objective of strategy was not to destroy an enemy's army but to occupy his territory, and the key for a successful occupation were the main towns, which were the seats of government and dominated communications.

The sieges themselves became lengthy affairs, strongly defended positions needing to be approached with care. A system of siegeworks had to be dug and manned until either the defenders surrendered or the trenches were advanced close enough to the defensive walls to risk an assault, the whole process taking months. In a complicated investiture, a double circumvallation needed to be built, one facing inwards to prosecute the siege, and one facing outwards to defend the attackers against a possible relieving force. Large numbers of footsoldiers were required for this form of warfare, to dig siegeworks, haul artillery, man trenches and ramparts, fend off counterattacks, and eventually carry through an assault. The cavalry on the other hand had a relatively limited role.

Finding sufficient troops, especially for a major campaign, was a constant headache, and in France the growing need for infantry was particularly difficult to satisfy. In the previous century Charles VII and Louis XI had created the *francs-archers*(2) but they were poorly trained, poorly armed and lacked motivation. The French nobility with their long traditions of knighthood were still prepared to serve in the gendarmerie and the

Compagnies d'Ordnance, but regarded the idea of serving on foot as demeaning. The first domestic French infantry organizations had to be recruited from the poor borderlands with their less powerful nobility, even though the population only partially regarded itself as French. The Bandes de Picardie were formed in 1480,(3) followed by the Bandes de Piemont in 1507. These Vieilles Bandes, even when extended to include the Bandes of Gascony and Brittany, still did not provide enough men, leading Francis I to another attempt to solve his infantry problem in 1534 by the creation of a new force which he optimistically called the Legions. Normandy, Brittany, Picardy, Languedoc and Guyenne were to provide one legion each, with two more formed from the remaining provinces. Each legion was intended to have a strength of 6000 men, divided into six bandes, each commanded by a captain, with a colonel appointed by the king in overall command. Recruits were to be volunteers and natives of the region forming the Legion.

The Legions proved most disappointing in practice and were no more satisfactory than the *francs-archers* had been. The plan was overambitious in terms of the administrative and financial support available. Finding and paying 42,000 men on a semi-permanent basis was beyond the resources of the realm. There were seldom sufficient volunteers so that the Legions were always under strength and suffered from poor discipline. They were merely the *francs-archers* under another name.(4) The legions were soon relegated to such secondary tasks as digging siege works and providing garrisons until they quickly disappeared after the death of Francis.

The failure of the legions still left the problem that 'Frenchmen were seldom eager to serve their king, and their king was not eager to employ Frenchmen.'(5) The answer was the Swiss, who offered France a large catchment area of available and willing footsoldiers, still the most highly regarded infantry in Europe. They provided the French with experienced well trained combat troops to strengthen the Vieilles Bandes, while lower grade legionnaires and militia were used for auxiliary duties such as garrisons.

The primary role of the Swiss was to form the centre of the battle line. While the cavalry provided the offensive shock, the infantry provided the resilience and staying power for the army to hold its position on the battlefield. Guicciardini's description from the Italian Wars still applied forty years later: 'The Swiss... would face the enemy like a wall without ever breaking ranks, stable and almost invincible.'(6) They were often brigaded with the gendarmerie with whom they had formed a healthy mutual respect at Marignano. The gravure of the battle line-up at Ivry, for example, shows the King and his gendarmerie in the centre of the line with two Swiss squares next to him on either side. The Swiss also had the task of defending the artillery, an honour held since they hauled the artillery over the mountains before Fornovo in 1495 and retained until a special artillery corps was created in 1671. At sieges, the role of the Swiss was to guard against and fight off excursions, take part in exchanges with relieving forces, and above all the honoured but highly dangerous task of storming the breach. Brantôme said: 'When we have a body of Swiss in our armies, we believe ourselves invincible.'(7)

The Swiss provided not only highly professional foot-soldiers but large numbers of them. There have been several attempts at estimating the number involved in mercenary service, these early years being the most difficult to quantify, being the least documented. An early estimate by May de Romain-motier in 1788 reached a total of 350,000 Swiss mercenaries employed as follows by the French kings during the sixteenth century:

Francis I	163,000
Henry II	81,100
Charles IX	40,900
Henry III	48,300
Henry IV	18,400
Total	351,700 (8)

The most recent estimate, by H. C. Peyer in 1978, came up with a total of 270,000 men for the sixteenth century, based the number of men in mercenary service throughout the period, with a percentage being replaced each year to cover losses due to death, injury, desertion or soldiers choosing to reside permanently in France.(9) Whatever the number it was undoubtedly very large and beyond the capability that France could provide from its own resources.

As well as the basic advantage of providing large numbers of skilled infantry, the use of the Swiss provided the French with several additional side benefits. Not least of these was that mercenaries could be sent home as soon as they were no longer required, either the war being over or the campaign season having ended. Warfare was a seasonal business that started in the spring as the roads dried out and forage became available and ended in autumn when the roads became impassable and the army could no longer live off the land. This hire and fire policy reduced the burden on the French Exchequer and avoided the social problems involved in caring for widows and orphans and in reabsorbing demobilized soldiers with their violent ways into the civilian population. Such problems were simply sent back to the Confederation.

The employment of mercenaries strengthened the position of the monarchy in less tangible ways. There was less need to arm potentially rebellious subjects, especially during a period of religious dissension. There was further consolidation of the authority of the Crown against a nobility that did not possess the same financial resources when it came to hiring mercenaries in large numbers and who could be passed by in the recruitment process. Lack of infantry for example consistently hampered the military operations of the Huguenots. From a strategic viewpoint, the alliance with the Swiss protected the French flank during the three centuries of wars between the Valois and Bourbons and the Habsburgs, while also depriving the Austrian Emperor of access to the pool of available Swiss mercenaries.

The French monarchs were well aware of all the advantages that accrued to them from the Swiss Alliance and went to great lengths to protect the relationship. When Henry II succeeded Francis I in 1547, one of his first acts was to invite the cantons to become godparents to his daughter. The personages that attended the christening, led by Andreas Schmid, the mayor of Zurich, were royally received and showered with presents.

In June, 1549, the alliance of 1521, which had expired upon the death of Francis I, was renewed with a slightly modified treaty. The terms remained basically unchanged except for the clause relating to termination, which was extended to five years after the death of the king. This extension proved to be invaluable in binding the Swiss to the crown through its three changes of heads during the Wars of Religion. Although Zurich and Berne refused to sign the new alliance because of repression of their coreligionists in France, their absence was compensated by the extension of the Treaty in 1550 to include the Grey Leagues as the equivalent of three cantons, with the same privileges as the Confederation and the right to provide a regiment as soon as the king's requirement for troops exceeded 6000 men. The inclusion of the Grey Leagues was recognized in the title of a new prestigious position established by Charles IX in 1571. Charles de Montmorency, Duc de Damville, was appointed the first Colonel-Général des Suisses et Grisons, in command of all the Swiss troops in the French army except the *Garde des Cent Suisses*. This much coveted position was held for 200 years until 1792 by fifteen French nobles of the highest rank. Their role was to act as protector of the Swiss, and they were charged with defending Swiss interests at court and with the French bureaucracy (see Appendix IV).

Four years after the renewal of the alliance, in June, 1553, a new agreement was reached at Baden between Ambassador Bassefontaine and the Diet. The Regulation of Baden was entitled *Capitulation Generale pour les Troupes Suisses au Service Royale*, and laid out the rules that would govern the Swiss mercenaries in French service until 1671. The main points of the Regulation of Baden were that in future the colonel would be elected by the captains and not chosen by the king; the officers and soldiers would receive three months' pay, which they would keep even if they became sick, were not used or were disbanded before the end of the three months; the pay of a soldier killed in service would go to his next-of-kin; the troops would not be separated and would be provided with decent lodgings; wages would be paid in gold or good currency to avoid losses in exchange; each soldier would receive a minimum of four crowns so that capable recruits could be found; the king agreed that his use of the troops would respect the alliances of the Confederation; the Confederation agreed to require the troops to serve until the end of their contracts and to apprehend and return any deserters. The Regulation of Baden continued to tighten up the organization of the Swiss troops. The barely controllable bands of *knaben* that had swarmed down from the mountains into Northern Italy in search of plunder at the beginning of the century had by the middle of the century been transformed into military organizations hired and regulated by contractual arrangements.

Starting in 1549, the contingents supplied by the Swiss were officially entitled regiments, each commanded by a colonel and carrying his name as the Regiment d'Erlach, Regiment Diesbach and so on. The regiment was divided into companies, the number and strength of which varied. While the aim was a regiment of 2400 men divided into twelve companies each of 200 men, the number of companies varied in practice between five and twenty and the strength between 100 and 300.

The company retained a strong identity with its canton, which negotiated a capitulation, selected the captain and was home to nearly all of the soldiers. These close ties largely explain the famous esprit de corps of the Swiss regiments. A Swiss recruit in the sixteenth century was not one of the dregs of society disappearing into the anonymity of army life. He was a member of his society temporarily away from home, and remained answerable to the standards of his society through his colleagues and officers while on service and through friends and relatives during his returns home between campaigns. Veteran soldiers cemented these relationships through their position as drill masters, training the next generation at the drill and shooting sessions which each village and town in the Confederation was obliged to organize. The democratic rights of a Swiss citizen still applied on service, so that within the company each soldier was treated as an individual. Although the rigid discipline upon which the efficacy of the pike square depended was strictly imposed in battle, the soldiers were otherwise permitted considerable freedom. The officers dressed the same as, lived with and fought with the men, general discipline being largely achieved by peer group pressure. The Swiss soldier in the sixteenth century was a proud professional, and the democratic and geographic roots of the Swiss contingents underpinned their continued reputation as the best infantry in Europe.

The colonel was originally elected by the captains but by the 1560s all the colonels were nominated by the crown through the French ambassador. He was responsible for overall military direction, general administrative matters, and hiring the regimental staff including chaplains, quartermasters, the Grand Juge and the Provosts. As an example of his remuneration, Pfyffer in 1562 received 600 livres tournois as colonel's pay. The colonel was also the owner of one company known as the Compagnie Colonelle. There tended to be a certain amount of friction between the colonel and the captains over areas of responsibility, with the position of the colonel gradually assuming more importance.

During most of the sixteenth century, however, day-to-day authority remained clearly in the hands of the captains. The captain had almost unlimited power over his company, of which he was the owner as well as the military leader. He formed the company, hired the men, provided their equipment, selected the officers and led them in the field. Although in theory the cantons selected the captains and the captains elected the colonel, in practice the French, through their ambassador, held the purse strings and had a decisive say in the choice of captains as well as colonel. The junior officers of the company generally included a lieutenant, a standard bearer, and one sergeant for every fifty men. There was also a music section of three drummers and a piper.

Once a capitulation had been agreed and the captain appointed, the recruiting process began. The captain would personally lead the recruiting drive, travelling from village to village with a few veterans as assistants, the small cortège moving about with flags flying, drums and pipes playing to attract attention and whip up enthusiasm. The arrival of the recruiters was an exciting event in village life. In the sixteenth century there were always more volunteers available than required and the captain could select the men he preferred from the rolls maintained by the canton. He could reckon on choosing a core of experienced professionals with some youthful enthusiastic first-timers mixed in.

The men selected would provide their own sword or dagger. The captain was responsible for providing armour, pikes and firearms, which he usually purchased from the cantonal arsenal. Once equipped, the company would assemble on a specific date at a central point such as the cantonal capital and march out to the location selected for mustering the regiment. For a regiment heading north to Paris or Picardy, this was usually between Chalon-sur-Saône and Dole, often the small village of Saint-Jean de Losne. The troops would traverse intervening cantons under the authorization of a prearranged travel permit. On arrival at the mustering point, the troops would be reviewed by French inspectors to check their numbers, to ensure they were capable, healthy soldiers and that they were properly armed. Once the company was accepted the men would swear an oath of allegiance to their captain before receiving their first pay.

The oath sworn by a regiment raised in 1552 by Nicholas Irmi of Basle included the following promises: to serve the king with honour and loyalty; to stop the flight of runaways by killing them if necessary; not to harm monasteries, churches, women, children, priests, mills, or bakers on pain of death; to settle all differences without delay through the justice of the regiment; not to mock others for their religion; not to blaspheme, get drunk, or gamble on feast days or Saturdays or on guard or in cemeteries; not to maltreat victuallers and to pay them; not to assemble or cause mutinies on pain of death; to obey the captain, judge, provost, sergeant and officers; on guard to obey the sergeant, keep the password secret, and not leave the post until relieved; not to insult the judge, provost or officers of the court for judgements rendered by them; not to let mules, horses, or the company's animals on to fields where they could cause damage; not to damage fields, vines or gardens; not to steal from private houses but on the contrary to purchase necessary commodities from markets or traders; only to butcher animals outside the camp; to live decently; to return with the patrols, not to tarry in taverns, not to discharge arms unnecessarily in camp, and not to take a colleague's quarters. This comprehensive list not only shows how discipline was administered but opens a window on the day-to-day activities of the soldiers and the concerns of their officers.(10)

The captain was personally responsible for payment of the troops. He received a lump sum from the French paymaster from which he paid the soldiers and the officers. All remaining amounts became his profit, but he also bore the risk of not being paid by the French, in which case he had to fund the company from his own financial resources. Wages started from the day the men left home and were paid at a monthly review. Base pay was a minimum of three ecus per month(11). The lieutenant and flagbearer received ten times base pay. Fully armoured pikemen received double pay and arquebusiers were paid a supplement of fifteen sous over base pay. A special battle payment equivalent to one month's salary was made until this practice was ended by Henry IV. The Swiss soldiers also benefited by exemption from French taxes, including those on specified quantities of alcohol and tobacco. Each soldier was responsible for his own subsistence, and was expected to pay for his provisions, unless the monthly pay failed, in which case he was permitted to live off the land. Finally, the soldier received a payment to cover his costs on the journey home at the end of his contract.

Irregularity of pay remained a constant problem. Rulers were well aware of the disciplinary problems that arose when pay failed. Nevertheless political ambitions continued to run ahead of financial resources or administrative capability. In the Swiss regiments the captains bore much of the burden imposed by lack of payments. Individual captains were owed as much as 20,000 livres and some such as Balthasar von Grissach of Solothurn were ruined despite an illustrious career in royal service. The officers of the fifty-two companies serving the crown in 1587 were owed over one million livres.

Relations between France and the Confederation were continuously soured because of arrears of pay and pensions, and of interest on loans raised by the king from some of the richer cantons. The Swiss authorities supported the cause of individual officers and soldiers who were owed money under capitulations that they justifiably regarded as binding contracts. The many politicians who had reached prominence through a military career ensured that the issue remained a priority for the Swiss authorities. In pursuit of their money, the cantons regularly threatened to call home the troops, without ever actually taking this final drastic step.

This constant wrangling over pay and debts preserved the reputation for avariciousness and disloyalty that the Swiss had won in the Italian wars. In fact there is more cause to wonder at the continued loyalty of troops that were only paid five years after serving the monarchy at Dreux and nine years after protecting the king in the retreat from Meaux.

Swiss troops were subject to their own discipline and to Swiss laws under the Caroline Code.(12) These rights were jealously guarded and the Swiss regiments insisted that the French authorities hand back any offenders for judgement and discipline. The staff of each regiment included a judge who acted as a legal adviser, in particular helping to decide whether an offence was a minor disciplinary matter that could be resolved by an officer or was serious enough that it should be brought before a tribunal. The latter comprised all the junior officers of the regiment plus one sergeant per company presided over by the youngest captain. It met in the open air in all weathers in front of the whole regiment. Its judgements were reviewed by a board, consisting of the senior officers of the regiment presided over by the oldest captain, which could reduce but not increase the punishments decided by the tribunal. A draconian series of punishments ran from fines and extra duties, through running the gauntlet of the regiment, to the death penalty for the severest offences which included raising a weapon against an officer, stealing a weapon from a comrade, encouraging desertion or other serious insubordination. Cowardice on the field would not reach the tribunal as every soldier was expected to kill on the spot any comrade trying to turn tail and run.

The Swiss regiments were also granted freedom to practice their own religion, a practical concession by the French to avoid limiting their recruitment possibilities to the Catholic cantons. Religious disputes within the regiment were forbidden in the strongest terms. A regiment usually had a Catholic priest and a Protestant chaplain on its staff. The exceptions to this religious freedom were the *Cent Suisses*, and later the commanders of the

Gardes Suisses. These positions were restricted to Catholics.

Once mustered the regiment marched off to join the main French army, covering about 15 kilometres each day. On the march each company kept together, with pikemen in front and rear and arquebusiers in the middle. If their route took them close to hostile territory a French cavalry detachment was occasionally despatched as an escort. Around 1550 the system of *ètapes* was introduced to move troops about the kingdom. Four *Grandes Lignes* were set out, with provisions and lodgings provided in advance at regular stages. This system considerably reduced marauding by the troops, at least when funds were available for the provisions requisitioned at each stage.

As described earlier, it is reasonable to assume that some 300,000 Swiss enrolled as mercenaries during the sixteenth century. Casualty figures are even more difficult to estimate, but recognizing that losses in a major battle could easily reach several thousand, together with losses in sieges and skirmishes as well as to sickness and disease, chances of survival were low. Total losses, including permanent emigrants as well as casualties, have been estimated at two-thirds of the total. The obvious question is therefore why hundreds of thousands of men would volunteer for a service in which their chances of survival were so low.

The answer is usually dismissed in the one word — overpopulation. Contemporary commentators and modern historians have described the high density and the high growth rate of the population in the Confederation at this time. The reasons advanced for this growth have included the simple lifestyle, lack of wars and plagues, local customs, and even the climate. It would apparently be self-evident that the overflow of population found its way into mercenary service. An eighteenth century English writer Abraham Stanyan commented in his *Account of Switzerland* (1714): "If they did not continually drain their country by keeping troops in foreign service, they would soon be so much overstocked in proportion to the extent and fertility of it, that in all probability, they would break in upon their neighbours in swarms or go further to seek out new seats."(13) The thesis that mercenary service was the only alternative to starvation in the harsh alpine environment still persists today. Pier Paulo Viazzo in his recent historical demography of Upland Communities described the traditional view as follows: "Most students of the Alpine world have taken it for granted that in the mountains population endemically tends to exceed the limits imposed by local resources, and have stressed the role of emigration as a way of disposing of surplus population. Therefore alpine emigration has been generally characterized and explained in terms of poverty and overpopulation."(14)

Certainly Switzerland was densely populated with around 600,000 inhabitants at the beginning of the fifteenth century, doubling to 1.2 million by the beginning of the eighteenth century. The growing population contained a large class of rural and urban poor existing on the borderline of starvation, and this group was readily available to the recruiting agents. In the mountain regions, however, the number of people remained broadly unchanged. Animal husbandry, which requires less labourers than the cultivation of crops, had already become the predominant economic activity by the middle of the fifteenth century. Again quoting Viazzo, it would be wrong to assume that "the inhabitants of barren high valleys were bound to be very poor, thereby confusing the poverty of the land, which was very real, with the poverty of the people in the mountains, which was simply potential".(15)

The position was more complex than the single word overpopulation does justice. Rather than just a solution for ridding society of unwanted children, thrust into the armies of foreign powers to avoid starvation, the mercenary profession was seen as a way of using special skills to expand local resources. The army was regarded as a profession, not a poorhouse. The lot of the Swiss mountain peasant was not significantly worse than that of the French or German lowland peasant, but the Swiss had a particular military expertise that they were able to market in the business of war. Schelbert comments: "The size of the population is basically... a function of practical, understood and utilized employment possibilities, one of which was mercenary service."(16)

To the individual soldier the basic mercenary wage provided an attractive income in the sixteenth century. The usual wage of four and a half guilders per month was about double that earned by a journeyman mason. Although subject to ever-increasing deductions and irregularity of payment, the base salary was considered competitive with that of other professional tradesmen. A careful soldier could at this time still reckon to save a reasonable portion of his wages.

In addition there was always the chance of a windfall. The fabulous spoils of the Burgundy Booty were unlikely to be repeated, although the *landsknechts* did sack Rome in 1527 and the Spaniards Antwerp in 1576. The Swiss themselves had severely reduced the possibilities of ransom by their custom of killing their prisoners. Nevertheless there was always the chance of spoils: weapons and equipment after a battle; sack of a town after a siege, especially if frustrated by a long siege or if the town had not surrendered before the besiegers had been exposed to the dangers of storming it; or by "liberating" the possessions of the civilian population despite the severe penalties inflicted by the Swiss code. One Moritz Stein of Olten looted 2000 gold crowns during the St Bartholomew's Night massacres, the Swiss mercenary's equivalent of winning the pools, an unlikely but not impossible dream.

Other than in Zurich where the influence of Zwingli was still felt, the profession was encouraged by the political leaders of the cantons, many of whom recognized the economic benefits which came to the Confederation in general and often themselves personally from mercenary service. French pensions, whether paid directly to the cantons or to individuals, represented an important part of the Confederation's income. Official pensions to Solothurn in 1632 came to 3900 livres with a further 7650 known payments to individuals, a total of 11,550 livres at a time when the cantonal budget was 81,000 livres. In the poorer cantons, where the number of soldiers was higher and other income lower, pensions could form as much as 20-30% of cantonal income. Deep-rooted power structures developed to protect the mercenary business.

The Confederation also enjoyed advantageous trade benefits from the alliance with France. Under Articles 5 and 9 of the Perpetual Peace of 1521, Swiss merchants(17) were granted freedom to trade in France without import duties and on the same terms as French merchants. The Confederation was also a net importer of grain as well as purchasing large quantities of salt from Aigues Mortes and the mines of the Franche Comté. Pensions and soldiers' wages provided the hard currency needed to support these purchases. The French Ambassador Moutiers estimated in 1668 that trade privileges were worth 100,000 ecus on top of the 300,000 ecus being paid annually in pensions. Peyer has calculated that the revenues from mercenary service formed about 6% of the Confederation's total income during the early sixteenth century.(18)

As well as the financial benefits, other motivations influenced potential recruits. To young men brought up on tales about the heroes of Morat and Marignano, the life of the soldier offered adventure and the chance to win fame and honour. Old soldiers' reminiscences about distant places, glorious victories and the cameraderie of life in the regiment provided stark contrast with the monotony of humdrum existence on the farm. For Colonel Henri Bouquet, future victor over the redskins of Ohio: "The military vocation stood out from an early age as the only way to satisfy his... need for action.... What other career could at that time satisfy his ambition and adventurous nature?"(19) As well as satisfying the restless spirit, recruitment offered the chance to escape adversity. Many peasants and town dwellers lived in such abject poverty that a mishap such as a failed harvest could mean starvation. We will see later the correlation in the eighteenth century between poor harvests and the number of recruits. Some recruits were running from judicial proceedings regarding a crime, and some from domestic circumstances such as a shrewish wife or a pregnant girlfriend. As Ulrich Mork, a 42-year-old labourer with a 54-year-old wife and no children wrote to his sister: "He liked war... what should he do at home, it was better away where he could eat and drink better and have more freedom."(20)

Many of the recruits were enlisting at 16 or 17 years of age when thoughts of casualty rates scarcely impacted the optimism of youth. In any case the thoughts of dying in battle might not have seemed too daunting to a youth whose life expectancy was only another twenty years even if he stayed quietly at home. A young man marrying between the ages of 25 and 30 would on average have only one parent at the wedding, and that would probably be one of the women. A census in the Zurich region in 1637 showed 46% men against 54% women and thirteen widowers compared with 151 widows in a survey of 4000 inhabitants. The temporary or permanent loss of so many young men to the military would have further tilted the naturally higher proportion of women and acted as a brake on the birth rate.

In summary, many men were pushed into mercenary service by poverty and unemployment which resulted from the existence of a larger population than indigenous resources could support. Many others, however, were attracted by a perception of military service as a profession or an adventure. Most were probably driven by a mixture of half-understood motives. A complex set of social mechanisms probably developed to keep the population broadly in balance with the available opportunities for employment whether those opportunities were at home on the farm and in the town, or abroad earning a living from a set of unique military credentials. Certainly, at this stage there was no shortage of eager recruits. The French Ambassador de Chauvigny wrote: "The majority know nothing other than mercenary service, which is well suited to their character, their genius and their taste."(21)

The French Wars of Religion

"Those whom one trusts more than anyone and without whom we would not have the courage to undertake the least thing."
Fourquevaux, *Instructions sur le Faict de Guerre* (1548)

Following the death of Henry II France suffered nearly half a century of civil war. It is not the objective of this work to follow the manoeuvrings of Catherine de Medici and her sons, nor the Guise and the Huguenots through the Wars of Religion. Rather, appropriate episodes have been selected that explain or illuminate particular aspects of the involvement of Swiss mercenary troops during this period.

One constant thread through the religious dissensions and political intrigues was the support of the Swiss cantons and their troops for the kings of France. The Confederation held steadfastly to the premise that its partner in the alliance was the King rather than the French State or any faction of the French people. The Diet expressed the position very clearly: "We only recognize in our treaties the alliance with the King. His subjects resolve in vain to dethrone him. Our oaths, which must bind us, forbid us from supporting rebels against him. The King is our sole ally and not his subjects. He is the only one we must defend."(1)

The original alliance of 1521 had been renewed in 1549 between the Confederation and Henry II for a period defined as the life of the King and five years after his death. After the unexpected death of Henry in a tournament accident in 1559, the important provision that extended the alliance to his successors ensured continuity in Swiss support for the French crown through the short reign of Francis II and the critical first years in the minority of Charles IX. From his first day on the throne a new French king was able to rely on a strong household guard for protection while he set about consolidating his hold on the Kingdom.

10. Ludwig Pfyffer (1524-1594), colonel in the French army and the most prominent Swiss of the second half of the sixteenth century, sometimes called "The King of the Swiss" (sixteenth century oil painting).

11. The Battle of Dreux, 1562, in which 6,000 Swiss infantry formed the core of the royal army against the Huguenots. The Swiss squares successfully defended themselves against cavalry and Landsknecht infantry (contemporary engraving by Jean Tortorel).

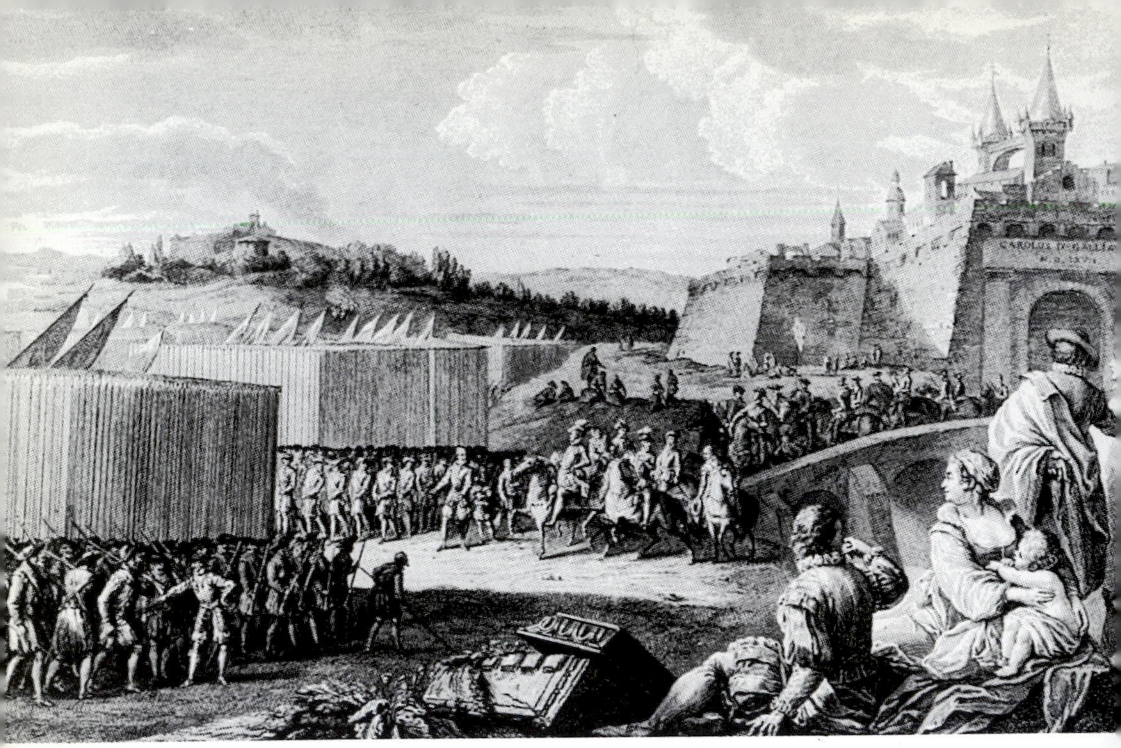

12,13,14. (opposite) Scenes of the Retreat from Meaux, during which the Swiss squares under the command of Pfyffer protected King Charles IX and his court from incessant attacks by the Huguenots while escorting them back to Paris from an exposed position at Meaux (from Zurlauben's *Tableaux Topographiques de la Suisse*, 1780).

15. The Battle of Ivry, 1590, in which the Swiss fought on both sides. The main squares on the royal side are shown in position next to the King's cavalry (contemporary engraving)

16. Kaspar Gallati (1535-1619), followed Fröhlich and Pfyffer as a senior colonel in French service serving four kings — Charles IX, Henri III, Henri IV and Louis XIII. Gallati was the first colonel of the Swiss Guards (from Zurlauben's *Tableaux Topographiques de la Suisse*, 1780).

17. Swiss Guard c1620. The Swiss Guards were formed in 1616. the first permanent Swiss regiment. They joined the French Guards in the Maison du Roi and took precedence over all other French and foreign regiments.

1620
Regiment des Gardes-Suisses
Officier

The relationship continued to be strained by the problem of the French debts, already 250,000 livres by the accession of Francis II and 35 million by the end of the century. In 1562, no pensions having been paid for seven years, the Diet resolved to withdraw its troops. Eventually a compromise was found and the alliance was formally renewed in 1564 for the life of the King and seven years after his death, and again in 1582 with Henry III for the life of the King and eight years.

During the Wars of Religion Swiss troops continued to serve the French crown through the system of capitulations. The regiment of 6000 men remained the basic unit for recruiting, sometimes raised in two units of 3000 men, and occasionally increased to 10 or 12,000 men. The regiments started to stay in service for longer periods rather than returning home each autumn after a single campaigning season. Throughout the period of the civil wars there were rarely less than 6000 Swiss serving in France at any one time.

The alliance with the Confederation meant that the royalist leaders could always rely on a strong force of Swiss to form the core of their army. The monarchy retained sufficient control of the country's finances and administration to be able to pay for the Swiss troops, or at least not slip so far behind with payments that the Diet recalled its men. The Huguenots, on the other hand, had sufficient support among the nobility to field effective forces of cavalry but were always short of enough funds to keep their hired *landsknecht* infantry in the field for sustained periods.

Since Marignano infantry alone had not been able to win a decision over a combined arms force. But equally a combined arms force with weak infantry could not force a decision against an opponent grouped around a strong infantry core. As Delbrück has pointed out, at this time "the decision in battle depended on the victory or defeat of the infantry."(2) During the Wars of Religion the Royalists were generally strong enough to win the major battles against the Huguenots, but they never managed to annihilate the Huguenot army nor to capture all the Huguenot fortresses and territorial strongholds. While the Swiss played a key part in ensuring that the Royalists avoided defeats and obtained important victories, not until after Ivry was the monarchy able to turn its battlefield successes into a lasting strategic advantage.

For a better understanding of the role of the Swiss troops in combat it is instructive to look in some detail at the Battle of Dreux, which took place during the first War of Religion. On 19 December, 1562, the royal army under Constable Montmorency had taken up a defensive position near the town of Dreux, blocking the route of the Huguenot army into Normandy where it intended to join up with the English army that had landed at Le Havre. The royal army totalled 18,000 men, including 6000 Swiss, 4000 *landsknechts* and 2500 Spanish infantry, but only 2500 cavalry. The

Huguenots under the Prince of Condé and Admiral Coligny had only 13,000 men, but including 5000 cavalry. Condé had carelessly allowed the royalist army to approach close enough to force a battle.

The Swiss were drawn up in the centre of the royalist line, probably in two squares each of 3000 men with a front of eighty men and thirty-six ranks. The company from Lucerne took the right hand files, with the companies from the Waldstaette and the other cantons to their left.

The Constable opened the battle with the command for the Swiss to advance against the Huguenots *landsknecht* infantry facing them. After kneeling to pray according to their custom, the Swiss moved forward, with small numbers of royalist cavalry supporting to either side. The advancing square received the full weight of a Huguenot cavalry charge against its right front corner. The riders broke into the square although not so far as the flags. The Swiss took many casualties(3) before the riders could be pushed out and the ranks reformed. The Huguenot charge drove off the supporting royalist cavalry leaving the Swiss flanks exposed to heavy arquebus fire. The Huguenot *landsknechts* then advanced to attack the halted Swiss, but seeing their hated rivals ahead the Swiss resumed their advance and drove the *landsknechts* back 200 paces until they broke. The Swiss captured twelve flags in this process.(4) Having driven off the royalist cavalry, the Huguenot cavalry had regrouped and resumed the attack on the Swiss square, this time from the rear. The rear ranks had worked loose during the long pursuit of the *landsknechts* so that isolated groups of ten or twelve men were detached from the main square, defending themselves as best they could even with stones from the battlefield. The Swiss Colonel, Gebhard Tammann of Lucerne, was killed at this point. Tammann had only recently taken over from Wilhelm Fröhlich, the victor of Cerisoles who had died two weeks earlier after forty years' mercenary service. Only at this stage, after the Swiss had been withstanding the full force of the Huguenot offensive for two hours, were the remaining royalist troops brought into the action. Eventually, after four hours' struggle, the longest battle since Marignano, the royalist forces gained the upper hand across the field and the Huguenots under Coligny(5) were forced to withdraw.

Swiss casualties were high. Besides the Colonel, twenty-one other officers and 1000 men were killed. The Swiss contribution to the victory was recognized as crucial and within four days Charles IX had written in glowing terms to the Diet praising the courage and steadfastness of the Swiss troops. Despite the fulsome praise, the soldiers finally received their battle pay in 1567, five years later.

As well as the troops from Dreux receiving their long overdue pay, the summer of 1567 also saw the Spanish general, the Duke of Alba, set off from Italy with a large army to put down an insurrection in the Spanish

Netherlands. His route along what became famous as the Spanish Road(6) took him close to the borders of both the Swiss Confederation and France, causing consternation in both countries and deep suspicion in France of Alba's real intentions. The French Ambassador in Solothurn, at that time Pompanne de Bellerive, was instructed to raise a regiment of Swiss troops that would be given the task of shadowing Alba and protecting the French border against any sudden incursion by the Spanish army. It is interesting to follow in some detail the progress of the Swiss regiment hired in this connection, both to illustrate the organization and activities of a typical mid-sixteenth century mercenary force, and because it resulted in a celebrated feat of arms, the retreat from Meaux.

The regiment consisted of 6000 men in twenty companies of 300 men, and was raised under the name of "The Swiss Guard Regiment of King Charles IX." The Colonel was Ludwig Pfyffer of Lucerne, one of the most famous Swiss captains, who became known as the "King of the Swiss" and dominated Franco-Swiss relations for a quarter of a century. At this time forty-three years old, Pfyffer already had two decades of military experience behind him and had been selected by his peers during the Battle of Dreux to take over as the senior Swiss officer after the death of Tammann. The captains of the twenty companies forming the regiment were also experienced officers, bearing the names of many of the Swiss military dynasties — Bircher and Segesser of Lucerne, Jauch and Kuhn of Uri, In der Halden and Reding of Schwyz, Wiesenbach of Unterwalden, Zurlauben of Zug, Tugginer of Solothurn and Studer of St Gallen.

The capitulation signed at Solothurn on 9 July, 1567, between the King and Captain Zurlauben for one of the companies of this regiment has survived. It contains the following clauses: the company would comprise three hundred men, all Swiss, thirty wearing armour and thirty armed with arquebuses; the king would pay nine hundred crowns for the recruitment; no soldier should receive less than three crowns a month and each arquebusier should receive an additional fifteen sous; the captain would receive a payment for himself, the lieutenant and the ensign equivalent to the pay of nineteen men; the captain would submit his men for review each month by controllers nominated by the king, and payment would be withheld for unjustified absentees; no blind or incapable men should be presented, no men should be presented twice, and sick men should be covered by certificates from the judge wherever they were hospitalized; the officers and soldiers would serve His Majesty against any of his enemies except the cantons and their allies, and they could not leave the King's service without his permission; officers of justice would be hired and paid according to custom; and, finally, officers would not beat, tax or demand money from victuallers, cooks or suppliers.(7)

With the capitulations signed, recruiting took place in early July. The troops were informed that pay would start on 21 July, that they should leave home on that date and travel via Geneva to the mustering point at Chalon-sur-Saône, where they arrived during the first week of August. The inspection by the French commissaires, who included the Governor of Burgundy, took place on 11 August, followed by the swearing of the oath. This oath has also survived and its provisions show the continuing concerns about the behaviour of the troops. The soldiers swore to abstain from blasphemy, drunkenness and eating meat on Fridays and Saturdays; to serve the king, except against the cantons and their allies; not to leave the regiment without the permission of a captain or colonel; to obey the officers and not mutiny; to remain at their guardpost until relieved by a sergeant; to defend their regiment, including the officers of justice and subalterns; not to pursue old grudges or ask the judges to arbitrate old disputes; not to take part in vendettas unless the life of a close relative were involved; to submit disputes to the judges; not to break or abandon their arms; not to disobey or rebel under pain of being brought before the High Judge; not to violate churches or butchers; not to attack peaceable persons; and that anyone killing a coward in battle or in assault would be exculpated. Pfyffer reported by letter to the authorities in Lucerne of the French satisfaction with the regiment, which was "a better looking and better equipped troop" than had been led into France for some time. The regiment marched out next day arriving on the 20th at Clairmont in Lorraine to await news of the Spaniards. On 9 September, the regiment moved on again to arrive in Château Thierry on the 19th.

By this time the services of the Swiss were needed to combat an even more pressing threat than the passage of Alba and the Spaniards. The court, including the King, his brother, and the Queen Mother, was on progress at the Palace of Monceaux when word arrived of a Huguenot plot to capture the lightly guarded royal party. The court hastily moved to a securer location in the town of Meaux and an urgent summons was sent to the Swiss camped forty-five kilometres away at Château Thierry. Pfyffer received the message just before midnight on 25 September, and before dawn next morning the Swiss entered Meaux, having marched at virtually stormpace all through the night.

After posting a strong guard, Pfyffer joined the debate among the royal party over whether to risk the fifty-kilometre journey from Meaux back to the safety of Paris. Constable Montmorency was for remaining at Meaux, believing the route to Paris across open countryside would be foolhardy without cavalry cover. Apocryphal or not, the celebrated intervention of Pfyffer in the debate won the day: "May it please your Majesty to entrust your person and that of the Queen Mother to the bravery and loyalty of the

Swiss. We are six thousand men and will open with the points of our pikes a path wide enough for you to pass through your enemies."

At dawn on the 28th the Swiss regiment formed up outside the gates of Meaux with the royal party in their midst and set off for Paris. At Legny in the Valley of the Marne, after about an hour of march, a Huguenot force of over a thousand cavalry led by Condé and Coligny appeared. The Swiss halted and formed a pike square with arquebusiers placed at the corners to await the attack. The Huguenot cavalry skirmished with the Swiss and fired from a distance but did not dare an outright assault on the pikes. Three times the Swiss marched on and then halted to reform the square when threatened with attack. Under the astonished eyes of the court, Pfyffer quietly gave his orders, the troops manoeuvred to present a wall of pikes against the cavalry swarming in all directions around the square, and, during ten hours under attack, not one man of 6000 broke ranks. The following is from the report of the Venetian Ambassador Correro who was with the French court: "When the relief force of 6000 Swiss arrived at Meaux, I swear I have never seen worse looking people; they looked incapable of carrying the weapons on their shoulders let alone using them. But when they formed up in order of battle they looked like different men. Three times I saw them front up to the enemy, throwing at him everything they had in their hands (including bottles which I saw flying through the air) before hurling themselves on him at full speed like mad dogs, with pikes lowered and without ever breaking ranks. They were so worked up to fight that the enemy did not dare to attack."(8)

Arriving at Le Bourget around five o'clock in the afternoon, the royal family slipped away on fast horses and reached the safety of the Louvre. The Swiss followed and finally reached their quarters in St Honoré around midnight, having lost only thirty men in the day's action. Next day the King reviewed the regiment and declared that he owed his life to "God and the Swiss." Pfyffer was honoured with the gold chain of the Order of St Michael but the men finally received their battle pay nine years later!

Two months later Pfyffer's regiment participated in the Battle of St Denis. This was largely a cavalry battle but the Swiss were involved in the later stages fending off an attack by the Huguenots' German *reiters* and overrunning part of the Huguenot infantry, for the loss of only ten men. The regiment also played a relatively minor role in the largely cavalry battle of Jarnac. At Moncontour, after first entering the battle through the unusual step of charging the enemy cavalry, the Swiss then held off several cavalry counter-attacks, before finally attacking and massacring the opposition's *landsknechts*. The regiment was finally disbanded in March, 1570. The men only received 140,000 ecus of the 800,000 owing them, and that after new loans were given to the French Ambassador by the towns of Berne, Zurich and Fribourg. Despite disbanding the regiment, the King retained one company as a personal guard which became the standard practice until the foundation of the Swiss Guard Regiment forty years later.

During the second half of the sixteenth century the French kings employed Swiss troops not to fight wars against other powers but to put down rebellious subjects, first the Huguenots and then the Guise. As shown in the previous examples, the Swiss were generally employed as combat troops to oppose the rebel armies on the battlefield, or in sieges. Occasionally they were used for police actions, however, and on two notable occasions they became unhappily embroiled in French internal affairs. During the infamous St Bartholomew's Night massacre of 24 August, 1572, several dozen Swiss soldiers played shameful parts. A number of Swiss guards, having been liberally plied with drink, were among the troops that cut down the Huguenot nobles within the Louvre itself. Others were part of the group that assassinated Admiral Coligny, in the process killing some of Henry of Navarre's Swiss bodyguard who were on loan to Coligny. One Moritz Koch received 10,000 crowns for his part in the affair, a Moritz Stein picked up 2000 crowns, and Captain Studer of St Gallen was able to buy two castles on his return home. Although only individuals were involved, their actions badly detracted from the otherwise generally honourable behaviour of the Swiss through the intrigues and machinations of the civil wars. Even Bodin, one of the apologists for the Swiss, had to admit that "that night the white cross suffered an unprecedented humiliation."(9)

The second occasion was the Day of Barricades on 12 May, 1588. Three days earlier at the head of 30,000 excited citizens, the Duke of Guise had taken over effective control of the centre of Paris. Henry III called on the Swiss to re-establish order in the capital, but tied their hands by forbidding them to use their weapons. 4000 Swiss under Gallati joined 2000 French Gardes on the Ile de la Cité. They were attacked by the mob, however, and sixty were killed before Guise could rescue them and allow them to withdraw. Meanwhile the King fled to Chartres. The whole episode was a precursor of 1792 and an example of the comparative ineffectiveness of the Swiss troops when used in a police action rather than a strictly military role.

If the unswerving loyalty of the Swiss troops to the crown was of inestimable value to Catherine de Medici and her sons, it was even more so for Henry IV. The assassination of Henry III in 1589 saw the end of the House of Valois and the controversial succession of the Protestant Henry of Navarre. Within seven days of his accession, Henry had written to the Diet to assure the Confederation of his friendship and confirm his expectation that the alliance would continue. Meanwhile, however, the King desperately needed immediate support and could not afford to wait for the Diet to deliberate and communicate its reply. The attitude of the 12,000 Swiss troops already in France, one-third of them Catholics, was vital to secure his tenuous grip on the throne. Nicolas de Harlay, Seigneur de Sancy, was sent to address the Swiss captains. He reminded them that their loyalty was to the King, pointed out that the King of France was never dead, and appealed for their support of Henry IV as the legitimate successor to the throne. The senior Swiss officer, Colonel Kaspar Gallati of St Gallen, the next in the illustrious line of Swiss captains after Fröhlich and Pfyffer, threw his weight behind these arguments. Without waiting to receive instructions from the Diet, the four regiments of Gallati, Wischer, Aregger and Hartmannis aligned themselves firmly behind the King.

The King was still in a precarious position. Unable to control Paris and not master over most of the kingdom, Henry needed to defeat the Guise-inspired League on the battlefield to secure his hold on the throne. With a shrunken army of 8000 men, 5000 of which were Swiss, Henry retired into Normandy and took up a defensive position outside Dieppe. Trenchworks were dug in the valley under the fortress of Arques with the Swiss Regiment Aregger defending a first ditch and the Regiment Gallati held in reserve behind a second ditch to secure communications with Dieppe.

The army of the League led by the Duke of Mayenne, the last remaining Guise brother, and with 20,000 men including a strong force of *landsknechts*, arrived outside Dieppe and tried to tempt Henry out of his defences. Mayenne finally decided to attack on the foggy morning of 21 September. Aregger's regiment was overrun following a trick played on them by the *landsknechts*. Several *landsknecht* companies approached the Swiss defences with their caps on their pikes to indicate that they wished to change sides, which was a not unusual occurrence and did not alarm the Swiss. When close enough, however, the *landsknechts* turned their weapons on the unsuspecting Swiss and stormed the first line of the royalist defences. Gallati's regiment stood firm on the second line, however. As the Duc d'Aumale wrote in his despatch, "Without the solidity of the Swiss Regiment Gallati the day was lost." Henry rallied his men around the Swiss with the famous cry, "Are there not fifty gentlemen of France willing to come and die with their King?' Enraged by the trick played on them, the Swiss of both the Gallati and Aregger regiments counterattacked and broke the *landsknechts*. At the same time the fog cleared enabling the royalist guns in the castle of Arques to bear on the retreating leaguers.

At Arques the King had held off the superior forces of the League and bought time for moderate opinion to rally to his cause. Having spent the winter gathering support, Henry in the spring of 1590 still had to defeat the army of the League in open battle to ensure his kingdom. The decisive encounter took place on 14 March at Ivry, which from the Swiss point of view is most interesting because Swiss troops appeared on both sides and is considered in the next chapter.

Ivry was the last major battle of the Wars of Religion and, other than the sieges of Paris and Rouen, finally brought these wars to an end. The loyalty of the Swiss troops to the reigning monarch, their performance at the heart of the royalist army in battles such as Dreux and Ivry and the defence of the King at Meaux and Arques were acts of decisive importance in the political as well as military history of France.

SECTION THREE

THE HEYDAY OF THE MERCENARY BUSINESS IVRY TO NEERWINDEN
1590-1693

X

Official Swiss Troops in Other Armies

'Those swisses fight on any side for pay'
John Dryden, *Works*, 1.99

To explain the development and organization of the Swiss mercenary system, it has been convenient to refer to the Confederation as one homogeneous entity. In practice, the consensus on which the Confederation depended was always a precarious balance between the interests and jealousies of the individual cantons. In relation to the supply of mercenaries, there were constantly two forces pulling at the alliance with France from separate directions. On the one hand the extreme Protestant cantons, especially Zurich, were against the mercenary system as a whole, and against supporting the Catholic kings of France in particular. On the other hand the Catholic cantons, especially Lucerne and the Waldstaette, were for expanding relationships with other Catholic states such as Spain, the Pope and Savoy rather than limiting support to France alone.(1)

In the Protestant cantons, the reformist preachers, particularly Zwingli, had consistently opposed the whole idea of mercenary service, to the extent that Zurich had not been a signatory to the original alliance with France of 1521 nor the renewal in 1549. Although Berne had been party to the original alliance there was considerable sympathy for the French Protestants to the extent of providing asylum to the children of Admiral Coligny after the St Bartholomew's Night massacres. Berne joined Zurich in not ratifying the further renewal of the alliance in 1564.

Throughout the Wars of Religion the Huguenots made strenuous efforts to mobilize the sympathy in the Protestant cantons and obtain levies of troops. While numbers of individual soldiers joined the Huguenot armies, on only three occasions did the Protestant cantons break ranks with Confederate policy and allow a formal or semi-formal troop movement.

In 1562 2000 volunteers from Berne under five members of the Diesbach family set out to join Condé but reluctantly turned back when envoys from the Berne Senate caught up with them at Lyons with instructions to return or face severe penalties. In 1575 two Bernese regiments with 6000 men under two more Diesbachs, Ludwig and Gabriel, again set out to join the Huguenots, this time ignoring entreaties from the Senate. This force joined Condé and spent most of its time quarrelling with the Huguenot's *landsknechts*. Peace was signed before it could have any impact on the battlefield. The leaders were imprisoned when they returned to Berne, but with mild sentences that did not satisfy the complaints of the Catholic cantons. The third outbreak was in 1587 when 4000 troops from Berne, Zurich and Basle were raised by Henry of Navarre to serve in the Dauphiny. Blocked from marching north by the forces of the League in Alsace and decimated by disease, the remnants of this sorry force were eventually incorporated into the official Swiss regiments. Zurich brought back three of the captains and executed them.

It is difficult to judge the extent to which the Protestant cantons supported these troop movements, turned a blind eye to them, or half-heartedly opposed them. Certainly Berne and Zurich never pushed their sympathy for co-religionists in France to the extent of causing a break with the rest of the Confederation. They were prepared to refuse ratification of the alliance and not to accept capitulations, but not to go so far as to despatch official troops to fight the regiments of the other cantons that were serving the king.

The loyalties of the Catholic cantons to the French were tested not by matters of religion, as they were after all serving the Catholic kings of France, but by financial and political considerations. Income from mercenary service was proportionately more important to the mountain cantons than to the richer cantons of the plateau. The preaching of Zwingli against the mercenary business has even been advanced as one reason why the Reformation did not spread uniformly across the Confederation, financial considerations outweighing matters of religious conscience. The constant threat to the income of the Waldstaette caused by arrears in payments was a running sore, especially when other Catholic powers, notably Spain, were able to distribute lavish pensions while the French coffers were empty.

The attitudes of the Catholic cantons were heavily influenced by the opinions of Ludwig Pfyffer, the famous mercenary leader who became mayor of Lucerne and was known as the "King of the Swiss". At the end of 1577 Pfyffer took umbrage at the hostile reception he was given in Paris when he tried to collect his pensions and arrears of pay, and he passed secretly into the camp of Spain. Nevertheless and despite an offer by

Spain to double pensions and pay off 800,000 crowns of French arrears, Pfyffer was still the head of the Swiss delegation that celebrated the renewal of the alliance in 1582. By 1585, however, Pfyffer was working openly with the Guise recruiting troops in the Waldstaette. That year he signed a formal capitulation with the representatives of the Duke of Mayenne to raise 8000 men. This was the first time that an official contract was signed to raise troops to fight the King of France and was viewed within the Confederation as a much more serious development than the officially-disowned Protestant troops supplied to the Huguenots. In practice the regiment only reached France in time to be disbanded after the Peace of Nemours but an important precedent had been set.

The following year the seven Catholic cantons met at Lucerne under Pfyffer's leadership and formed the Ligue d'Or. This League concluded an alliance with Philip II of Spain, which included the provision for Spain to raise between 4 and 13,000 troops. Subsequently, Solothurn, the site of the French embassy and one of the Cantons most dependent on mercenary service, had second thoughts about this separatist move and withdrew from the Ligue.

In 1589 and again in 1590 Mayenne raised troops in the Waldstaette, and on the second occasion Swiss troops came face to face on the battlefield for the first time. After the defensive action at Arques, Henry IV still needed to break the army of the League. The decisive action took place on 14 March, 1590, at Ivry. Henry's army had increased to 15,000 men, including 9000 Swiss in four regiments. The royalists took to the field with the Solothurn Regiments Aregger and von Grissach on the right, the Wischer Regiment of Glarus and the Hartmannis Regiment of the Grey Leagues on the left, and the King and the cavalry in the centre. Mayenne again had a larger force, 20,000 men including a large force of *landsknechts* and a 3000-man Swiss regiment commanded by Ludwig Pfyffer's brother Rudolf and Sebastian von Beroldingen of Uri.

As the battle unfolded, the royal cavalry defeated the cavalry of the League and then the Swiss infantry overran the league's *landsknechts*. Suddenly in the middle of the battle the Swiss came face to face with Pfyffer's regiment. They ceased their advance and raised their weapons. Not understanding why they had halted, the King urged the Swiss to press on. When it was explained to him why the Swiss had halted, the King, in response to impassioned pleas from his own Swiss captains, reluctantly accepted the surrender of the Pfyffer regiment, "in consideration of the respect for which he held the Swiss nation". The King returned their flags and instructed that they be taken back to the Confederation as proof of his goodwill.(2)

Although Swiss spilling Swiss blood was avoided on this occasion, Ivry marks an important transition in the history of the Swiss mercenary. For most of the sixteenth century the Swiss had served as loyal allies of the kings of France. Other than the brief period from 1510 to 1516, the Confederation had been diplomatically tied to France since 1474, and formally allied with France since 1521.(3) The Swiss troops were as much allies of France as mercenaries in the service of the wealthiest paymaster.

With the semi-official levies in support of the Huguenots and the official capitulations of the Catholic cantons with Spain, however, the clearcut relationship with France started to break down. Although France remained the formal ally of the Confederation for another two centuries and the majority of Swiss mercenaries continued to serve the kings of France during this time, increasingly important contingents appeared in other armies. For example, 4000 men under Walter Roll of Uri served under the Duke of Alba in the Netherlands, and three times in the 1590's the Catholic cantons supplied the Duke of Savoy. Eventually, the Swiss would show none of the reticence about fighting each other that had caused them to lower arms at Ivry.

Meanwhile, for the remainder of the reign of Henry IV, the close relationship between the King and the Confederation continued. Both the King's conversion to Catholicism in 1593 and the death of Pfyffer in 1594 helped to stabilize the relationship. Further regiments were raised for the siege of Paris and experienced captains such as Gallati and Reding were persuaded to lead the men despite their being practically ruined financially. On one occasion, as guarantee of payment, the French Ambassador Harlay had to deposit his entire fortune in Geneva.(4)

In 1597 the alliance expired and the issue of the French debts again came to a head. At the King's request, his chief minister Sully calculated in a document 280 pages in length that the staggering and surprisingly precise total of 35,823,472 livres and six sous were owing to the Swiss for pensions, arrears of pay with interest at eight per cent and interest on loans at five per cent. After five years' hard bargaining a repayment schedule was agreed, with one million livres to be paid immediately, followed by 400,000 livres per year. Henry, always cognisant of the role the Swiss had played in securing his crown, thanked his ambassadors for succeeding in reaching an agreement, thereby "placing the throne on a sound footing for myself and my successors".(5) In 1602 a delegation of forty-two Swiss notables celebrated the renewal of the alliance at an imposing ceremony in the cathedral of Notre Dame. Even Zurich signed the new alliance in 1614, for the first time in a century.

Before turning to developments in the seventeenth century and the "military revolution" one specialized role of the Swiss mercenary needs to be mentioned, the provision of bodyguards. Rulers have often chosen for their personal protection large foreigners, speaking strange languages, who could be relied on to stay apart from palace intrigues. The Swiss met all these criteria, and during the sixteenth century many Italian and German princelings had Swiss guards as well as the Pope and the Kings of France.

La Compagnie des Cent Suisses had been formed by Charles VIII in 1497 as a personal bodyguard. Its Captain-Colonel was a high-ranking French noble.(6) The position was held by the de la Marck family from the beginning of the sixteenth century until 1653 when they sold it for 100,000 livres. The Captain often had difficulty communicating with his German-speaking subordinates,(7) and effective command was in the hands of a Swiss Captain-Lieutenant. These Swiss officers often developed a close personal relationship with the King. Wilhelm Tugginer, for example, was bodyguard, taster and confidant of Charles IX, and it was Tugginer who was alone with the King when he died in the seclusion of the Palace of Vincennes in 1574. Famous colonels such as Pfyffer and Gallati held a position in the *Cent Suisses* as well as command of their regiments. Service in the *Cent Suisses* was recognized as an honour, as well as being paid one livre per month more than an ordinary soldier.

The *Cent Suisses* largely performed a parade function, preceding the king on ceremonial occasions, dressed in their brilliant uniforms and with drums and pipes playing. In 1585, however, Henry III sought to reinstate their role as bodyguards. A new regulation specified that twelve Swiss should always accompany him both within and outside the palace and by night they should occupy a guardroom next to his chamber. The Swiss had mixed success as guards, preventing an assassination attempt on Henry II in 1557 but failing to prevent the assassination of Henry III by a fanatic Jacobin in 1589. Henry IV was also assassinated under mysterious circumstances in 1610 while inexplicably riding in the streets of Paris without any guards.

At the time of his death Henry was planning to raise a new army of 50,000 men, to support the cause of the Protestant claimants to the Duchy of Cleves.(8) 6000 Swiss had already marched to the Moselle when news of the King's death reached them. Sully's *Memoires* claim that at the time of his death Henry had grandiose plans for a United States of Europe in which his good friends the Swiss would play a major role.

The Military Revolution

"The Swiss sell the liberty of their bodies in order to retain the liberty of their country."
  Duc de Rohan

A generation of English-speaking historians has been much concerned with debating whether the innovations introduced by Maurice of Nassau and Gustavus Adolphus of Sweden at the beginning of the seventeenth century deserve to be described as a Military Revolution. In relation to the Swiss Mercenary it is appropriate to consider the changes in warfare that took place around this time and their direct and indirect effects on the Swiss troops.

The new infantry tactics developed by Maurice of Nassau were based on a new battlefield unit, the 500-man battalion. The intention was to enable more men to be brought into effective action by releasing the passengers hemmed uselessly in the centre of the 6000-man Swiss square or Spanish *tercio*. The new battalion consisted of 250 pikemen arranged five deep on a front of fifty men, flanked by platoons of musketeers arranged ten deep. The musketeers were trained to execute the countermarch whereby each rank filed to the rear to reload after firing. Maurice's shallow battalions were ranged in two or three lines. These changes considerably improved the manoeuvrability of the infantry but at the expense of increased vulnerability to attack from the flank or the rear.

Employment of the new tactics required a high level of training and discipline in order to maintain the alignment of the formation during an advance or when facing about to protect against a flank attack. Furthermore, the musketeers had to be trained to perform the countermarch and to load and fire their weapons effectively and safely. Until the time of Maurice, training had been limited to the demonstration of weapon-handling and combat techniques to new recruits, and discipline had meant the prevention of the worst excesses of the men by the threat of punishment. Maurice's solution for obtaining the disciplined performances he required was the introduction of drill. Manuals such as Jacob de Gheyn's *Exercise of Armes* broke down the operation of loading and firing the musket into forty-two separate movements and illustrated thirty-two positions for the pike. These actions were drummed into the men by multiple repetition at twice-a-week sessions of drill. Discipline came to mean obedience to orders.

As well as teaching simplified weapon-handling techniques, the introduction of drill implied many other far-reaching changes for the infantry. Individual skills and courage became less important than the ability to follow orders and repeat routine tasks. As second-class recruits could have repetitive actions drilled into them, and even the dregs of society could have the routines beaten into them, a much larger pool of labour became available for the army recruiters. This in turn supported a further expansion in the size of armies. A higher proportion of officers and non-commissioned officers was needed to impose stricter disciplines on lower-grade recruits. The investment in training meant that it was worth retaining the men for longer periods, rather than releasing them at the end of each season only to train new recruits at the beginning of the next. On the other side of the coin, the combination of longer service, less vocationally motivated troops and dislike of more stringent discipline meant that desertion became a serious problem.

Improvements in weaponry allowed Gustavus Adolphus to expand on the Dutch system during the early part of the Thirty Years War. Progressive replacement of the arquebus with new lighter-weight muskets and the introduction of paper cartridges with a premeasured charge increased the rate of fire. Although only one round a minute was still considered a good rate, this was sufficient to allow the number of ranks that could keep up a continuous fire to be reduced from ten to six. Gustavus also increased his firepower by the introduction of volley firing and the use of light horse-drawn field artillery. The infantry part of a battle in which the participants employed the new tactics generally consisted of the two sides advancing towards each other slowly enough to maintain their lines. When about a hundred yards apart they would start to blaze away at each other, hopefully in volleys. The opposition, needing to stand upright to reload, offered presentable targets even to inaccurate muskets fired in the heat of action. The battle terminated when one side broke and fled. Cavalry could attack, fight and flee. Guns could be positioned, fired and captured. But the battle was only finally decided when one side's infantry was driven from the field.

In such a battle the pikemen performed the purely defensive role of protecting the flanks and rear against a cavalry charge. The heavily armoured cavalryman charging home armed with a lance had given away to lightly armoured *reiters* armed with pistol and sword and wheeling in front of the pikes to fire.(1) Defence against such cavalry needs fewer pikemen (and shorter pikes, which reduced in length from sixteen feet to eleven feet). Firearms rather than cavalry or pike squares now provided the infantry shock weapons, with pikes available to provide protection. This was the opposite of sixteenth century practice. Although there were different opinions between military leaders about the optimum proportion of pikes to firearms, a combination of the two remained necessary until the invention of the flintlock with bayonet towards the end of the seventeenth century. Hand-to-hand fighting virtually disappeared and close-quarter weapons such as the halberd were no longer carried.

Clearly these were important developments in weapons and tactics that took place during the first half of the seventeenth century. However, a number of arguments have been advanced against giving these developments the title of Military Revolution: firstly, that earlier changes such as the introduction of the stirrup and the invention of hand-held firearms were far more revolutionary; secondly, that the changes described above were gradual and evolutionary rather than suddenly occurring at one point in time; and thirdly, that proponents of the new revolutionary tactics cannot be demonstrated to have gained any decisive battlefield advantage, superior size continuing to be the main determinant of victory or defeat. Black has summarized the concept of the Military Revolution as "provocative but ultimately unconvincing."(2)

Earlier writers such as Oman and Delbrück pay particular attention to the Swiss-led development of the pike square, that allowed infantry to hold their own on the battlefield against cavalry for the first time in half a millenium. Taylor comments that "the Swiss introduced a revolutionary change into the art of war by evolving a shock tactic for unmounted troops". The "originality and permanence of the Swiss contribution"(3) deserves the description revolutionary far more than the refinements in tactics introduced by Maurice and Gustavus Adolphus. As well as Black's arguments, it should also be remembered that these were basically battlefield reforms during a period when battles were much less important to military strategy than sieges. A commander in the early seventeenth century rarely set out on campaign to search out and destroy his opponent's army. His concern was to besiege and take key locations that controlled communications and a large enough area to feed his army.

There must also be some doubt as to the extent to which such refinements were pioneered by the Dutch. Lynn has pointed out that even before Maurice's reforms the standard French infantry unit had been gradually reducing to battalion size of four to five hundred men. "The French had independently evolved units of similar size, composition and disposition before they came under the influence of Dutch practices."(4) This is not to say that Maurice of Nassau had no influence on the French; after all he was the future Marshall Turenne's uncle. Publication of manuals and the movement of mercenaries ensured both the ready dissemination of new ideas and that changes tended to take place in several armies at about the same time. Dutch-style weekly drill was introduced into the French army (including the Swiss regiments) under the Code Michaud of 1629 and increased to twice a week in 1661. In 1667 Jean Martinet, whose name has become synonymous with disciplinarian, was appointed Inspector General of Infantry.

Among the Swiss regiments themselves, only relatively minor changes occurred at the beginning of the seventeenth century. The 300-man company had always been the building block for the regiment and each company could readily be deployed independently. Only much later were battalions formed from joining companies and brigades from regiments. The Swiss had also long been renowned for their iron discipline on the battlefield. While not previously carrying out drill routines, the Swiss formations had always marched to the beat of the drum, and they handled themselves with the professional expertise of long-serving veterans. The discipline and manoeuvrability of Pfyffer's Swiss had been the wonder of the French court during the retreat from Meaux fifty years earlier. It is difficult to perceive any "revolutionary" impact on the Swiss as a result of developments in the Dutch or Swedish armies.

During the seventeenth century the Swiss regiments continued to perform two roles for the French. Firstly, they provided large numbers of infantry. Even during the relatively quiet years of Louis XIII's minority and early reign, there were seldom less than 6000 men serving in France. In 1635 when France declared war on Spain, four regiments of 12,000 men were raised and by 1640 there were more than 20,000 Swiss in the French army. Richelieu declared: "It is practically impossible to wage major wars successfully with the French alone. Foreigners are absolutely essential to make up the strength of the French army."(5)

Secondly, the Swiss continued to provide élite combat troops, particularly as the new drill techniques enabled supplementary regiments of lower grade recruits to be raised for the more mundane tasks of siege warfare and garrison duty.

On the battlefield the Swiss, together with the older French regiments, formed the backbone of the infantry, the solid unmovable mass that hopefully kept the army on the field until the cavalry, artillery, infantry pressure or superior generalship won the decision. In the event of a defeat the Swiss could be called on to provide a disciplined rearguard that could make the difference between the army surviving to fight another day and a disastrous rout.

In 1616 the first permanent Swiss regiment was formed as the Swiss Guards, which joined the French Guards in the Maison du Roi and took precedence over all other regiments of French and foreign infantry. The Guards always had the honour of occupying the centre of the line of battle and being first to storm the breach at a siege. Louis de Marvel of Neufchâtel wrote to his parents how he was first to storm the breach at Reims in 1653 "in front of the entire army" and was presented to the young Louis XIV and the Queen Mother in honour of his bravery.(6) The Guards took part in 150 major battles over the next 176 years. They formed the king's bodyguard outside the palace and were quartered in the suburbs of Paris. Kaspar Gallati, having served four kings of France, was the first colonel until his death in 1619 at the age of eighty-four (one of many Swiss captains who lived into their eighties, presumably benefiting from a constitution able to survive the rigours of battle and camplife). The Swiss Guard regiment contained ten companies, each canton providing either one whole or half company. The company contained 300 men, initially two-thirds armed with pikes and one-third with firearms. With the colonel's pay of 13,920 livres, 8176 livres per captain, and 104 livres and eight sous per soldier, it cost nearly half a million livres a year to keep the Guards in service. The king generally took an active interest in his guards, whose officers were formally presented to him each New Year's Day, the colonel even being given the signal honour of a royal handshake.(7)

The Swiss regiments continued to be raised in accordance with the capitulation system. Elsewhere in Europe the first half of the seventeenth century was the heyday of the Military Enterpriser. Large-scale contractors such as Mansfeld, Wallenstein, Bernhard of Saxe-Weimar and the Swiss Hans Ludwig von Erlach undertook to fund and raise regiments and even whole armies. Within the Confederation, however, the canton acted as the General Enterpriser, working with the French Ambassador to select a colonel for the regiment and allocating capitulations for companies in an orderly businesslike manner.

Originally the companies had been assigned to captains who raised the troops and led them in the field. The captains had then taken over the financial responsibility for the company, receiving a gross income from the French crown, meeting the company's costs, and taking the difference as their own profit. The captain effectively became the owner of the company. Gradually the financial risks became so great that a new type of company owner came into being. These were prominent local businessmen who accepted the capitulation as a speculative business venture, hiring military leaders to take command of the troops in the field. Redlich has estimated that there were about twenty such local Enterprisers operating in the Confederation.(8)

The capitulation specified the revenue from which the Enterpriser was expected to pay his officers and men according to agreed wage rates. This left him a basic profit of around 600 livres. There were many opportunities to augment this income, however, some more unscrupulous than others. Tricking the king's inspectors to include more men on the muster rolls than were actually present was standard practice. Ruses such as passing the same men twice (known as *passe volants*), passing off lowly-paid injured or crippled men, or hiring temporary men for the muster all provided additional profits, as could delaying payments to the men in the hope that they would die or desert. Profits could be made on the sale of weapons and equipments. The Enterpriser would naturally expect to receive pensions and business benefits appropriate to his position. Opportunistic profits were always possible, from gifts such as the gold chains traditionally dispensed by the French kings at the end of a campaign, or plunder from a defeated enemy. Ownership of a company could be highly profitable, and lead to great wealth. It was also a highly risky business as not only did it need luck on the battlefield, but also because payments from the shaky finances of the French crown were extremely unreliable. Many Swiss captains, including Gallati, were brought to near or actual bankruptcy.

The lines became increasingly blurred between political, military and business leadership within the Confederation. Ownership of a company became the perquisite of influential political figures, particularly those with a seat on the cantonal Diet where the important decisions were taken. Equally, a wealthy business background or an illustrious military career were ideal qualifications for the more lucrative political positions. Political, military and business success went hand in hand and were passed on to the next generation thereby forming the politico-military dynasties that ruled the Confederation during the next century as the Patriciat.

The affairs of the Swiss military enterpriser, Kaspar Jodok Stockalper of the Valais, have been studied in detail.(9) The French Ambassador wrote to Mazarin that Stockalper was the "most important man in the Valais". A wealthy businessman with, among other interests, a highly successful salt trading company, a member of the cantonal Diet for virtually his whole adult life, and a military enterpriser for thirty years from 1640 to 1670, Stockalper was an archetypal local grandee of the period. Steffen has calculated that Stockalper made a net profit of 250-300,000 livres from his mercenary business, even without inestimable side benefits from special concessions to his other businesses. He needed, however, to be financially sound enough to stand a 75,000 livre loss during one period in his career as an Enterpriser.

The military lobby in the Diet acted to protect its business interests by passing laws to punish deserters and hinder illegal recruiting. Finding enough recruits was starting to become a problem. The ever-increasing armies demanded more men, yet military service was starting to be perceived as a less attractive prospect. Recruiters needed to offer a signing-on bonus, initially only a thaler or two but by the middle of the century equivalent to half a month's salary. Drink flowed freely during recruiting sessions in the back rooms of taverns and many a recruit was persuaded to sign up under the heady influence of too much wine and the stirring tales of old veterans recounting glorious battles, plunder won and the fraternal atmosphere of camp life. The authorities tried to prevent the worst abuses in the recruiting process, though these were by no means all one-sided. Many a prospective recruit took the shilling and enjoyed a convivial boozy evening before disappearing with the bounty in his pocket.

Mercenary wages around the middle of the seventeenth century were at first sight still competitive. A study of a regiment raised in 1654 showed an average wage of 220-230 crowns per month, which was about fifty per cent higher than the average construction worker's wage at the time. Pikemen earned two crowns more and experienced soldiers had some chance of promotion to non-commissioned officer, as each company had three corporals, a provost and a sergeant. These positions were in the 240-300 crowns range, and were almost invariably promoted from the ranks. Some soldiers earned additional income by continuing trades such as cobbling or smithing as a sideline, or by working as labourers while billeted in garrisons.

Less than a quarter of the soldier's wage was handed over in his weekly pay, however. This was intended for his food and drink. The rest was retained by the company captain on account to cover various stoppages. This practice had two side benefits for the captain, as not only did he have less immediate cash to find if payments from the French were slow in coming but also that a credit in the company's account was a significant disincentive against desertion. The most important stoppages were for repayment of recruiting costs and for uniforms and weapons.

Captains started to provide standardized clothing at about this time.(10) Uniforms were doublets and hose in whatever design took the Captain's fancy, and cost about three to four months' salary. Weapons were generally procured by the captain from the cantonal armoury and charged to the soldier. A musket with a bandolier cost about half a month's salary, a pike and cuirasse cost about one month's salary. It was nearly a year before the soldier had paid back his initial costs and the minimum signing-on period therefore came to be a year and a day. After the first year it was possible for a careful soldier to save money, despite continued outgoings for additional clothing such as shoes and stockings, possible doctor's bills, barbills and so on. The testament has been found of an ordinary soldier called Kaspar Rudolf of Solothurn who died in 1624 leaving some 560 crowns to various beneficiaries. Mostly the soldiers left service with either a small saving or a small debt to the company account. Those leaving in credit were either paid cash or more probably received a promissory note.

At any one time about two-thirds of the men had served for less than three years, their predecessors having either left or been killed. The one-third with more than three years service included veterans with twenty years or more. These had usually been promoted to become NCOs. Unlike the German armies, the Swiss regiments still kept strong regional ties. For example one of Stockalper's regiments was nearly all from the Valais, and contained only thirty-four non-Swiss among 522 men, and eleven of these were from neighbouring Savoy.(11) Desertion was not yet a serious problem. One company recorded only ninety-eight deserters during a twenty-year period from 1649 to 1668, of which 53 were on three specific occasions (one related to a pay dispute, one after a battlefield defeat, and one for unknown reasons). On eleven of the twenty years there were three desertions or less.(12)

The Confederation largely managed to avoid becoming embroiled in the Thirty Years War. Despite continuing internal tensions between the Protestant and Catholic cantons, whose sympathies were drawn to one side or another, the Confederation and the individual cantons succeeded in maintaining a policy of strict neutrality towards the various combatants. The authorities appreciated the threats to the territorial and political integrity of the Confederation that would result from being drawn into the conflict by the various belligerents. They had also been forced to recognize that the Confederation's military system had become seriously outdated. The vaunted Swiss infantry could not compensate for lack of artillery and cavalry or an effective command structure if it became necessary to defend the homeland.

The continued prosperity that resulted from the policy of armed neutrality, especially in contrast with the spreading destitution to the North, was the cause of wonder for Grimmelshausen's *Simplicissimus*: "The country seemed to be completely different from other German counties, as though I were in Brazil or China. I saw the people living in peace; cattle stood in the cowsheds, the farmyards were full of chickens, ducks and geese. There was absolutely no concern about being attacked, no anxiety about being looted, no fear of losing life or possessions."(13)

A few alarms were raised when foreign armies transgressed the northern frontier of the Confederation. In 1633 the Swedes under Horn crossed into the Thurgau to attack Constance from the Swiss side, and the same year an Austrian army marched through the territory of Basle. Basle was traversed again in 1638, on this occasion by a French army under Bernhard of Saxe-Weimar. The main threat to Swiss neutrality, however, came in the South, due to the strategic position of the Alpine passes, especially the Valtelline.

The Valtelline, which had belonged to the Grey Leagues since 1513, is a valley leading north-west from Lake Como towards the Tyrol. It formed at this time a stretch of the most important military corridor for the movement of troops between the Spanish possessions in northern Italy and Habsburg territory in Austria.(14) Also from a French viewpoint the valley had an important strategic significance, both as the link with its Venetian ally and to block off enemy troop reinforcements.

Great Power stratagems were complicated by clan rivalries in the region. The Planta family supported the Austrians and Spaniards, while the Salis family, prominent mercenaries over many centuries, supported the French. The whole pot was stirred up by an adventurer and intriguer called Georg Janatsch.

The Valtelline affair opened in 1620 when Catholic soldiers under Pompée de Planta massacred a number of Protestants and then, supported by Spanish troops, defeated at Tirano two regiments sent by Berne and Zurich to the aid of their co-religionists. In 1621 a pact was signed by all the Powers concerned, including the Confederation, confirming the sovereignty of the Grey Leagues over the Valtelline but granting the Austrians and Spaniards rights of passage. Janatsch then brutally assassinated de Planta,(15) and war again broke out. This time the Austrians invaded and annexed the Valtelline. Richelieu at this point decided that it was time for the French to intervene and an army of 3000 French and 8000 Swiss joined Janatsch and Ulysses von Salis in driving the Austrians out. In 1626 the independence of the Valtelline under the Grey Leagues was again declared. The territory gradually drifted back under Austrian influence, however, until the French intervened a second time. In 1635 a small Franco-Swiss army under the Duc de Rohan fought a brilliant campaign of mountain warfare and again evicted the Austrians. Despite the assassination of Janatsch, irregular hostilities continued in the region until the Peace of Westphalia.

The Thirty Years War ended with two important steps in support of the Confederation's policy of armed neutrality. In 1647 the Defensionale of Wil specified measures to improve Swiss defensive capability. Arrangements were made for 12,000 men to be immediately available to defend the frontier with two further levies each of 12,000 men in reserve if required. The effectiveness of the new measures was proved the same year when rapid mobilization dissuaded the Swedish army from transgressing Swiss territory. In 1648 the Peace of Westphalia(16) finally confirmed the legal separation of the Confederation from the Empire and its independence as a sovereign state.

While maintaining its policy of neutrality throughout the war, Swiss troops had of course been heavily involved in the conflict through mercenary contracts, especially with France. During the early part of the war Richelieu had kept France out of the conflict in order to quell the remnants of internal dissension and to improve the financial position of the state. Around 6000

Swiss troops were generally in French employ at this time and took part in the sieges of La Rochelle, Montauban and other Protestant strongholds. When France finally declared war on Spain in 1635, military expenditures were doubled and the number of Swiss troops likewise to 12,000 in four regiments. By the death of Louis XIII in 1643 there were over 21,000 Swiss in the French army. 3400 were in the Swiss Guards and the rest in seven other regiments dispersed around the French borders in Flanders, Lorraine and Catalonia. The Swiss took part in every significant French action during the war, including the two most important — Rocroy and Lens.

Taking place on 19 May, 1643, five days after the death of Louis XIII and five months after the death of Richelieu, the Battle of Rocroy marked the end of the long supremacy of the Spanish infantry. 15,000 French infantry and 7000 cavalry under the 23-year-old Louis de Bourbon, Duc d'Enghien and future Grand Condé, faced a Spanish army of 26,000 men, including 16,000 of the famous *tercios*.

The Swiss Regiment de Molondin under Colonel Jacques d'Estavayer-Molondin of Fribourg was in the centre of the French first line with the Regiments of von Wattenwyl and von Roll in the second and third lines. The battle opened with a cavalry engagement on both wings. Then Enghien, having defeated the Spanish cavalry on his right, cut through the Spanish centre isolating the Spanish infantry in the first line from the Italian and German troops supporting them. The outnumbered Spanish *tercios* were then annihilated by repeated infantry and cavalry attacks. 8000 of the Spanish army were killed and 7000 captured. Although not of lasting significance to the course of the war, Rocroy saw the effective end of the Spanish *tercios*as the preeminent European infantry.

The Swiss had been at the centre of the action. Yet only a month later Enghien was writing to his father the Prince of Condé from the French camp at the siege of Thionville: "The Swiss regiments in this army are at the end of their resources and have begged me to write to you requesting their pay. They serve so well, especially the Regiment de Molondin, that I could not refuse their request. I assure you they provide the best infantry of my army."(17)

On 20 August, 1648, 16,000 French under Enghien (now Condé) faced 18,000 Spaniards under Archduke Leopold of Austria at Lens. At the height of the action, the French, Swiss and Scottish guards in the centre of the French line had broken through their opponents' front line and found themselves isolated by their advance. At this critical moment the Swiss General Hans Ludwig von Erlach attacked from the right flank with 4000 troops from the army of Weimar and saved the day. Two months later Condé introduced Erlach to the young Louis XIV as: "Sire, this is the man whom you should thank for the victory at Lens."(18)

XII

No Money, No Swiss

"Point d'argent, point de Suisse"
Racine, *Les Plaideurs*, 1.1

The perception of the mercenary profession has been heavily influenced by the strictures of Machiavelli:

"Mercenaries are disunited, thirsty for power, undisciplined, and disloyal; they are brave among their friends and cowards before the enemy; they have a fear of God, they do not keep faith with their fellow men; they avoid defeat just as long as they avoid battle; in peacetime you are despoiled by them, and in wartime by the enemy. The reason for all this is that there is no loyalty or inducement to keep them on the field apart from the little they are paid, and this is not enough to make them want to die for you. They are only too ready to serve in your army when you are not at war; but when war comes they either desert or disperse." (1)

These accusations were largely merited with respect to mercenaries at the time Machiavelli was writing. The bloodless battles of the Condottiere, succeeded by the marauding bands of Swiss and *landsknechts* that swarmed over northern Italy at the beginning of the sixteenth century, created a justifiably negative impression on the author of *The Prince*. As discussed in Chapter VI, the Swiss troops at that time fully deserved their reputation for cruelty and disloyalty. They often refused to fight at the most inconvenient moments in order to obtain arrears of pay.

As the sixteenth century progressed, however, the activities of the Swiss mercenaries were increasingly organized through the capitulation system. The plundering *knaben* of earlier times had been replaced by professional soldiers. Within the Confederation, the mercenary was regarded as a respectable craftsman, employed in the biggest industry in Europe. Military service was considered an integral part of the Swiss economy.

As in any other business, the Swiss expected to be paid. As we have seen, arrears of pay and pensions, and defaults on repayment of loans reached enormous sums. The French kings' inability or unwillingness to pay their debts regularly strained Swiss loyalty to breaking point. From the Swiss point of view, the constant disputes were in pursuit of money they had been promised in formal contracts but never paid. They regarded the contract as binding on both sides and expected the French to keep their side of the bargain. It is worth stressing that on no occasion did the Swiss seek to obtain an increase in pay over the level previously agreed in a Capitulation. The problem was basically caused by French kings hiring troops they could not pay for. "No money, no Swiss" was as much the perception of the hirer as the hired.

The assertion by Kiernan that "if the paychest gave out they changed sides or marched off home" (2) is appropriate as a description of mercenary troops in Machiavelli's time but gives a misleading impression of the mercenary profession as it subsequently developed, at least as far as the Swiss are concerned. Without being excessively apologetic about the Swiss, whose forces undoubtedly contained as many rapacious and untrustworthy individuals as any other, there was no occasion on which the Swiss "changed sides", either during a campaign or during the period of a capitulation. The *landsknechts* regularly did so, to the extent that their ruse at Arques was successful because the willingness of German troops to change sides even in the middle of battle was accepted as normal. Turncoat was not, however, a description that could fairly be applied to the Swiss.

Similarly, during the Italian Wars the Swiss armies would regularly disappear back into the mountains. But after the middle of the sixteenth century, the Swiss troops never "marched off home". They threatened to do so on many occasions, most notably in 1571 and 1650, but never actually carried out the threat, which was really a bargaining counter to obtain at least partial payment of the French debts. Equally, although the Spanish army in the Netherlands mutinied forty-six times between 1572 and 1607, (3) and although mutiny was a serious problem in the Elizabethan army, (4) there was no occasion on which the Swiss troops mutinied before the peculiar circumstances of the French Revolution.

Rather than turncoat, deserting mutineers, the most remarkable characteristic of the Swiss troops was their steadfast loyalty to the French alliance, a unique 300-year relationship in the history of Europe. Indeed it is reasonable to question whether the Swiss troops in French service were mercenaries or allies. They have justifiably been described as "an army within an army". (5) Unlike Scots, Irish, Italians, Hungarians and all the other foreign troops in French service, the Swiss remained under the control of their country of origin. All the renewals of the Alliance and all capitulations preserved the right of the Swiss authorities to call the troops home if the Confederation needed them. This right was a cornerstone for the preservation of Swiss neutrality. Until Napoleon no power dared to attack a nation that could call 50,000 elite troops home to its defence (and incidentally cut off the assailant from future supplies of recruits). The Swiss regarded the French as allies and not once in all the official correspondence between the two countries is the word mercenary used.

The dual loyalty of the Swiss troops in their curious position as half-mercenaries, half-allies is illustrated in the oath sworn by each soldier: "I swear to serve loyally and with honour his Most Christian Majesty the King of France, to obey the colonel and the officers in all their commands, to maintain the honour of the Swiss Nation in all circumstances, to be loyal and obedient to the Swiss authorities. May God, Our Lord Jesus, and all the saints help me."

Swiss loyalty to the French alliance was guaranteed by the clear practical advantages that the relationship provided to both parties. The French could rely on recruiting large numbers of skilled infantry while the Swiss made financial profits from their export business in professional soldiers. An anecdote about an exchange of words between the French Minister of War Louvois and Colonel Stuppa in front of Louis XIV encapsulates the complexity of the relationship. Louvois commented to the King: "Sire, with all the money Your Majesty has paid to the Swiss, once could pave the road to Basle with coins." To which Stuppa replied: "Sire, with all the blood that my countrymen have spilled for France, one could fill a canal from Paris to Basle." (6)

Despite the close ties of the French alliance, there were three categories of Swiss mercenaries that served in other armies. The first were individual soldiers following a military career that could take them through several armies. This was not considered unusual or reprehensible at the time, and was commonplace among the officer class of all nations. For example, Hans Ludwig von Erlach, to whom the French victory at Lens was attributed, was a member of a renowned Bernese military dynasty whose ancestors included the Rudolf von Erlach who had commanded the Swiss troops at Laupen in 1339. Erlach started his career in the Swedish army in which he was already a colonel at the age of twenty-nine. Returning to Berne he became a senator and was instrumental in designing the Defensionale to update the Swiss defensive system. He raised a regiment for the French in 1630 before joining the army of the large-scale military enterpriser Prince Bernhard of Saxe-Weimar. Erlach took command of this army on the death of Prince Bernhard in 1639 and spent the rest of his career in French service.

A similar career was followed by Ulysses von Salis, born in 1594 into a military family from the Grey Leagues that had played an important part in Swiss history since the eleventh century. Already a page to the Duke of Bouillon at the age of twelve, he was commanding a company in the service of Venice in Dalmatia by the age of twenty. He fought in Mansfeld's army at Mingolsheim and Fleurus before taking command of a company of the Swiss Guard in Paris in 1628. Salis rushed home to serve with Rohan in the Valtelline campaign and then served the rest of his career with the French, becoming the first Swiss to reach the rank of Maréchal de Camp. He eventually died at the age of eighty.

As a last example, Hans Rudolf von Werdmüller of Zurich had already served France, Sweden, Venice and Austria when he became a captain in the Swiss Guard in 1654 at the age of forty. He fought under Turenne at the Battle of the Dunes, became a General in French service, then commander of the artillery for Venice and died as a Field-Marshal for Austria.

Swiss officers crisscrossed Europe, gaining experience and popping up in curious places. An Erlach even became an Admiral in the Danish navy. Countless common soldiers also wandered through the armies of Europe but their histories are less traceable than those of the officers.

The second category of mercenaries serving other than the French were those motivated by religious sympathies. During the French Wars of Religion, the Swiss authorities had been largely successful in limiting the extent to which troops actually served the enemies of the French crown. Nevertheless on three occasions Protestant troops joined the Huguenots and the Catholic cantons signed capitulations with Spain. Similarly during the Thirty Years War, Swiss troops again served in the armies of co-religionists, although not directly against the French. The Protestant cantons, especially Zurich and Berne, supplied troops to the Swedish army, the regiments of Weiss and Escher fighting at Lützen and Nordlingen. Catholic regiments from the Waldstaette regularly served Savoy, Spain and Venice, service for the latter being considered as defending Christendom against the Turks. The military enterpriser Kaspar Jodok Stockalper, for example, although closely tied to the French as we have seen, also at various times had companies serving Savoy, Venice and Naples. (7)

The third category of mercenaries not tied to the French alliance were those recruited unofficially or semi-officially by other powers on a straightforward contract-hire basis. Wherever conflicts broke out, the representatives of the belligerents swarmed over the cantons enlisting the willing recruits still available after the official capitulations had been filled. Although the Diet thundered against secret recruiting, suitable presents to influential politicians ensured that the recruiters could pursue their activities without too much interference. The continuous repetition of bans on recruiting shows how little they were heeded. A network of recruiters and their agents covered the Confederation. The recruiters were usually veteran soldiers and their agents were prominent members of the local community, especially innkeepers. For a secret or illegal levy, the recruiter moved from a table outside an inn to the back room, often at a location near the borders of the canton so that he could quickly disappear if threatened. Mercenaries for hire from the surrounding regions, especially southern Germany, gravitated to the known recruiting grounds in the Confederation to add to the pool of local labour and add fuel to the whole process. How many were recruited unofficially outside the capitulations is unknown but the amount of discussion among the authorities about the problem would indicate that the numbers involved were significant.

Free Companies were companies not incorporated into regiments. They operated uneasily between the official and unofficial troops. Sometimes they were the remains of regiments, the rest of which had been disbanded for the winter. The practice started of retaining one or two companies garrisoned in potential trouble spots to ensure the internal stability of the kingdom. These companies were then incorporated in the new regiments raised the following spring. This practice was a step along the way towards a standing army. Additional Free Companies were recruited by captains from disbanded soldiers returning home. Such companies were sometimes recognized by the cantons and sometimes not. When recognized they were called "*companies avouées*" or authorized companies. The French ambassadors were also known to raise Free Companies when the French debts were so high that they could not negotiate the placement of official capitulations.

The position in the middle of the seventeenth century may be summarized as follows. The vast majority of Swiss mercenaries were employed by the French crown under capitulations raised in line with the alliance between the two countries. The loyalty and commitment of these troops was never questioned. Some mercenaries served semi-officially or unofficially for other powers. These included men not selected for the official capitulations and therefore some less reputable and less trustworthy elements. Because of the secrecy of many of the unofficial arrangements, the numbers involved are difficult to estimate but were significantly less than those serving France. The introduction of standing armies and the increasing acceptance of capitulations from other powers changed this picture during the second half of the seventeenth century so that by 1701 the proportion serving France was equalled by the proportion serving other powers.

XIII

The Introduction of Standing Armies

"The Swiss army is the main nerve of the French army"
The Prince of Orange

A standing army is a force of regular soldiers that exists in peacetime as well as in wartime. During the second half of the seventeenth century the advantages of such a force over the prevailing custom of hiring troops for one campaign at a time became apparent. Instead of disbanding the troops in the autumn, the soldiers could be drilled and trained through the winter months. A cohesive body of experienced disciplined troops was then ready the following spring to incorporate the relatively small number of raw recruits hired to replace the previous year's losses.

The introduction of standing armies had a symbiotic relationship with the growth of absolutism. On the one hand, the expenses of the regular army could only be met as the administrative framework was built up to collect sufficient taxes. In France (concentrating on the main employer of the Swiss troops), a group of formidable bureaucrats developed the necessary administration. Colbert provided the finances and Michel Le Tellier, War Minister from 1643 to 1666, and his son the brilliant and ruthless Marquis de Louvois, War Minister from 1666 to 1691, undertook a thorough reform of the military organization. Civil bureaucrats, the *Intendants aux armées*, were introduced to take charge of logistics and ensure that the troops were paid regularly, the prerequisite for good discipline. Improved logistics provided the further benefit of reducing the wastefulness caused by the troops living off the land, which in turn increased the capability of the peasantry to pay the new taxes.(1) Better administration also ensured that a higher proportion of the available finances found its way to the troops and not into the pockets of the Military Enterprisers. The Le Telliers were able to clamp down on such abuses as absentee officers and unacceptable numbers of *passe-volants* that had crept into the army as a whole, including the Swiss regiments. Reliable financing and military reform enabled another sharp increase in the size of armies. The French army that had numbered 70,000 men on the death of Henry IV had expanded to 150,000 men under Louis XIII and now increased to 250,000 under Louis XIV. Under the Le Telliers the French army was transformed into a modern, centrally controlled organization, and became the largest yet seen in Europe.

The other side of the relationship was that the standing army provided the absolutist monarchy with a solid defence against internal dissension. Disciplined loyal troops could quell rebellions, guarantee law and order, assist in the collection of the taxes that fed the system, and generally ensure political control. The uprising of the Fronde had created an indelible impression on the young Louis XIV and he was determined that such a challenge to his authority should not be repeated. As a side benefit, the army also provided a useful career to keep the nobility occupied and out of mischief. The standing army has justifiably been called the cornerstone of absolutism.(2)

Long-term enlistment allowed the standardization of armaments and equipment, which was especially useful as important changes in weaponry took place at the end of the seventeenth century. During the middle years of the century an infantry regiment was typically armed with one-third pikes and two-thirds matchlock muskets. The matchlock was then replaced by the more efficient flintlock musket, which required only three ranks to maintain a continuous fire and which, by doing away with the dangerous lighted match, allowed the musketeers to be placed closer together. During the same period the bayonet was invented. The plug bayonet, introduced in the 1650s, fitted into the barrel of the musket, theoretically allowing it to be used either as musket or as pike. In practice it was not very effective, tending to jam in the barrel. The socket bayonet, however, was a genuinely revolutionary development. Invented in the 1690s(3) the socket bayonet locked onto the outside of the barrel, allowing the weapon to be used both as musket and pike at the same time. It was noticed at the battle of Fleurus that German regiments armed with bayonets could fend off French cavalry attacks at least as well as other German regiments armed with pikes. The musketeer could now defend himself and the redundant pike quickly disappeared from the battlefield. In the winter of 1703-4 the Swiss regiments were the last to give up the weapon on which their military reputation had been founded two hundred years earlier. As General Susane has commented on the changes: "It is only necessary to say one word to give the highest praise: namely that they were adopted by the Swiss troops who thereby abandoned the tactics which had been their strength and glory during two hundred years."(4)

The Swiss regiments also joined the rest of the army in introducing

18. Fusilier of the Swiss Guards. The Swiss Guards adopted in 1703 their famous uniform of red coat, with blue lining, facings, breeches and stockings, the exact reverse of the French Guards.

19. Swiss fusilier. In 1703 the Swiss regiments finally gave up the long pike on which their reputation had depended for two hundred years, and changed to flintlock muskets with socket bayonets.

20. Peter Stuppa (1620-1701), Colonel of the Swiss Guards, confidante of Louis XIV and founder of the first permanent Swiss regiments (painting by Nicholas de Largillière).

21. François de Reynold (1642-1722), Lieutenant-General, Colonel of the Swiss Guards during the War of the Spanish Succession and Colonel General des Suisses et Grisons (oil painting by Hyacinthe Rigaud).

22. Bivouac of the Swiss Guards, the senior Swiss Regiment. Throughout the eighteenth century at least ten percent of the French army consisted of Swiss regiments.

23 and 24. Departure and Return of the Soldier — a somewhat romanticised view. Foreign service became decreasingly popular during the eighteenth century, sharp recruiting practices multiplied and the period of enlistment lengthened (by the Bernese painter Freudenberger).

25. Regimental flag of the Karrer Marine (1719-1763), showing the design of multicoloured wavy flames radiating from the centre that was used by all the Swiss regiments.

26. Review of the Swiss Guards by Louis XV on the Plaine des Sablons, their main parade ground in Paris, c1760 (oil painting by Lenfant).

companies of grenadiers. These were handpicked troops operating in front of the lines with the dangerous task of hurling their grenades at the enemy from close positions. In this role they could trace their ancestry back to the *enfants perdus* which had skirmished in front of the Swiss squares at Novara and Marignano. Initially men from each company were handpicked for this dangerous but coveted role. Later a separate grenadier company was formed in each regiment, but with the men still on the strength of their original companies so that the financial risk of these positions was spread among the captains. As usual the conservative Swiss were the last regiments to make this change, the line regiments in 1691 and the Swiss Guards in 1696.

During the last quarter of the century the wearing of uniforms was introduced for the first time. Some standardization of clothing had taken place through the bulk buying of Military Enterprisers when they were responsible for outfitting their men, but the troops still tended to be a ragged collection wearing a sash to identify themselves from the enemy.(5) 1688 was the year that the Swiss regiments started wearing uniforms, most prominently the red coat that would be their proud trademark for the next hundred years.(6) The individual regiments were recognizable by different combinations and colours of buttons and accoutrements. Finally, in 1703, the Swiss Guards adopted their famous uniform of red coats with blue lining, facings, breeches and stockings, i.e. the exact reverse of the French Guards uniform. Headgear for all the troops was the tricorne hat.

The military reforms took place following a difficult period in the relationship between the Swiss and the French after the accession of Louis XIV. In 1649 Mazarin had suddenly dismissed sixteen Swiss companies without pay and many of the men died of cold and hunger while struggling to return home. The ill-will in the Confederation caused by this episode brought to a head yet again the long-standing problem of payments and debts. The following year the Diet went so far as to order all the troops home in an attempt to precipitate an agreement on the payment of the debts. Neither side wanted a final break and yet another compromise was patched together. It was eventually agreed that a total of 4,600,000 livres would be paid over six years. As guarantee, the French crown jewels were handed over to five Swiss colonels for transportation to Zurich, where they remained in safekeeping for the next fifteen years. Happily this was the last major dispute over pay and thereafter payments were made regularly. Louis himself wrote to Colbert on 28 March, 1677, telling him to pay the Swiss because "it would be good ... that these people are content".(7)

The alliance expired in 1651, and only in 1663 did the French succeed, through intensive diplomatic efforts and the lavish award of honours and pensions, in negotiating a renewal. The new alliance was for the life of the king plus eight years, and included all the usual clauses as well as two new appendices. The first accorded Swiss officers the same opportunities as were enjoyed by French officers for advancement to the highest ranks, including that of General Officer. The second assured the Protestant cantons that their troops would be free to practice their own religion and could be withdrawn if another religious war broke out in France. An embassy of nearly one hundred prominent Swiss leaders joined Louis XIV in renewing the alliance at a formal ceremony in the Cathedral of Notre Dame followed by a huge troop review at Vincennes.(8)

The renewal of the alliance was, however, followed by further disputes during the 1660s, this time over the issue of Free Companies. The key personality in this issue was Peter Stuppa, at that time Colonel of the Swiss Guards. Stuppa, born in Chiavenna in the Grey Leagues in 1620, served in the Guards at the age of sixteen, was a captain at the age of thirty-two and colonel at the age of thirty-eight. He enjoyed the full confidence of the King(9), and went on to become acting Colonel-General des Suisses et Grisons during the minority of the Duc de Marne, a Lieutenant-General, and remained Colonel of the Guards until his death in 1701. Stuppa conceived the plan to rehire recently demobilized troops together with troops from areas that were close allies of the thirteen cantons without actually being members of the Confederation.(10) The troops were hired at reduced rates of pay into Free Companies and kept outside the capitulation system. The French ministers were attracted by the financial benefits of the plan, enabling them to obtain more troops for the same outlay. There was uproar in the political and military establishment of the Confederation, however, who saw both their business cartel and their officer caste threatened by outside competition. Protests were made to the French Ambassador and Stuppa's effigy was hanged in Lucerne. Nevertheless, Stuppa installed himself secretly in the Jura near Basle with his agents. 12,000 men flocked to join the Free Companies despite the efforts of the Swiss authorities to block the activities of the recruiters. For these men, the Free Companies provided possibilities of employment and advancement not available to them through the regular companies licensed by the cantons and reserved for their favoured sons.

In 1671 the picture changed completely. The French were preparing for war with Holland and it became urgently necessary both to secure new levies of Swiss troops and to prevent their being available to the Dutch. The same Stuppa therefore came up with the new plan of establishing permanent Swiss line regiments. Stuppa himself was sent to negotiate the new arrangements becoming a French ambassador to his own country. By the end of the year he had signed capitulations for four new regiments, each consisting of 2400 men in twelve companies. The capitulations, much to the satisfaction of the Swiss authorities, reverted to the previous system with the important new provision that a company would be paid as a full 200-man company provided it consisted of a minimum of 180 men. The twenty missing men were known as *places-mortes*.

Four regiments were mustered in front of the *Commissaires de Guerre* at Gex on 17 February, 1672. These were the Regiments Erlach, Stuppa, Salis-Zisers and Pfyffer. The Regiment Erlach was allocated entirely to Berne and restricted to Bernese citizens. The others were allocated to several cantons, Pfyffer for example comprising companies from Lucerne, Glarus, Fribourg and Solothurn. The ties between the regiments and their home cantons were weaker than earlier but still present. The fifth Swiss Regiment, the Greder from Solothurn, was formed in 1673. The sixth was formed in 1677 by the younger brother of Stuppa and was known as Stuppa-Jeune with the earlier regiment known as Vieux-Stuppa. The seventh and eighth were formed in 1690, the Salis consisting of twelve Free Companies and the Courten from the Valais. These regiments remained in service until the French Revolution, changing their names as their ownership and the name of their colonels changed. Pfyffer for example became Hessy in 1689, de Burky in 1729, de Tschudi in 1737, de Vigier in 1740 and de Castella in 1756 (see Appendix VI). Despite the agreement to revert to the capitulation system, the French also continued to recruit Free Companies clandestinely, more than sixty being recruited between 1670 and 1690.

The Swiss Guards, numbering around 3000 remained the senior Swiss regiment. Fusiliers in the Guards had to be a minimum of one metre seventy-five centimetres in height, and grenadiers one metre eighty-two. When not on active service, the Guards were quartered in such suburbs of Paris as Suresnes, Rueil, Nanterre, Colombe, Saint-Denis and Satrouville, with one battalion in the city itself in the Rue Grange-Batalière. In some of these districts the Swiss formed a quarter of the population. While their fiscal privileges brought prosperity to the local economy, the presence of such a large group of foreigners also caused social tensions. Each day the regiment was literally on guard outside the royal palaces at Versailles, Fontainebleau and the Louvre, or exercising on the Plaine des Sablons.

The new regiments were quickly in action during the war with Holland participating notably in the siege of Maastricht and the battle of Seneffe. By the time the war ended in 1678, ten per cent of the French forces were Swiss. There were 2900 men in the Swiss Guards, 2400 in each of six line regiments and 8000 men in forty free companies, a total of 25,000 men.

The reforms of the army caused some significant changes in the relationships of the officers and the men, both from a military and a business point of view. The officers of the Swiss regiments had traditionally been very close to and often barely distinguishable from the men, living and fighting together and wearing practically the same clothes. In the standing army, however, the requirements of discipline by drill imposed a clear separation between officers and men. Informal group discipline was replaced by strict discipline according to the rule book. Furthermore, instead of being a neighbour from home who left to campaign each year, the captain now spent years at a time in foreign service and recruited his men through agents and relatives back home. The new recruit might no longer know his captain before he joined up. He was no longer treated as an individual *knecht* or *knabe*, proud of his skills and freely choosing to enrol to carry out his trade. The soldier was now expected to be the anonymous member of a drill squad carrying out orders promptly and without question.

Under the new capitulations the captain remained the proprietor of the company as well as its military leader. As the state had taken over many of the supply functions, however, the financial rewards were much slimmer than in the heyday of the military enterpriser during the first half of the seventeenth century. The initial investment to form a company of 200 men was 20-22,000 livres. Nearly half of this was for the new uniform which cost over 50 livres per man.(11) In addition, the captain needed capital to fund his recruitment costs and travel expenses. He was relieved of the cost of weaponry, which the State had taken over in order to ensure standardization of arms and ammunition, but other than a 4000 livre advance had to provide the rest of the investment himself. To spread the risk the captain sometimes took on only a half-company, a practice which the French permitted as it bound one more officer to the French cause. The captain charged the recruit for the uniform, docking the cost from his pay over a two-year period. During that time he stood the risk of losing his investment if the recruit deserted, or was killed or captured in action.

The 1673 capitulation of the Greder Regiment shows the sums involved in operating the company. The captain received 18 livres per man monthly for the 200-man company to give an income of 3600 livres. He paid 180 men an average of 14 livres per month, in a range from 10 livres for a non Swiss to 18 livres for a specially regarded soldier with influence on the hiring of more recruits. The majority were paid 13, 14 or 15 livres. The salaries for the men, therefore, totalled around 2500 livres. Officers' and NCOs' salaries came to another 4-500 livres per month, leaving the captain a net income of 6-700 livres. He would also make a profit on food and uniforms that he sold to the troops but he would have additional recruiting costs to replace deserters and casualties. All being well the average income for a company captain was around 8000 livres per year. At least the payments from the king had become much more regular following the reform of the French administration systems, and he no longer suffered the huge payment arrears of the past. The overall profitability of the business hinged on keeping the company intact long enough for the initial investment to be returned, which depended on the captain's luck in action and his ability to keep desertion under control.

For the men, the terms were less attractive than those enjoyed by earlier generations of mercenaries. The average pay was 3-4 livres less than at the beginning of the century and the cost of the uniform had also now to be deducted. In addition, the opportunities for looting under the new disciplinary rules were much reduced. Nevertheless, mercenary pay was still higher than the wages from equivalent semi-skilled occupations, payment could now be relied on, and the experienced soldiers often obtained a supplementary income from some sideline such as selling fruit and vegetables from a small garden that they cultivated.(12)

Apart from the lower pay, mercenary service was starting to become less attractive for other reasons. The three-year signing-on period required a more serious commitment than the adventure of a season's campaigning. The drill and stricter discipline were not at all popular, especially compared with the previous easy-going camaraderie of the Swiss troops. The reforms of the Le Telliers aimed to improve the effectiveness of the troops, not their wellbeing. Plenty of recruits were still available but less than before, and at the same time armies were increasing in size. For the first time demand overtook supply.

As an illustration, of the 6038 men newly recruited as replacements for the Solothurn regiments between 1639 and 1730, only 2763 or 45% were inhabitants of the Canton of Solothurn itself 2422 or 40% came from other cantons, especially Berne, Lucerne and Basle. The remaining 853 or 15% were non-Swiss, mainly German-speakers from southern Germany, Austria and Alsace but with a smattering of many nationalities including two Irishmen.(13)

Armies continued to recruit by voluntary enlistment but, now that soldiers were becoming more difficult to find, the incidence of sharp recruiting practices multiplied. Waverers were seduced with flowing wine, the favours of barmaids and strumpets, and a recruitment bounty of up to 12 thalers (at a time when a labourer's wage was 4 thalers a month). The cantonal authorities devoted much effort to organizing the recruiting process more fairly, and incidentally to protecting the business in which many of them had interests. Complaints and disputes over recruiting nevertheless continued to mount.

Once he had the men in harness, the captain made every effort to keep them as long as possible in order to avoid additional outlay on recruiting replacements. The normal period of service was three years. The captain tried to hang on to his men for additional periods by paying them in such a way that they were permanently in debt, by prevaricating over providing them a demobilization pass without which they were technically deserters, or by persuading them to re-sign, using the same promises and tricks as practised by the recruiting agents. The majority of the troops remained for at least twice the minimum period and many for their whole adult life.

The average company still lost about thirty men each year, for whom replacements had to be found. Firstly, sickness and disease carried off many, especially if they were exposed to the insanitary conditions of a campaign. Then, some did manage to leave the service after completing their time. Most importantly, for the first time, desertion was becoming a problem. The singing of folksongs(14) had to be forbidden as it promoted melancholy and homesickness. Deserters were leniently treated by the authorities at home and there were many cases of two- and three-time offenders. It was regarded as the captain's business to recover and punish his men, a task not made easier by the general public sympathy for the deserter rather than the officer. Finally, the main risk, of course, not just to the captain's livelihood but to life itself was participation in a major battle. The Greder Regiment, whose finances were used as an example above, was almost wiped out in 1708. The possibility of death in action had to remain the most important consideration in both the soldiers, and the captain's choice of occupation. The Swiss regiments were still regarded as elite troops and therefore tended to be used at every opportunity. There was hardly a single major battle or siege in all of Louis XIV's many wars in which Swiss troops were not in the thick of the action.

At the end of the Dutch War in 1678, the French decided to retain all the Swiss regiments, but arbitrarily cut the soldiers' wages by four crowns per month in order to save on costs. This reduction brought wages in the standing regiments down to the same level as in the Free Companies. The company strength was also reduced to 160 men, ie. below the level of 180 which triggered payment of the full 200-man complement. In 1688, however, pay and company strength were brought back to the previous level in preparation for the War of the League of Augsburg.

For this war the Swiss provided not only an average of 25,000 men but also invaluable strategic protection for the centre of France's eastern frontier against an otherwise complete encirclement by her enemies. The six campaigns of the war included three major battles and innumerable sieges, but neither side was able to win a decisive advantage. Although Marshal Luxembourg was successful enough in the battles to decorate Notre Dame with the flags he captured,(15) he was unable to annihilate the army of the league. This was largely due to a serious tactical disadvantage in the infantry formations of the late seventeenth century. Unlike the Swiss squares which had marched into combat in the formation in which they would fight, infantry now needed the best part of a day to manoeuvre laboriously from line of march into line of battle. During this time, an opponent not wishing to fight would simply march away. This happened at Fleurus in 1690, for example, where a flanking movement by the French and Swiss guards won the battle but could not reform in time to prevent Waldeck retreating with most of the allied forces intact.

Nevertheless the French claimed two famous victories. At Steenkerque in 1692 the French were surprised by William and the Duke of Wurtenburg broke through the French first line destroying the Regiment Bourbonnais. The Swiss Brigade Polier, consisting of the Regiments of Salis-Zisers and Vieux-Stuppa, advanced and held the line for an hour against four furious onslaughts by the allies. Finally the Guards, with four princes of the blood at their head and supported by the Swiss regiments Greder, Stuppa-Jeune, Courten and the remains of the Brigade Polier, were ordered to advance with blades drawn. The Guards' attack won the day. The Swiss lost ninety officers, including Colonel Polier, and 2000 men during the battle. It was said that the Regiment Salis-Zisers won such fame at Steenkerque that for many years people would come five or six leagues just to see it march past.

At Neerwinden the following year, having withstood three allied attacks, the Guards were finally ordered to advance and took the village of Neerwinden in a house-by-house fight. The Guards were supported by a brigade of Vieux-Stuppa and Greder, and Susane writes that all contemporary accounts agree that the great victory that day was due above all to the extraordinary bravery displayed by this brigade.(16)

The war also saw several lengthy sieges, including those of Mons in 1691, Namur in 1692, Charleroi in 1693, Brussels in 1695 and Ath in 1697. Louis granted the captains of the Swiss Guards the rank of colonel in perpetuity for their actions at the siege of Mons. Siege warfare had become so sophisticated, however, that there was simply not enough time available during the campaigning season to take several fortified places and thereby occupy and dominate a province. The war therefore stuttered on inconclusively before petering out with neither victor nor vanquished.

SECTION IV

THE DECLINE OF THE
MERCENARY BUSINESS
BLENHEIM TO SAVANNAH
1704-1779

XIV

Service for Holland

"The Swiss preserved as they do today their liberty without attempting to oppress others. They hired their forces to neighbours richer than themselves."
Voltaire, *The Age of Louis XIV*

After the ending of the War of the League of Augsburg, the French retained only four companies in each of the Swiss regiments. The Swiss were quickly brought back to full strength, however, for the War of the Spanish Succession When war broke out again in 1701 there were 24,600 Swiss serving in the French Army.

There were as many again serving with the armies of the Grand Alliance — 11,200 with the Dutch, 5400 with the Spanish, 4800 with the Austrians and 4800 with Savoy. The Swiss participated in all the campaigns of Marlborough and Prince Eugene, including the battles of Blenheim, Ramillies and Oudenarde. The stage was set for the inevitable clash of Swiss on the battlefield that had been avoided for two hundred years despite close shaves at Novara and Ivry. Swiss finally met, fought and killed Swiss at the bloody battle of Malplaquet in 1709.

The Protestant cantons had always been sympathetic to the aspirations of the Dutch in their struggle for independence. In 1599-1600 Hans Krieg von Bellikon had led five companies from Zurich in the service of Maurice of Nassau, and several individuals and small groups fought with the Dutch over the years. When William III landed in England in 1688 he was accompanied by his Swiss bodyguard. The cantonal authorities, however, considered themselves bound by the alliance with France and consistently refused Dutch representatives the right to proceed with the hiring of troops, despite the attractive pay and conditions offered by the Dutch and despite the deep-seated suspicion of the French that had existed in Zurich in particular since the days of Zwingli.

Shortly after the outbreak of the war between France and Holland in 1672 an incident occurred which strained the loyalty of the Protestant cantons even further. The Erlach Regiment from Berne was ordered forward to cross the Rhine. When the officers protested that the articles of their capitulation prohibited their use against a Protestant power, Condé turned the guns of his French regiments on the Swiss and forced them to obey. The incident was only defused by transferring the Erlach Regiment to the front in Catalonia where it fought with honour for the next twenty-four years(1). Despite uproar in Berne, the Protestant cantons continued to refuse the overtures of the Dutch. Individual officers, however, such as Jean de Sacconay of Berne and Johann Heinrich Lochmann of Zurich resigned their commissions in the French army and joined the Dutch.

A series of French actions after the end of the War with Holland exacerbated the already tense relations between France and the Protestant cantons. Having acquired Burgundy under the Treaty of Nijmegen, thereby removing the previous buffer zone between France and the northern cantons, France immediately started building the fortress of Hüningen, right across the river from Basle. As a further provocation, in 1681 France annexed Strasbourg, which had formal defensive pacts with Zurich and Berne. Finally, in 1685 when Louis revoked the Edict of Nantes, many of the 400,000 Huguenot émigrés found their way into the Confederation, especially to Berne and the Vaud. Anti-French feeling was stirred up by Protestant pastors, who railed from the pulpit against the antichrist Louis XIV, and by two skilful ambassadors — Peter Valkenier of Holland and Thomas Coxe of England. They found a sympathetic hearing from Niklaus Daxelhofer, the most important politician in Berne at this time, who felt he had been personally snubbed when Louis had refused him an audience during a earlier visit to Paris.

In 1690 the five Protestant cantons(2) signed a defensive alliance with England and several companies served under William of Orange at the Battle of the Boyne. In 1693 Valkenier finally also succeeded in raising five regiments from Zurich, Berne and the Grey Leagues. These were led by Lochmann, Tscharner, Mülinen, Muralt and Cappol. A sixth regiment from Vaud under Sacconay came into Dutch service after three years with the English in Piedmont, and a seventh in 1702. Formal capitulations were concluded in 1701 specifying similar if somewhat more generous terms than the capitulations with the French. Each regiment consisted of 1600 men in two battalions, each battalion comprising four companies of 200 men. The total strength of the Swiss regiments at the beginning of the War of Spanish Succession was then 11,200 men. The Dutch were not entirely satisfied with the quality of the troops, complaining about the

126

number they considered either too old or too young. They nevertheless awarded a special payment of 3000 guilders to the troops that participated in the siege of Naumur for "extraordinary services".

Before looking at Malplaquet, it is worth briefly mentioning some of the activities of the Swiss troops involved on both sides in the earlier battles of the War of the Spanish Succession. At Blenheim in 1704, the two Swiss regiments Hirzel and Albemarle(3) formed part of Marlborough's right, while Lieutenant-General Zurlauben of Zug was unsuccessful in preventing the collapse of the French centre. At Ramillies in 1706 10,000 Swiss fought with the allies, Colonel Werdmüller leading two Swiss regiments in the first attack on the French right. The young Captain de Constant from Vaud led two battalions in the rescue of Marlborough when the latter was thrown from his horse while somewhat foolishly taking part in a cavalry mêlée. On the French side two brigades of Swiss troops despatched to the right flank to stem the allied breakthrough were completely unsuccessful and took flight with the rest of the French army. The Swiss Guards lost 200 men while covering the French retreat. Following the allied victory at Ramillies, two Swiss officers were given command of captured cities – Hirzel in Brussels and Werdmüller in Courtrai. At Oudenarde in 1708 the Swiss formed the core of Overkirk's encircling force that attacked the French right, while on the other side the Guards with five other Swiss regiments covered the French retreat. Meanwhile the Regiment Courten had suppressed the uprising of the Camisards, participated at the Siege of Barcelona and then joined the Regiment Hessy under the Duke of Berwick for the French victory at Almanza.

On 11 September, 1709, nearly 200,000 men met on the battlefield at Malplaquet, the largest number involved in any European battle before the Napoleonic Wars. The left flank of the allied army was occupied by the Dutch under the command of the Prince of Orange and included six Swiss regiments. Having been repulsed once, the Prince, taking the flag of the Regiment May in his hand, urged the Swiss into a second attack. Sweeping away the French Regiments Navarra and Piedmont the Swiss found themselves face-to-face with the redcoated Swiss of the Brigades Brendle-May and Chandieu-Greder forming the French second line. There was no repeat of the hesitation at Ivry. The Regiment May of Holland fell on the Regiment May of France in a murderous fratricidal frenzy. When the Dutch attack was driven back 100 officers and 2000 men lay dead. Further heavy Swiss losses occurred when the Guards covered the French retreat from the field, several Guards companies disappearing completely. Altogether the French lost 14,000 men and the allies 20,000 at Malplaquet, in a slaughter which shocked the whole of Europe. No less than 8,000 of the losses were Swiss. It has been pointed out (4) that the involvement of the

Swiss troops was instrumental in preserving the Swiss neutrality during a war that involved the whole of Western Europe — but at what cost!

As well as the Swiss serving in the Dutch army, the long-standing ties of the Waldstaette with the Spanish also developed into formal capitulations. Fourteen regiments were raised during the seventeenth century, a total of 47,000 men. No less than nine of these regiments were commanded by members of the Beroldingen family of Uri. Konrad von Beroldingen died in 1638 aged 80 having commanded seven regiments during his long career. In addition, Savoy and then Naples started regularly to recruit troops from the Confederation. The Bürkli Regiment of Zurich joined the Austrian army. Francis Lefort of Geneva was entrusted by Peter the Great with rebuilding the Russian army.

As the seventeenth century closed, another four hundred thousand Swiss had served as mercenaries in the armies of Europe. The vast majority served the French under the terms of the alliance, but increasing numbers accepted capitulations in other armies.

Louis XIV could well comment to Colonel Reynold of the Swiss Guards after the Battle of Denain: "Listen well, Monsieur Reynold, I am very pleased with the Swiss, very pleased." But the exclusive relationship with France that had withstood serious strains on several occasions during the sixteenth and seventeenth centuries would no longer be exclusive during the eighteenth.

XV

The Ancien Régime

"No product here the barren hills afford,
But men and steel, the soldier and his sword."
Oliver Goldsmith — The Traveller 1764

Throughout the eighteenth century the firepower of the flintlock musket made it supreme on the battlefield, despite its inaccuracy.(1) The line of infantry, which allowed the maximum firepower to be deployed in a forward direction, was the standard tactic and shock action by infantry or cavalry was relegated to second place. Because of the slow rate of fire(2) each line initially consisted of four ranks. The introduction of iron ramrods and prepacked cartridges speeded up the rate of fire and allowed the ranks to be reduced to two. In theory each line marched towards the enemy, maintaining ranks until close enough to fire a murderous volley. The two lines then stood blazing away until one side broke and ran. In practice there were many flaws with this theory and the most effective deployment of the infantry remained a subject of considerable debate.

Firstly, it was an extremely difficult and lengthy process to change the army from column of march to line of battle. Marlborough needed seven hours to accomplish this preliminary before Blenheim. This meant that the opposition needed to fight only in what it considered favourable circumstances, otherwise it simply marched away while the other side was forming up. There was in any case a reluctance to risk expensively recruited and trained troops, so that open battles again became quite rare. Even such an aggressive commander as Marlborough only succeeded in engaging the enemy in four battles during ten campaigns.

Secondly, moving the line of battle forward without opening gaps that could be exploited by enemy cavalry was tricky in parade ground conditions and almost impossible on uneven ground or on a battlefield covered with physical obstructions such as trees and streams. A ploughed field or a churned-up meadow was enough to break up the line, which therefore advanced at a snail's pace, constantly pausing to redress its ranks. The cadenced step introduced in the 1750's helped but the thin line several miles long remained notoriously difficult to control.

Thirdly, although the infantry were trained to fall back in a square and defend themselves with their bayonets in an emergency, and although a second line advanced a couple of hundred paces behind the first and ready to advance and plug any gaps, the line was extremely vulnerable to being broken by the opposition's artillery and volley firing as well as by its own wavering. The enemy cavalry were poised to exploit any breaks.

Finally, it was difficult to prevent the men from firing too soon. The most effective method of fire was the volley at short range, for its impact on morale as well as the physical casualties it caused. At Fontenoy in 1745, the French officers insisted with misplaced chivalry on the English firing the precious first volley, which had been loaded carefully and calmly before the battle. Ninety officers and 600 men of the Swiss and French guards were killed on the spot. To be really effective the range needed to be fifty paces or at most one hundred paces, and even then only one round in two or three hundred actually caused a fatality. The troops, however, were understandably anxious to start firing before coming within range of the enemy's guns. Although they marched forward with muskets shouldered, some troops would start firing too soon, and as firing while moving was virtually impossible, chaos quickly ensued. The two lines would blaze away until in the noise, smoke and confusion one side broke and ran.

The French infantry were generally recognized as the least inclined to stand their ground if the engagement came to exchanges of fire in the front line. Whether due to the claims that the French "national genius" thrived on attack, or to lack of discipline and leadership, French military thinkers were encouraged to look for other tactics, and there was much heartsearching about the relative merits of the column and the line.(3)

Eighteenth century military tactics required ever more precision taught by ever more drill. Discipline became correspondingly draconian, both to drum in elementary manoeuvres and weapons-handling techniques and to shackle increasingly reluctant troops to the colours.(4) Armies became increasingly divorced from the daily life of most of the population. The peasants and the bourgeoisie paid their taxes for the king to wage war. Aristocratic officers on the one hand and the riffraff in the ranks on the other hand had ever less in common with the bulk of the citizenship.

All armies relied on a large proportion of foreign mercenaries to make up the numbers and provide a core of experienced well-trained troops. Among the foreign troops, the steadiness of the Swiss regiments in a firefight was well recognized. The sight of the redcoats marching forward through the dense smoke that covered the battlefield gave waverers renewed confidence to hold their positions. Although a position in the first line was considered the most prestigious, the Swiss Guards were nearly always positioned in the centre of the second line where they could provide most support.

Despite the increasing number of lower grade troops in their ranks, the Swiss regiments maintained their reputation for discipline without resorting to Prussian extremes. The ranks still contained a high proportion of career soldiers who strictly adhered to a code of conduct that stressed personal honour, bravery and devotion to duty. The geographical basis for recruitment ensured maximum peer group pressure from colleagues who were comrades on the battlefield and neighbours at home. Keegan has pointed out that: "when a soldier is known to the men who are around him, he ... has more reason to fear losing the one thing he is likely to value more than life itself – his reputation as a man among other men."(5) The personal code was reinforced by a clearcut set of regulations covering all aspects of behaviour, and a swift and rigorous judicial system to punish transgressions. The Swiss officers lived with the men, especially on campaign and were careful not to neglect the mundane tasks of providing supplies, billeting, hygiene and training. They led by example, especially on the battlefield, where leadership entailed willingness to accept the risk of death or injury. The traditions of the regiment and the uniqueness of the Swiss were assiduously cultivated. The whole structure combined to form troops of high morale and esprit de corps, who demonstrated iron discipline under even the severest of combat conditions.

Four new Swiss regiments were raised by the French during the eighteenth century to add to the Guards and the eight line regiments already in existence. Regiment Karrer was formed in 1719 specially for service in Louisiana and was responsible to the Department of the Marine. Karrer was discharged in 1763. Regiment Travers from the Grey Leagues was formed in 1734, Lochmann in 1752 (the first company from Zurich in French service since 1690) and d'Eptingen from Basle in 1758. By the time the last was formed there were therefore eleven Swiss regiments in total, excluding Karrer. As the name of the regiment changed each time there was a new colonel, following their progress can be confusing. In 1760 they were known as follows, with their original name and foundation date in brackets: Jenner (Erlach 1672), Boccard (Vieux Stuppa 1672), Reding (Salis-Zisers 1672), Castella (Pfyffer 1672), Waldner (Greder 1673), D'Arbonnier (Stuppa Jeune 1677), Diesbach (Salis 1690), Courten (Courten 1690), Salis (Travers 1734), Lochmann (Lochmann 1752), and D'Eptingen (D'Eptingen 1758). A full listing of the regiments and the guards under their different names is shown in Appendix VI.

The Swiss regiments, including the Guards, all wore the famous red coats coloured with bright red madder dye. All the regiments wore white waistcoats and breeches, except the Guards who wore blue. Officers had silver epaulettes on their coats and carried an eight-foot pike known as an esponton. The regiments were distinguishable from each other by the colours of their facings, cuffs and collars as shown in the table below, as well as differences of buttons and pockets. With battle consisting of marching openly to within 100 paces of the enemy to fire, bright colours that would enhance the morale of the troops and intimidate the enemy were more important than camouflage.

Original Name	Facings, Cuffs and Collars
Guards	Blue
Erlach	Black
Vieux Stuppa	Lemon
Salis Zisers	Sky blue
Pfyffer	Royal blue
Greder	Brown
Stuppa Jeune	Yellow
Salis	Sky blue
Courten	Royal blue
Travers	Royal blue
Lochmann	Royal blue
Eptingen	White

The regimental flags were all of similar design, a white cross dividing the flag into four, and each quadrant filled with multicoloured wavy flames radiating from the centre, where the regimental motto was inscribed in gold.

Twenty years of relative peace followed the Treaty of Rostadt and the ending of the War of the Spanish Succession. For the brief War of the Polish Succession 1734-5 the Travers Regiment was raised in the Grey Leagues and 25 companies added to the existing regiments. The Swiss participated notably in the Siege of Philippsburg where the Swiss Guards were charged with storming the breach. At the head of the Guards were members of three of the great patrician families – Erlach of Berne, Castella of Fribourg and Besenval of Solothurn.

During the War of the Austrian Succession 1741-8, the King at one stage decided to join the army in person which led to two issues for the Swiss troops. Firstly the *Cent Suisses* demanded and were granted the honour of marching at the head of the army. Secondly, when the King decided to participate at the siege of Freiburg the Guards decided that their obligation to protect the King superseded the prohibition on their serving outside France and crossed the Rhine with him.

The Swiss were prominent as usual at the Battle of Fontenoy in 1745. The French and Swiss Guards held the centre of the first line. As the Swiss troops quietly awaited the start of the battle, twenty paces ahead of the first line stood their commander. This was Colonel Zurlauben who later wrote the first comprehensive account of the Military History of the Swiss in the Service of France.(6) Next to the Guards was the Valaisan Regiment Courten and further to the right were Bettens and Diesbach. As Cumberland drove forward with the famous advance of his 16,000-man column, the Swiss held two positions critical to stopping the advance. The main redoubt on the left was held for six hours by the Guards grenadier company under Rodolphe de Castella, losing four of their seven officers in the process. On the right Bettens and Diesbach held three hastily erected redoubts for the duration of the battle.

The following year at the Battle of Laufeld the Regiments Monnin and Diesbach were almost annihilated with 1200 casualties in taking the village after six assaults with fixed bayonets.

After a respite France went into the Seven Years War of 1755-63 thoroughly unprepared to face Frederick the Great's Prussian army at its height. The French officer caste was notoriously lax and more interested in preserving a lavish and luxurious lifestyle than in pursuing its military calling. The troops were poorly equipped and trained, and, since the recent death of Marechal de Saxe, the army lacked an outstanding General.

At Rossbach on 5 November, 1757, the 22,000-man Prussian army comprehensively routed the French. As Soubise attempted to encircle the Prussians in an ambitious and carelessly executed manoeuvre, Frederick ordered a sudden attack against the flank of the advancing French column and destroyed it in less than an hour. With the whole French army in flight, only the Regiments Planta and Diesbach held the field despite the loss of 400 men.

They finally retreated in orderly squares bringing back the French artillery under constant attack from Seydlitz' cavalry. Impatiently watching from a hill Frederick turned to an adjutant and demanded: "What are these red walls that my cavalry cannot breach?" "Sire, they are the Swiss," came the answer, to which the King did not comment but gravely raised his hat in salute.(7)

The Regiments Reding, Salis, Jenner, Planta, Lochmann and Waldner participated in the various campaigns, maintaining the Swiss reputation for solidity and reliability at Hastembeck, Krefeldt, Bergen and the defence of Kassel by the Regiment Diesbach. At one point the Zurich Regiment Lochmann refused to cross into Prussian territory in accordance with the terms of its capitulation. In answer to Marshal Soubise's scornful query as to what use were the Swiss in that case, Colonel Lochmann replied, "To cover your retreat across the Rhine, Sir". Lochmann was temporarily arrested for insubordination but the incident quickly blew over as the regiment distinguished itself at Hastembeck and Krefeldt.

The failures of the Seven Years War provided the catalyst for a series of much-needed reforms introduced by the War Minister, Choiseul. The number of infantry regiments was reduced and, except for the Swiss regiments which kept the names of their colonels, took the names of provinces; the bloatedly excessive number of officers was severely pruned, and officers were expected to have minimum levels of experience and live with their commands; the Ecole Militaire was created; the uniform was changed to incorporate the epaulette and the Prussian collar; and regular changes of garrison were introduced to accustom the troops to the march.

As Choiseul also held the rank of Colonel General des Suisses et Grisons, he inevitably also turned his attention to the Swiss troops. A new General Capitulation with 51 clauses was signed on November 3, 1764, that resolved many old grievances and clearly stipulated the rights and obligations of the Swiss. Some of the more important clauses specified the following: each regiment would consist of two battalions, each of eight companies of fusiliers plus a grenadier company recruited from among the fusiliers; each company would have a minimum of forty soldiers and a maximum of 80, and at least two-thirds were to be Swiss; each company should be commanded by a captain, lieutenant and sub-lieutenant with two junior officers, while the regiment was commanded by a colonel, a lieutenant-colonel and a major (all appointed by the King) with a staff of twenty; the captain received 1200 livres for recruiting in time of peace and 3000 livres in time of war, and an annual salary varying between 1600 and 3000 livres depending on the size of the company; the captain became essentially an employee with his business role limited to recruiting and the provision of equipment; officers were promoted within the regiment rather than the company and would receive a pension; the Swiss troops could not be used at sea, nor against the Pope, the Empire, Austria or Florence.

The Swiss regiments continued to preserve jealously their rights to be subject to the Swiss system of justice and to freedom of religion. In the 1730's Franz Adam Vogel, Grand Judge of the Swiss Guards, published the Caroline Code and a collection of documents referring to the privileges of the Swiss. Other than the regiments from the Valais which were entirely Catholic and those from Berne and Zurich which were Protestant, all the Swiss regiments were of mixed religion and two chaplains practised side by side. Arguments over religion were expressly forbidden in the regulations.

The term of the General Capitulation was 25 years and it therefore governed the employment of all Swiss troops in France until the Revolution.

All the other foreign troops had become simply regiments of the French army with a history of recruiting from particular countries. The Swiss, however, retained their unique position as Swiss citizens licensed by the cantons and allied with France but serving under the command structure of the French army.

The most controversial aspect of the new capitulation was the preservation of the privileges enjoyed by the oligarchy of military families. "His Majesty retains certain regards for those families which have raised companies for his service and if, when those companies become vacant, one of the descendants of the family has the right age and qualities to command the company, he shall be given preference over others."(8)

The alliance had not been renewed since it lapsed in 1715. Shortly after his accession, Louis XVI set in motion negotiations for a formal renewal of the alliance. A new treaty which cited the Perpetual Peace of 1516 and the original Treaty of 1521 was signed in Solothurn on 28 May, 1777. The Treaty specified the right of the King of France to raise troops in preference to any other power. The new alliance together with the General Capitulation governed the relations between France and the Confederation until the Revolution.

XVI

Reduced Attractiveness of Mercenary Service

"Around him wide a sable army stand,
A low-born, cell-bred, selfish servile band,
Prompt to guard or stab, to saint or damn,
Heav'ns Swiss, who fight for any God or man."
  Alexander Pope — *The Dunciad, 1728*

While somewhat reduced in numbers from the army of Louis XIV at its peak, the French army during the Seven Years War that started in 1755 still totalled 400,000 men. The administrative reforms carried out by Colbert and the Le Telliers had created an effective national militia for the first time, and about one Frenchman in six was directly involved in the defence of the realm. Nevertheless, foreign troops were still considered an essential component of the army for their two traditional purposes, to provide additional numbers and to furnish élite combat troops. About 20% of the army was normally enrolled in the foreign regiments and about half of these were Swiss.

Some 300-400,000 Swiss were employed as mercenaries during the eighteenth century.(1) Although the number of Swiss mercenaries in the eighteenth century was broadly similar to each of the previous two centuries, the population of the Confederation had increased in the meantime so that the number of men becoming mercenaries each year had declined from three per thousand to two per thousand. The mercenary business was under pressure from two sides. Firstly the profitability of the enterprise was sharply reduced. Secondly the pool of labour was drying up as a result of unpopular service conditions and unattractive levels of pay compared with new employment opportunities available in expanding industries. The overall impression is of a mercenary business in decline.

The dislike of the service conditions associated with the introduction of standing armies intensified. The following list covers only the major dislikes. The period of service, nominally four and later six years, became ever longer as the captains used fair means and foul to keep their men in order to protect their investment. There was little room for individual prowess or heroic deeds in an army that prized machine-like precision in weapons handling above all else. Uniforms were provided but were of poor quality, ill-fitting and generally designed for the parade ground rather than for campaigning. Barracks started to be built but were insanitary and a breeding ground for disease.(2) They also set the troops apart from the local community in which they had previously lived. Food was rarely adequate — the reluctant but literate recruit Bräker recounts that even a group of soldiers pooling their rations and cooking together did not eat the minimum officially considered desirable.(3) A comment from Marechal de Saxe describes the miseries of the soldier's lot: "Once the rainy season has arrived his head is seldom dry. As for his feet it cannot be doubted that his stockings, shoes and feet all rot together."(4)

While the Swiss troops were never treated as brutally as the wretches in the Prussian army, Swiss justice remained swift and severe. In the Bernese regiment in French service between the years 1701 and 1787, 30 men were executed, 75 had to run the gauntlet, 11 went to the galleys and 6 to the chain gang. The crimes resulting in these punishments were mainly stealing and desertion while on guard duty.

In fairness it needs to be pointed out that the soldier was not much worse off than the average peasant. Indeed he enjoyed certain social security benefits that were generous for the time. The capitulations stipulated that care be given to the sick and wounded, that arrangements be made to transport invalids home, and even that they should be paid on arrival rather than risk being robbed en route. Generally, however, conditions were a deterrent rather than an attraction to recruitment.

As we have seen, during the seventeenth century the mercenary had been transformed from a wild freebooter into a disciplined soldier. During this transition the opportunities for a windfall from looting had all but disappeared, leaving the soldier's pay as his sole income. During the eighteenth century this pay sank to the lower end of the wage scale. An average monthly pay of 8 guilders around 1750 was comparable to but not much better than a textile worker with 8-9 guilders or a day labourer on 7 guilders. Out of this, moreover, he received only 60% to meet his daily needs. This was handed over every ten days and called his Pret. The other 40% was held back against his account in the Company Book to repay the money advanced by the captain for his recruiting costs, and his uniform, together with the cost of eventual replacement of the uniform(5), repairs to equipment, and so on. The company account was agreed with the soldier once a year. The captain tried to keep the soldier in debt so that he was forced to sign on for repeat terms of service, but not so far in debt that he was encouraged to desert. The soldier was still open to being cheated by unscrupulous captains over costs of food and equipment. At least the regularity of pay had improved in the French regiments, although six-month delays were still the norm in other armies, including the Dutch.

As the incidence of desertions increased, captains became less willing to allow soldiers to pursue profitable side occupations. These were popular as a means of earning supplementary income, but often required a freedom of movement that facilitated desertion.(6)

As well as the less attractive pay and conditions offered to a mercenary recruit, the expanding textile industry provided alternative employment opportunities. Northern Switzerland, especially Zurich and St. Gallen, had introduced techniques brought by Huguenot refugees to become one of the centres of the European textile industry. At this time, prior to the Industrial Revolution, visitors described Switzerland as one of the most industrialized countries in Europe. Some 200,000 people were employed in textiles alone, and although many were women and children there were also opportunities for young men who might otherwise have joined the colours. Industry had to a large extent taken over from mercenary service the role of mopping up the population overflow.

Emigration also drew off potential recruits. Large groups of emigrants had periodically left the Confederation, usually seeking freedom to express their religious beliefs. In the eighteenth century about 50,000 emigrated in three waves. At the beginning of the century Brandenburg was the main destination, followed by Prussia in the 1770's, both linked to periods of agricultural crisis. In the period 1734-44 the Amish and Mennonites established their settlements in Pennsylvania and Carolina.

This is not to say that the mercenary business suddenly died out. Despite the alternative opportunities offered by industry and emigration, 6% of the adult male population of Zurich was working abroad, mainly in military service, in 1748 (representing about 2% of the total population). This already high proportion of the population of an industrialized canton increased to 12% after the harvest failures of 1770 and 1771.(7) Military service clearly remained an important element in the economic life of the community.

The most desirable recruits were those who regarded the army as a career or a vocation. In many military families, and not just of the officer caste, one generation after another automatically followed into the regiment. Joseph Addison wrote in *The Tatler* in 1709: "The inhabitants of this country are as curious as the country itself. They usually go into military service young and if they remain bulletproof to their fiftieth year, they bring the money they have saved and their remaining limbs back home to spend the rest of their lives amidst the mountains of their homeland. One of the men, who had just lost an eye, proudly told me that there were seven wooden legs in his family and that none of his relations throughout four generations had gone to his grave with his body whole."(8)

The mass of recruits, although having some sense of adventure, probably saw mercenary service more in terms of a way of earning a living and keeping the wolf from the door. One study showed that 40% of recruits described themselves as without profession, 25% as professional soldiers, 20% as textile workers, and 15% as handworkers of different types.(9) Poverty and destitution were widespread and parish records are full of men joining up "to win a piece of bread". Whether motivated by vocation or necessity, however, there were less and less suitable volunteers to meet the demand.

The difficulty in finding sufficient suitable recruits was not made easier by the increasingly outspoken opposition to the mercenary system led by articulate writers and churchmen. Pastor Ruchat of the Vaud wrote of "the miserable commerce in human blood, concealed under the name of alliances and foreign service."(10) Rousseau commented: "I think that everyone owes his life and his blood to his country, that he is not permitted to attach himself to princes to whom he owes nothing, nor even less to sell himself in the least noble calling in the world, that of a vile mercenary."(11) Waser calculated that up to the time of his writing France had employed 1,110,798 Swiss who had earned 1049 million florins in pay and 86 millions in pensions and other payments. He translated this into an average of 122 guilders per soldier which he compared with a contemporary statistic that a Swedish citizen produced an average income for the state of 704 guilders. Waser questioned: "Should not a warm Swiss lad be worth at least as much as a cold Swede? Yes he is when he works hard and faithfully in his fatherland, marries sensibly and leaves numerous descendants. Why then must he be sold at such a poor price and hunted at the point of a sword into foreign service?"(12)

The opposition to mercenary service in general was aimed particularly at service for France. As well as the anti-Catholic feelings in Zurich and Berne, there was also a belief that the simple healthy lifestyle of the Swiss was being corrupted by soldiers returning from France. The ways of camplife with swearing, fornicating, drunkenness and gambling and the affectation by the officers of fine clothes and fancy manners were all seen as attacking the fundamental strengths of Swiss society. Troops returning from Dutch service were considered as remaining closer to the values of society than the "libertines" returning from France. There had also long been a general uneasiness about the corrupting effect of French pensions. The Diet wrote to the French Ambassador in 1697 that the Swiss officers "instead of continuing to enjoy excessive luxury in clothes, equipment and horses, should revert to following the example of their ancestors."(13) These outspoken criticisms did nothing to facilitate the search for mercenaries.

To meet the shortage in recruits, captains turned to three sources — dubious and criminal elements of the population, foreigners and strong-arm recruiting tactics.

While it had long been common in other countries to use the army as the dustbin of society, and some misfits had always been pushed into the army in Switzerland as well, only in the eighteenth century did this practice become widespread in the Confederation. The physically disabled were enrolled and those short in stature.(14) Petty criminals were sentenced to military service. A Zurich captain, Lochmann, was given permission to recruit three men provided he also took one Niklaus Grob then in prison. Serious offenders from Zurich were sent to the regiments serving in Holland with the recommendation they be shipped onward to companies serving in the East Indies. Beggars and paupers were pushed into the arms of the recruiters. While providing much needed men, the practice of recruiting the outcasts of society also suffered a major disadvantage. Healthy honest farm workers were even less inclined to sign up knowing they would sleep and fight with thieves and beggars.(15)

The second way of meeting the shortage was to recruit foreigners. This group included half-Swiss (basically second or third generation sons of Swiss mercenaries who had married or settled in their country of service) and non-Swiss. Hungarians, Poles, Swedes, Russians, Greeks, Englishmen, Irishmen, Frenchmen and Germans of all sorts were to be found in the Swiss regiments. German speakers from southern Germany, Austria and Alsace were preferred as they understood the language of command and were easier to pass off as Swiss. French deserters also were easy to pass as Suisses Romandes. But in the end all nationalities were accepted. Despite the harsh discipline, the Swiss regiments were popular because of the higher pay. In 1750 a soldier in a Swiss regiment serving in France was paid 11 sous 5 deniers a day while his French counterpart was paid 8 sous 8 deniers. The zone along the Rhine below Lake Constance centred on Stein-am-Rhein was the chief recruiting ground in Europe, channelling foreign recruits into the Swiss regiments.

The French in particular took exception to paying a premium for Swiss regiments only to be provided with a motley collection of nationalities. There was nevertheless an appreciation that the disciplines and traditions of the Swiss regiments, and the professionalism of their officers, still produced elite troops even when they included a minority who were not native-born Swiss, and that this was still worth a premium price. A compromise formula came into practice whereby a certain percentage, usually two-thirds or 75% of the men had to be Swiss. For example, the General Capitulation of 1764 specified that at least two-thirds of the soldiers should genuinely be Swiss. A French ordinance of 1696 confirmed the right of the Swiss regiments to recruit Germans, which in particular included Alsatians. This practice was reconfirmed in 1726 by the Duc de Marne, Colonel-General des Suisses et Grisons "that by the word Germans one also understands all those who speak German and that Alsace has always been considered under the general denomination of German."(16) An analysis of Bernese regiments in the first half of the century showed an average of 20% non-Swiss rising to one-third during wars.(17) The numbers may well have been much higher, however, as a whole new area of chicanery and sharp practice developed. Now, not only were there *passe-volants* but all sorts of nationalities masquerading as Swiss with false papers and curious accents. The captains, whose overriding objective was to keep the regiment up to its proper strength, connived in the deceptions. Many actually preferred to use non-Swiss who were both lower paid and less able to complain to the Swiss authorities of abuses. One can also suppose that in times of war the mustering commission was willing to turn a blind eye to many tricks. In 1763 the French Minister of War Choiseul declared with some exaggeration: "One is astonished to realize that of the 18,000 Swiss that the King pays, there are only 3000 true Swiss."(18)

The percentage of non-Swiss was higher in the regiments serving in Spain, Savoy or Sardinia which were much less popular than service in France or Holland. As a result, the premium paid for the Swiss regiments serving these countries started to disappear. A comparison of the annual costs per year of a soldier serving in regiments of different origin showed a considerable narrowing of the gap between the Swiss and the rest.(19)

Origin	1715	1749
	livres per man	livres per man
Savoyard	171	171
French	190	231
German	220	237
Swiss	228	234/261

Just to complete the picture, there were generally a few hundred Swiss serving in French regiments, some willing to trade lower pay for less strict discipline while others were seeking specialist careers in the cavalry or the artillery.

The third way to enhance the supply of recruits was by turning up the wick on the recruiting process. The network of recruiters was intensified. Each regiment appointed one and then two fulltime recruiters rather than rely on infrequent visits by serving subalterns. The recruiters, based in the regiment's home territory, in turn employed a network of agents. In some cantons individual agents were given exclusive territories but in others they competed vigorously with each other. In Berne for example, which always had 50 to 60 companies in French, Dutch and Sardinian service, each with an average of two recruiters per company, there were 100-120 active recruiters, plus all their agents, plus the secret recruiters for Spain, Naples, Prussia, etc. Signing-on bonuses were increased and the trickery that had long been part of the recruiting process was intensified to a level falling not far short of the press.

The recruiting agents were also made responsible for delivering the recruits to the mustering points – Chalon-sur-Saône for France, Genoa for Sardinia and Marseilles for Spain. It was during the march to the mustering point that the most desertions occurred, as many of the recruits sobered up and had second thoughts and as tricksters tried to slip away with their recruiting bonus. The agents therefore guarded the volunteer recruits like prisoners and sometimes even bound them like a chain gang. As with the hiring of social outcasts, the often brutal and underhand recruiting methods eventually worked against themselves by further increasing the unpopularity of mercenary service and making volunteers even more difficult to find. The authorities were constantly torn between their duties to protect their citizens from the worst excesses of the recruiters and their need to keep the Canton's regiments up to strength.

Hand-in-hand with the difficulty of finding recruits went the difficulty of keeping them. Desertion became a serious problem in the Swiss regiments during the eighteenth century. Deserters were fleeing any number of abuses – sharp practices in their recruitment, barely subsistence levels of pay, squalid conditions, more trickery in the signing-on process. The Swiss were also notorious for their tendency to homesickness. The singing of nostalgic songs was forbidden and the captains often intercepted letters from home. Authorities and public opinion at home was sympathetic to them and regarded the captain as having the responsibility of recovering his men. Where local authorities did intervene to send back deserters, it was less to uphold the law than to get rid of troublesome vagabonds. The captains themselves were always tempted to rehire deserters as they were not only a name for the roll but were already partially trained.

Desertion was a cancer that affected all the armies of the eighteenth century, and this despite the fact that desertion was no easy matter. Troop movements and choice of quarters were planned around the prevention of desertion, so that the would-be deserter had to wait his chance. This often arrived during the confusion of battle.(20) It needed courage for him to take the plunge, determination being gradually whittled away in watching the severe punishments meted out to recaptured deserters. Then he had to find the right opportunity that would not get him killed in the process, before finding his way back home across hundreds of miles avoiding his own troops, enemy troops and a hostile peasantry. That so many did desert despite such daunting obstacles is a testament to the slavery from which they were escaping.

Meticulous research into the records of the Bernese regiment and guard company in French service between 1701 and 1788 has revealed that one quarter of the troops deserted.(21) In Sardinian service the position was even worse, with 40% of the troops deserting. To put the problem into perspective, half as many men again deserted as were killed during the same period.

Half the deserters left either en route to their regiment or during their first year. The rest deserted at differing times and included long service soldiers and even NCOs. As might be expected, desertions peaked in war years.

The following table shows the total number of recruits to the Bernese regiments in France and Sardinia in the eighteenth century together with the numbers of casualties and deserters.

	Total Recruits	Casualties	Deserters
1701-87 France	1868	306 16%	498 27%
1738-97 Sardinia	1711	471 27%	670 39%
	3579	777 30%	1168 45%

Of the casualties, half the men died during their first two years of service. Although there were high casualties in years when the regiment was involved in battle, there were overall as many deaths from sickness and disease as from battle wounds. Entry to hospital for whatever reason was regarded as a death sentence. Medical skills could cope with bullet wounds to limbs by extraction or amputation, but could do nothing for internal wounds. In any case the insanitary conditions usually led to the patient's death no matter what the treatment.

If a soldier managed to survive and not desert through to retirement age, the process for a foreign soldier to obtain a pension was lengthy and complicated. In the case of French service, the regiment had to apply to the French Ambassador in Solothurn, who forwarded the request to Paris where the applicant's rank, service record and religion were all taken into account. Of the Bernese regiment considered above, only 29 actually obtained a pension in the whole century, lower than average as this was a Protestant regiment but still pitifully small.

Such examples demonstrate the fate awaiting recruits and the reasons why they were increasingly difficult to find. Nevertheless throughout the eighteenth century there were regularly 50,000 men or more serving in the

Swiss regiments in the different armies of Europe. The system was in decline but was not dead. Instead of a surplus of willing volunteers, troops were difficult to find and many were not Swiss. But the demand was as great as ever and the Swiss regiments managed to meet it, albeit with difficulty.

The captains who owned the companies had to cope not only with the declining popularity of mercenary service but also a squeeze on the profitability of their business. In principle owning a company was still a lucrative affair. A new company required around 20,000 guilders investment, mainly for recruiting costs and uniforms. From the difference between the income he received and his payments to his officers and men, the captain could theoretically expect to amortise this investment in about three years. The possibility of losing men in battle had always made this a risky business, but now the additional steady seepage of men from desertion seriously affected the financial viability of the enterprise. Costs of recruiting replacements came out of the captain's expenses, and as mercenary service became increasingly unpopular recruitment costs increased proportionately. The real amortisation period was more likely to be a minimum of six years, not a high return for such a risky investment.

Other opportunities for profit were also closed to the captain as the new state bureaucracies took over many of the functions he had previously performed. Weapons were issued by the state(22) so that supplementary profits were not available from this sideline. At the beginning of the century, the captain could buy uniforms privately at low costs, but later had to buy from state magazines at listed prices. He was no longer needed to provide finance as states could deal direct with bankers such as Joseph Bauer et Fils of Geneva who loaned 5 million pounds to Sardinia during the War of the Austrian Succession. His main opportunities for additional profits came from the income on the *places mortes*, by successfully sneaking through *passe-volants* and by shaving the amounts he was supposed to pay his men according to the capitulation. By the end of the century the captain had virtually disappeared as a business entrepreneur and effectively became an employee of the state. Two incidents demonstrate the reduced attractiveness of the business. Of the 36 new companies raised by France in 1743, only 8 captains took a full company, while 56 took a half company each. In 1749 the officers of the Regiment Bettens wrote to the Minister of War d'Argenson: "One can risk one's life many times in the service of the King, but one can sacrifice one's welfare only once; we see absolutely no hope nor possibility of recovering during the peace from the debts which the war has plunged us into."(23)

Nevertheless, the military families that had come to dominate the political and social direction of the Confederation owed their wealth and prestige to their participation over many generations in the mercenary business. Some families developed interests in textiles and other industries, but most continued to cling tenaciously to the activity on which their social and economic prominence had been built. Despite the much reduced profitability of the business, the military dynasties continued to provide captains and colonels to own and operate the companies and regiments.

The military families had become an oligarchy known as the Patriciate. Thirty-five families in Berne accounted for over 300 members of the Cantonal Council. There were sixty-seven such families in Fribourg, thirty-four in Solothurn, and twenty-nine in Lucerne. Names such as Diesbach, Erlach, Wattenwyl, Mulinen, Bonstetten in Berne, Zurlauben in Zug, Reding in Schwyz, Salis in the Grey Leagues, Pfyffer in Lucerne, repeat in the histories of the Swiss regiments over more than three centuries. In Vallière's index of the most famous officers there are thirty-three Diesbachs, twenty-seven Erlachs and thirty-three Salis. The lieutenant of the Cent Suisses was a Diesbach from 1644 to 1733. During the siege of Tournai in April 1745, eleven members of the Reding family, from cadets to generals, were in the trenches.

In theory companies could not be inherited. When a company owner retired or died the canton appointed a successor. In practice the closely knit military caste ensured that the company was granted to a suitable member of the next generation of the ruling families. A typical career of the son of such a family saw him leaving school aged 14-16 and joining the family regiment. As a cadet, he wore an ordinary soldiers uniform with a badge of a white feather and a silver dagger. He would follow a military career for several decades, providing the tradition and continuity for which the Swiss regiments remained famous despite the increasing numbers of non-Swiss in the ranks. Provided he was lucky enough to remain alive, he would then return home to protect his family's interests in the political institutions of the Confederation. As a magistrate he would then perpetuate the system by ensuring the smooth flow of the necessary authorizations to those officers reciprocating with the offer of a choice appointment for a favoured son or nephew.(24)

The Patriciat was strongly influenced by the culture and autocratic political structure of the state in which they mainly pursued their military careers, the France of the Ancien Régime. There were also close financial ties. In the year 1740, the Burgomaster of Berne, Thormann von Diesbach and his wife received secret pensions from France to the value of 6620 livres, and it must be supposed that the Patriciat was affected by the venality and dissipation that crippled the officer caste of the French army in the eighteenth century. The Confederation had come to be dominated by a hereditary aristocracy that owed its power to the mercenary business. All the military families were politically influential, and conversely there was scarcely an influential politician that did not have close connections with mercenary enterprises. Under the guidance and protection of the Patriciat the business retained its importance to the social and economic life of the Confederation throughout the eighteenth century despite the new stresses which it faced.

The power and wealth that these families enjoyed can still be seen today in the imposing castles they built(25) Mercenary chateaux are found throughout Switzerland, mostly luxurious mansions but including a few real palaces. Schloss Marschlins built by the Salis family, the Freulerpalast at Näfels, Schloss Waldegg built by the Besenvals, the Werdmüllers' Schloss Elgg, are a few of the more imposing. These ornate buildings continue to provide a reminder of the social and economic power of the mercenary dynasties.

Another anecdote demonstrates the pervasiveness of the mercenaries in Swiss life. The regiment Vieux-Stuppa included a lieutenant named Jean Jacques Hebdenstreit of Basle. Louis XIV once described this officer as solid as the rocks of the mountains and bestowed on him and his successors the right to call themselves La Roche. This name is now known throughout the world through the giant chemical company Hoffmann-Laroche.

27. Baron de Besenval (1721-1791), Marechal de Camp, who was the military commander of Paris during the days leading up to the storming of the Bastille (portrait by Danloux).

28 and 29. The massacre of the Swiss Guards at the Tuileries on 10 August, 1792, when 760 Swiss soldiers died defending the royal palace against the mob.

30. Antoine-Henri Jomini (1779-1869), General in the French and then
the Russian army, author of classic texts on the Art of War (portrait
by Ch. Gleyre).

31. Swiss guards — ivory toy soldiers that actually belonged to the Dauphin (the uncrowned Louis XVII) during the French Revolution.

32. The Crossing of the Beresina, 1812, where four Swiss regiments formed the rearguard defending the crossing with eight separate bayonet charges. The Swiss lost 1200 out of 1500 men.

XVII

Service in all the Armies of Europe

"Law, logicke and the Switzers can be hired to fight for anybody."
Thomas Nash – *Christ's Tears over Jerusalem 1594*

	1690	1701	1748	1787
France	32000	24700	23100	14100
Holland	11200	11200	20400	9800
Naples	-	-	6700	5800
Austria	7300	4800	2500	-
Savoy/ Piedmont-Sardinia	3500	4900	10600	2950
Spain	10800	6400	13600	4900
Others	200	2300	100	2350
Total	65000	54300	77000	39900

The table shows the main countries for which Swiss troops served during the eighteenth century.(1) The fluctuations by year partly reflect whether or not the continent was at war. 1690 was during the War of the League of Augsburg, 1701 was in the brief lull between that war and the War of the Spanish Succession, 1748 was the last year of the War of the Austrian Succession, and 1787 was a year of peace. Despite the variations by year, however, it is clear that the French share of the Swiss troops was in decline, from half in 1690 to less than a third in 1748 and 1787.

The next most numerous after the French were the Swiss troops employed by the Dutch. Chapter XIV describes how the Swiss first signed capitulations with the Dutch at the end of the seventeenth century. During the eighteenth century, however, the United Provinces had finally established their independence after nearly two centuries of struggle, and the Dutch were largely able to avoid the conflicts of the time.

In 1712 an alliance between the Confederation and the United Provinces was signed, largely as the result of the diplomatic endeavours of General de Saint-Saphorin of Vaud. The Swiss troops were established in seven regiments of 1600 men for a total of 11,200. An eighth and a Guards regiment were formed in 1748 under Colonel Wattenwyl.(2) The Dutch varied the strength of the regiments quite significantly. In 1748 for example the Swiss regiments were brought up to 20,400 men in preparation for the War of the Austrian Succession. While in 1716, 1737, 1751, and 1788 reductions of over 2000 men within the space of a few months were ordered to reduce costs.

All the Swiss troops in Dutch service, including the Guards, wore royal blue coats with red linings, and white waistcoats and breeches. The Stürlers, Constants and Wattenwyls were prominent families in Dutch service. Many of the officers had connections with the freemasons.(3)

On two occasions Swiss troops were lent to the English. In 1715 Jean Jacques Goumöens led a regiment to Scotland to help suppress the Jacobite rebellion.(4) The Regiment Hirzel fought at the Battle of Culloden in 1746. Otherwise, the Dutch were able to stay neutral during the Seven Years War and the Dutch army experienced a long period of peace during the second half of the eighteenth century. After fighting in the French Revolutionary Wars, the six Swiss regiments still in Dutch service were finally disbanded in 1797.

During the War of the Spanish Succession five Swiss regiments served with the Spanish Army in Italy. At the end of the war, however, Spain was financially ruined and dismissed all its foreign troops. In 1724 a new Swiss regiment was raised under Colonel Niederöst, followed by regiments Aregger and Sury in 1734 and Dunant, Old-Reding and Young-Reding in 1742. For most of the eighteenth century, the Swiss formed about ten per cent of the Spanish army.

The Swiss regiments were hired under capitulations, similar to those governing French service, but with the important difference that the regiments were not officially recognized by the Cantons. The capitulations were signed by the King of Spain and individual colonels. Deprived of the political support of the cantonal authorities, the Swiss officers were exposed to constant abuse and harassment by Spanish bureaucrats. By 1750 the Swiss officers were claiming a total of 25 million guilders in arrears and many families were financially ruined. Schwyz wrote to Baron von Reding in 1753: "No one knows better than yourself and the other colonels in Spanish service that the reason for the poor state of your regiments is in fact because Capitulations were solicited by the colonels and concluded with individuals instead of being agreed with the cantonal authorities in the old way."(5)

Although the capitulations allowed one-third non-Swiss and one-third Protestants, the colonels always had the greatest difficulty filling their quotas. Unreliable pay and poor conditions of service meant that Spanish service was always less popular than with the French or the Dutch. Often the regiments contained closer to one-third Swiss born, many of the rest being sons of the regiment born to Swiss soldiers who settled in Spain with local girls.

The problems caused by the normally lax Spanish administration were at their worst during the War of the Austrian Succession. The proximity of the main war zone in Northern Italy to the Confederation led to new recruits being mustered at Thonon on Lake Geneva and escorted direct to Italy without receiving proper training in Spain before being thrust into battle. The rate of desertion and casualties was far higher than usual. For example the complement of the Old- and Young-Reding regiments dropped from 5,600 men in 1742 to 1300 men in 1747, despite having recruited 8,000 men in the meantime. Most of the officers were ruined trying to keep their men fed during an almost total breakdown of pay and provisions. The Sury regiment of Solothurn managed to keep going only with the aid of thousands of small loans from the citizens of the Canton, which were only finally repaid forty years later.

During the second half of the eighteenth century, the Swiss troops fought for Spain in Portugal, Algeria and in Minorca. Two additional regiments were raised to fight the French Revolutionary Armies along the Northern Spanish border — Regiment Jann from Nidwalden in 1793 and Regiment Courten from the Valais in 1795. A new General Capitulation in 1804 finally gave the Swiss regiments in Spanish service the equivalent status and financial protection as the regiments in French service. The improved pay and conditions, and the availability of troops from the regiments dismissed by the French in 1792, enabled a significant improvement in the quality of the Swiss regiments in time for them to prove their worth against Napoleon.

Seven Swiss regiments served in the Austrian army for various periods during the first half of the eighteenth century.(6) The first capitulation was signed with the Protestant cantons in 1690 and the last in 1742. Several of the capitulations restricted the Swiss regiments to garrison duties in the Rhineland although others allowed the troops to be used more freely. In the latter case they were generally employed against the Turks. Heinrich Bürki of Zurich, for example, took part in nine campaigns on the Austrian/Balkan frontiers and reached the rank of General Fieldmarshal. The Swiss troops wore white coats with red waistcoats and linings. No Swiss regiments fought with the Austrians in the Seven Years War, but several Swiss officers reached high rank in the Austrian army, including Tillier and Sprecher.

Although 800 Bernese troops had fought for the Duke of Savoy in 1243, only in 1577 did Swiss troops start to serve Savoy on a regular basis. In 1597 the *Cent Suisses de la Garde* were formed, serving without interruption until

1831. Otherwise Swiss regiments served intermittently through the seventeenth century under such colonels as Karlbermatten and Amrhyn as well as the usual Diesbachs and Erlachs. The first permanent Swiss regiment was formed under Colonel Hackbrett in 1708, later becoming known as the Regiment Valaisan. This was joined by Regiment Bernois in 1733, the Regiment Romand in 1735 and the Regiment Grisons in 1742. These regiments served Savoy and its successor, the Kingdom of Piedmont-Sardinia until the French Revolution. The troops were uniformed in royal blue, with collars and facings of yellow for the Regiment Valaisan, orange for the Regiment Bernois, and red for the rest. Three additional regiments were raised in 1783 in response to the threat from revolutionary France. One regiment passed into English service in 1794 as a result of being shipwrecked on Corsica. The six remaining regiments passed into French service in 1798 as the Legion Helvetiques d'Italie.

Two other small bodies of troops served under capitulations. The Montenach Regiment remained in Genoese service from 1686 to 1786, while several regiments served Venice intermittently, the last being four regiments that returned home in 1719 after destroying a pirate stronghold at Dulcigno. Service for Venice was initially seen as adventurous and romantic, but because of poor administration and the isolation of the main war zone in Dalmatia, this service eventually became quite unpopular.

Although not covered by formal capitulations, numerous other Swiss served with distinction in all the armies of the eighteenth century, in Europe and beyond. Many sought out the Prussian army in order to pursue their military careers under the most illustrious commander of the time, Frederick the Great. High-ranking Swiss officers in the Prussian army included the four Dohna brothers of Coppet, Jean-Louis Rossier of Vevey who became Frederick's adjutant, Emmanuel Warnery of Morges, and most renowned of all Robert Scipio von Lentulus of Berne. Lentulus, son of a Swiss General in Austrian service, was persuaded personally by Frederick to leave the army of Maria Theresa in 1745 and join the Prussian army. He was given the task of reorganizing the Prussian cavalry, which he commanded at Rossbach, Leuthen and Zorndorf, becoming Lieutenant General of Cavalry in 1767. Seven foot tall, master of several languages and married to a Prussian countess, Lentulus became a confidant of the King and was entrusted with several diplomatic missions.

Further East, in Poland, King August II formed a bodyguard of Hundred Swiss under Hubert von Diesbach in 1733. The Russian Tsars were served by the Lefort family of Geneva for several generations. Francois Lefort was entrusted by Peter the Great with the creation of the Russian navy, building a fleet of 28 ships on the Black Sea. His nephew Pierre Lefort took part in over 40 battles in Persia, Turkey and Finland; while another nephew Jean followed his uncle by becoming a Russian admiral. Two generations of the Vaudois family Ribaupierre were officers and ambassadors for Catherine the Great. Philippe de Landerset of Fribourg served Portugal in the East Indies and then as Portuguese ambassador in North Africa.

These examples show just how numerous, widespread and esteemed were the Swiss officers in mercenary service during the eighteenth century. On the eve of the French Revolution the following 34 Swiss officers were serving with the rank of Lieutenant General or equivalent, and a further 102 Swiss held the rank of Major-general, Brigade-general or Marechal de Camp.

Swiss Lieutenant Generals on the eve of the French Revolution:

France:	D'Affry, Beausobre, Pestalozzi, Diesbach, Reding, Hartmannis, Erlach-Riggisberg, Castella, Besenval, Pfyffer-von Wyher, Zurlauben, Courten, Maillardoz
Holland:	Sandol-Roy, Steiger, May, Escher, Bouquet, Chambrier
Naples:	Tschudi, Wirz, Jauch, Burckhardt
Austria:	Tillier
Savoy:	Courten, Sury, Kalbermatten, Pictet
Spain:	Buch, Dunant
England:	Haldimand, Prévost
Prussia:	Lentulus, Erlach

Of this total of 136 general officers half were from the five cantons of Berne (18 generals), Vaud (17), Fribourg (14), the Grey Leagues (12) and Solothurn (8). They included five members of the Salis family from the Grey Leagues, four Erlachs from Berne, four Courtens from the Valais and three Diesbachs and three Castellas from Fribourg.

During the seventeenth and eighteenth centuries Swiss soldiers also started to appear outside Europe in the armies of the colonial powers. One Daniel Moginié led an adventurous career in the service of Persia and Afghanistan before remodelling the army of the Emperor of Hindustan on European lines. He died in 1749 still aged only 39. The French Regiment Karrer that later became Hallwyl served the French in Louisiana fighting the Indians, in India fighting the British and in the East Indies. The Swiss were also active in the Dutch colonies. A Jakob Steinmüller commanded the Dutch forces on the island of Java, while a Louis de Mellet fought the English in Guiana.

The majority of the Swiss outside Europe were, however, in the service of the British, particularly in India and North America. In July, 1751, the Court of Directors of the British East India Company resolved: "To treat with Sir Luke Schaub for obtaining four companies of Swiss soldiers for the Company's service in India of 139 men each, including therein 19 officers."(7) These companies were secretly recruited and arrived the following year in India where they formed the core of Clive's army in the campaign against the French. Although the companies were disbanded in 1755, most of the men remained and fought with Clive at Plassey two years later. It has been remarked that these few hundred Swiss with their strict discipline and fire control defeated both the French and the numerically much larger local armies and were responsible for winning India for the British.(8)

A number of Swiss officers played an influential role in the history of North America during the second half of the eighteenth century. The British formed the Royal American Regiment in 1754 consisting of two Swiss battalions, one Scottish and one Dutch. The Regimental Commander was Jacques Prévost of Geneva. The two Swiss battalions were commanded by Henri Bouquet of Rolle and Frederic Haldimand of Yverdon, and two of Prévost's brothers served as officers. All were to leave their mark on American history.

In 1763 the Indian chief Pontiac led a general uprising of all the tribes in the central and north-eastern part of North America against the colonial invaders. Only three of the inland fortresses were able to hold out — Detroit, Niagara and Fort Pitt.(9) In July, 1763, Bouquet set out with a force of 1000 men to relieve Fort Pitt. On 4 August the relieving force was attacked by the Red Indians at Bushy Run. An audacious counterattack by Bouquet surprised the Indians and put them to flight. Six days later he reached Fort Pitt and the uprising melted away. The following year Bouquet negotiated a peace settlement with the Indians that brought a lengthy period of stability to the whole hinterland. In 1765 Bouquet was transferred to Florida where he died of fever within a few days of arriving. The location of his grave is unknown.

Meanwhile Haldimand had served under General Abercrombie in the campaign to occupy Canada, including the taking of Montreal, before taking over as Governor General of Florida following the tragic death of Bouquet. Called back to London in 1775 to brief George III personally on the American Revolution, Haldimand returned in 1778 as Governor General of Canada. With one English regiment and 20,000 Hanoverians under his command he put energetic measures in hand to shore up the defences of the colony.

Meanwhile one of the Prévost brothers, Augustin, distinguished himself in the South, holding Savannah in 1779 against Generals d'Estaing and Lincoln. His son Sir Georges Prévost fought in Guiana, the Antilles and Martinique, before becoming Governor General of Nova Scotia and then of the whole of Canada.

SECTION FIVE

LAST THROES OF MERCENARY SERVICE
THE BASTILLE TO THE VATICAN
1789-TODAY

XVIII

Loyalty and Honour

'Indifferent to politics, republicans ready to fight the Republic, these men were motivated by discipline and by honour. They would die for their word and not for an ideal nor for patriotism. But loyalty is a virtue in itself; this indifference of the Swiss to the cause of the King or of the people made their heroism not only more pure but more military. They showed the devotion not of a patriot but of a soldier.'

Lamartine – *Histoire des Girondins*

During the twenty years leading up to the French Revolution, as the Ancien Régime disintegrated and France lapsed gradually into chaos, the Swiss regiments came to be treated increasingly as the agents of the King. Instead of being quartered harmoniously in the suburbs of Paris and the other cities, the Swiss troops became isolated like the garrisons of an occupying power. On the eve of the Revolution, the Guards were garrisoned in Paris and the other eleven regiments in Aix en Provence, Arles, Saarlouis, Troyes, Strasbourg, Bitche, Lille, Valenciennes, Corsica, Colmar and Dunkirk. The Swiss were by this time the most distrusted of all the foreign regiments, partly because they were the most different with their German language, high pay and special privileges. The Swiss were also not entirely innocent of causing trouble, bored and sometimes drunken troops often provoking incidents with civilians and other regiments. In particular, however, the Swiss were disliked because of their use in repressing civilian disturbances. The royal army had always been employed as police, but political disturbances and food riots dramatically increased this function after the disastrous harvest of 1788. Because of their strict discipline and lack of ties with the local population, the Swiss were used in an exceptionally large number of actions to control civilian disturbances. After the other foreign regiments were dismissed in July, 1791, the Swiss remained to become even more the focus of the revolutionaries' antagonism. Every day brought

155

quarrels and street fights between the soldiers and the people, and increasingly serious riots had to be put down.

A Swiss grenadier, Gamaliel Fonjallaz, has described his role in quelling a disturbance in the streets of Paris in 1788: 'A battalion of French guards and a battalion of Swiss guards were ordered to disperse the rebels, who numbered more than 8000 armed with forks, stones and pikes...The French guards entered the area ahead of us as they were barracked in Paris while we were in Courbevoie. The rebels killed several French guards with cobbles thrown from windows...Then we received the order to fire on anyone in the streets or the windows. We advanced firing against the rebels and several were killed or wounded...We patrolled the streets of Paris for several days. When the rebels realized we would hound them out, they met and decided to fall on us at night and take our arms. Someone betrayed their plans to us and we shared the intelligence with the French guards. We were all ready when they came at midnight. At the agreed signal, three taps on the drum, we fell on them with swords drawn. Within half an hour the street was covered with dead and wounded. The rest fled and order was restored; all has remained quiet since. The French guards lost seven dead and eleven wounded. I took a sword thrust in the right thigh that cost me five weeks in hospital.'(1)

By May, 1789, the unrest was so serious that the King and his advisers decided to order large numbers of troops into Paris to restore order. The arrival of the troops only increased the tension, however. The Swiss regiments Salis, Reinach, Lullin and Diesbach marched into Paris and were camped on the Champ de Mars and in front of the Ecole Militaire along with thousands of other French and foreign troops. Tensions continued to mount in the summer heat as the troops, bored and without adequate rations, were harangued by demagogues during the day and shot at by night. Lieutenant General Baron von Besenval of Solothurn, the effective military commander of Paris as well as the senior Swiss officer, confined the troops to camp in an attempt to reduce the friction. On June 24th, however, two companies of French guards mutinied and left the camp to carouse in the local bars. Over the following days the French guards disintegrated as a military organization and mingled with the revolutionaries eventually to become the core of the National Guard.

On 12 July, enflamed by Camille Desmoulins, the mob turned on the foreign troops camped in front of the Ecole Militaire and the next day sacked the Hotel de Police. With no direction coming from Versailles, Besenval decided on the 13th to order all 8000 Swiss troops back from their guard positions around Paris to the camp on the Champ de Mars, effectively ceasing the policing of the capital. As he explained later in his memoirs: 'If I had employed the troops in Paris, I would have ignited civil war.'(2)

On the morning of the following day, 14 July, 1789, the mob plundered thousands of muskets and several cannon from the Invalides, and streamed towards the Bastille, the fourteenth century fortress that symbolized the repression of the Ancien Regime. Within the fortress Governor de Launay commanded a small force of 82 invalides (retired soldiers) and 32 fusiliers of the Swiss regiment Salis-Samade, led by the young lieutenant Nicholas von Flue of Unterwalden. This small force had spent the previous days shoring up the defences of the castle as best they could and transferring all the gunpowder stored in the Arsenal into the Bastille for safekeeping.

At ten in the morning on the 14th about fifty armed citizens arrived at the Bastille to demand the surrender of the fortress, which de Launay predictably refused. A couple of hours later the mob arrived on the scene and forced their way into an inner courtyard. An exchange of fire drove back the crowd with 83 casualties, but when the revolutionaries brought up cannon some of the invalides opened the gates. The mob stormed in, disarmed the soldiers and occupied the fortress. Von Flue and his men were led away through the throng amid cries that they should be strung up. In von Flue's own words from his later report to the Swiss authorities: 'With threats and insults and a clamour from the whole mob that we ought to be hanged...swords, bayonets and pistols were continually pressed against me. I did not know how I would die but felt that my last moment had come.'(3) Governor de Launay was massacred by the mob, but von Flue and his men were eventually released, losing only two men during the whole action.

The following day the King took another step down the slope towards losing his crown by agreeing to withdraw all troops from Paris and Versailles. Then on October 5th, the day of the market women, the royal family escorted by the Cent-Suisses were forced to move from Versailles to the Tuileries, the royal palace attached to the Louvre in the centre of Paris.

For the next two years the twelve Swiss regiments maintained their discipline as best they could amid the turmoil. The Swiss Guards were the senior regiment in France following the mutiny of the French Guards in 1789. Their official complement of 2165 men was reduced to 1500 in 1792, serving in four battalions each of three fusilier and one grenadier company. The Cent-Suisses were disbanded on 16 March, 1792, after nearly three hundred years protecting the kings of France. The senior officer of the Guards was the 79-year-old Lieutenant-General Louis d'Affry of Fribourg, who had followed a glittering career since becoming a captain at the age of twenty but was by this time much enfeebled by old age. Effective command was exercised by his deputy Lieutenant-Colonel Maillardoz of Fribourg and by Major Bachmann of Näfels in Glarus. The officers were stretched to maintain discipline under the constant bombardment of revolutionary pamphlets, tracts and harangues.(4)

The other regiments were garrisoned throughout France and faced similar pressures to throw down their arms and join the revolution. There were serious incidents between the Swiss and the civilian population, the Courten regiment in Douai and the Vigier regiment being involved in disturbances. But, at least some local authorities appreciated their presence. In August, 1790, the Municipality of Lyons petitioned the Ministry of War not to transfer the Regiment Sonnenberg without which it would be impossible to maintain order. On the whole discipline was maintained, but one of the regiments cracked, the only example of a mutiny in the long history of Swiss regiments in French service. In August, 1790, soldiers of the Regiment Chateauvieux based at Nancy broke into the regimental treasury and refused to obey the orders of their officers. The Regiments Vigier and Castella marched on Nancy and put down the mutiny after a bloody three-hour battle in the streets. A few days later a court martial condemned the ringleader to be broken on the wheel, twenty-three others to death by hanging, forty-one to thirty years each in the galleys, and seventy-four others to regimental discipline. Revolutionary France was stunned by the severity of Swiss justice and a year later the Assembly freed those in prison. Their red caps from Brest prison became one of the symbols of the Revolution.

Another incident occurred in February, 1792, when the Regiment Ernst in Aix en Provence was surrounded by a crowd of 10,000 Marseillais and forced to surrender its arms. The officer in charge, Major Wattenwyl, justified his decision with the statement that the 'Regiment stands for the defence of the King but not for the massacre of French citizens.'(5) Some weeks later the Regiment regained its weapons and returned to Berne, where it was received with acclaim for its cool behaviour under impossible circumstances.

Meanwhile the position of the Guards, the only regular troops in the whole of Paris, was becoming ever more difficult. The royal family was blockaded in the Tuileries, not even daring to walk in the gardens for fear of the mob. On 1st August, 1792, the guard on the Palace was doubled to two companies and Captain Erlach wrote to the Burgomaster of Berne: 'The volunteers from Marseilles have made clear that their aim is to disarm the Swiss Guards, but we have all decided to retain our arms, at the cost of our lives if necessary.'(6) The Regiment was barracked in the suburbs, the First Battalion in St Roch and Montmartre, the Second in Rueil and the Third and Fourth in Courbevoie. On 4 August the whole Regiment marched secretly at night to the Tuileries where it passed the day under arms before dispersing back to its barracks at dusk. On 7 August a detachment of 300 men was reluctantly dispatched into Normandy to escort a food convoy. During the night of 8 August the whole Regiment was again ordered back to the Palace, one thousand men marching quietly through the deserted streets of Paris as though through enemy territory. Only a small guard and the sick were left in barracks, together with the regimental flags in anticipation of the probable outcome.

Throughout the 9th the city buzzed with preparations for an attack on the Tuileries while the defenders made what dispositions they could. The thousand Swiss troops were joined by 2000 National Guardsmen of doubtful loyalty and 200 gentlemen who had come to the defence of the King. The combined force was under the command of the Marquis de Mandat of the National Guard until he was called before the National Assembly and summarily shot. The Guards were stationed around the gardens and buildings but the Tuileries was not a fortress and was difficult to defend. The four courtyards of the main building – the Cour des Princes, Cour Royale, Cour de Marsan, and Cour des Suisses – had no clear field of fire. To make matters worse the Regiment was short of ammunition.

Lamartine has described the scene as the troops settled down to pass the night of 9 August: 'The Swiss were massed in the hallways with their flags. Seated on benches and stairways, guns in hand, they passed the hours of the night in a deep silence. The reflection of the lights on their arms, the noise of their gunbutts echoing from time to time on the marble, the low sound of the guards' challenges created the atmosphere of a camp on the eve of battle. The red uniforms of the 800 Swiss sitting and lying on the landings and the staircases looked ominously like a river of blood.'(7)

Around six in the morning, without food, the men stood to their posts as the sound of the approaching mob reverberated through the streets. The crowd of 100,000 outnumbered the Swiss by one hundred to one. At eight thirty the King was persuaded to throw himself on the mercy of the representatives of the nation. Captain Erlach organized an escort of 150 men and forced a passage for the royal family through the crowd from the Tuileries to the National Assembly. The royal family was incarcerated and the two senior Swiss officers, Lieutenant-Colonel Maillardoz and Major Bachmann who had accompanied the King, were arrested. Only Erlach and the escort were allowed to regain their regiment. With the departure of the King the National Guard promptly deserted to join the mob and by nine in the morning only the Swiss, the 200 gentlemen and various palace servants were left in the Tuileries.

Following the detention of Maillardoz and Bachmann, Captain Jost von Dürler of Lucerne took charge of the defence. Deciding that the perimeter of the gardens was too long to defend, he shortened his lines to cover the palace buildings only.(8) At nine thirty the crowd broke down the gates to the Cour Royale and came face to face with the Swiss Guards, silently waiting in battle order. After a brief and futile attempt to persuade the Swiss to surrender, cannons were rolled up by the insurgents and fired on the guards from a distance of fifty metres. The Swiss immediately returned fire clearing the courtyard and capturing the cannon.(9) But the mob quickly returned pressing from all sides and desperate hand-to-hand fighting was joined.

In an attempt to stop the massacre the King sent a handwritten note that the Swiss should return to barracks, which was verbally transmitted, however, as a message that the Swiss should join him at the Assembly. About 200 guards formed up under Dürler to fight their way through to the King, while the rest continued to defend the Palace. With the loss of 50 men the relief column did succeed in reaching the Assembly, where several deputies, not expecting to be involved in the front line, promptly took flight through the windows. The King, also taken aback at the arrival of the Swiss, ordered them to lay down their arms. Protesting fiercely with tears of frustration in their eyes the guards obeyed and were immediately mobbed and dragged off to prison. Many were hacked to death en route including Captain Erlach whose head was sawn off and paraded on the end of a pike.(10)

Meanwhile at the Tuileries the 450 remaining guards continued to resist. But pressed back by weight of numbers through the courtyards and up the staircases, ammunition virtually gone, they lost more and more men until the last pockets of resistance were silenced and the last men hunted down and slaughtered. One spectator, Napoleon Bonaparte, was later to write in his *Memoires de Sainte-Hélène*: 'Never since, on any of my battlefields, have I seen anything like the number of bodies as those of the Swiss that day.' The bodies were mutilated by the mob with the most inhuman atrocities, Napoleon observing that in particular the women committed 'the worst indecencies on the bodies of the Swiss.'(11)

246 officers and men, mostly those disarmed in the National Assembly on the orders of the King, had been imprisoned in the Abbaye de St Germain and the Conciergerie. Nearly all were murdered in their prisons on 2 and 3 September, victims of the September massacres. Major Bachmann escaped the butchery but only as far as the guillotine.

About 200 Swiss escaped Paris by diverse routes, many helped by moderate Frenchmen appalled by the excesses of the mob. Dürler managed to reach Switzerland the following February. Some of the men captured were forced into the Paris battalion of the Revolutionary Army.

The Swiss Guard Regiment that had served France for nearly 200 years in 71 campaigns, 154 battles and 30 major sieges was exterminated. There is some doubt about the exact numbers killed, but the monument overlooking Lucerne specifies that 760 Swiss were killed on 10 August, 2 and 3 September, and that 350 survived. A special medal was issued to the survivors with the cross of the Confederation on one side and the words *Treue und Ehre* (loyalty and honour) on the other.

The news of these events caused suffering and revulsion throughout the

Confederation. The Diet immediately recalled the remaining Swiss regiments which were all back in Switzerland by the end of October.

XIX

For and Against Napoleon

"The first Swiss Regiment is composed of men who have served France and will be loyal to you...What troops would you like? The Swiss will give you all you could wish for. They are good soldiers and will not let you down."
Napoleon Bonaparte — letter 30 July 1806 to his brother Joseph

Until 1792 armies had consisted of volunteers and mercenaries. Along with its many other changes, however, the French Revolution introduced the concept of the citizen army. Answering the call to defend the motherland, conscripts swelled the ranks from 360,000 in February, 1793, to 670,000 in January, 1794, and 1.1 million by the autumn of 1794. Although the Swiss regiments had been discharged in 1792, the availability of experienced troops to train and stiffen this mass of new conscripts could not be ignored and between 3 and 4000 Swiss were quietly persuaded to enroll in the Revolutionary Army.(1)

Five years after the massacre at the Tuileries, the new rulers of France were regarding the Swiss Confederation itself with covetous eyes. For a new French leadership unencumbered by the ties of previous alliances, the temptation to seize the legendary treasures of Berne, Basle and the other cities; the Swiss arsenals; rich pastures for the quartering of armies; strategic control of the Alpine passes and the centre of France's eastern frontier, was irresistible. In 1798 the Directory, by that time dominated by Napoleon, ordered the invasion of the Confederation.

The Club Helvetique de Paris still existed and its leaders, Frédéric-César de la Harpe of Vaud and Peter Ochs of Basle, were the quislings who provided a spurious request for help as an excuse for the French invasion.

In March, 1798, Generals Brune, Schauenberg and Pigeon invaded Swiss territory and on the 5th entered Berne, the first invaders ever to do so. The Confederation should have been able to field an army of 50,000 men stiffened by experienced mercenaries returned from France. The attack by France, however, the 300 year ally and cultural partner of the Patriciate, seemed to paralyse the leadership. With no preparation and no cantonal direction a weak force under General Hans Ludwig von Erlach won a minor victory at Neuenegg, but the Confederation was quickly overrun. Only in the Waldstaette was there any serious resistance. Alois von Reding, Landamman of Schwyz and a former colonel in Spanish service, put together a force of 7000 men, but despite spirited resistance centred on Rothenturm was defeated by General Schauenberg's superior forces in May. An uprising by 2000 Nidwalians was crushed on the Drachenreid in September. Pockets of resistance continued to fight the French and the country was never completely pacified. The following year, 1799, Switzerland became a battleground for the first time in centuries. The Austrians defeated the French at the first battle of Zurich in June, but then Massena beat the Russians at the second battle of Zurich in September forcing the desperate retreat of General Suvarov across the eastern Alps.

Meanwhile, the puppet Republique Helvetique had signed in November, 1798, a capitulation to raise 18,000 men for France. The terms were similar to those of the capitulations signed with the Ancien Régime. There was a very low response to the request for troops as the French were regarded as an occupying power and the massacre at the Tuileries was still a recent memory. Thousands of young Swiss emigrated rather than be forced into the French army. Many joined the Regiment of Ferdinand de Rovérea harassing the French from across the borders, and others joined the three regiments in English service, whose history is briefly described below.

The Regiment de Meuron had originally been recruited by the Dutch in 1781 and served in South Africa and Ceylon. In 1795, faced with considerable uncertainty after the French invasion of Holland and unpaid for three years, de Meuron secretly negotiated to transfer his regiment into British service. The island of Ceylon, which was otherwise defenceless, followed de Meuron into the British Empire. Meuron's Swiss Regiment as it was called then served in India, taking part in the victory over the Tippoo of Mysore at Seringapatam. Subsequently the Regiment transferred to Malta and Sicily, and then on to Canada to serve under General Sir Georges Prévost in the war against the United States. The Regiment was disbanded in 1816, though several officers and men remained in Canada to join the Red River Colony.

The second Swiss Regiment in English service was that formed by Colonel von Roll of Solothurn in 1795. The first commander of the Regiment was the Jost Dürler that had led the defence of the Tuileries before escaping with the aid of sympathizers. The Regiment von Roll served in Egypt from 1801-7, then in Sicily and Spain until disbanding on Corfu in 1816 after being decimated by disease.

In 1801 Colonel von Wattenwyl of Berne formed a third Regiment for English service, largely from the remains of de Rovéréa's partisan unit. Uniformed in bulls-blood red like de Meuron and von Roll, the Regiment von Wattenwyl served in Egypt until 1804, Sicily until 1807 (participating in the landing at Santa Eufemia and the battle of Maida), Spain until 1814, then Canada until being disbanded in 1816. In the war with the United States, the Regiment took part in the defence of Canada in the area of Niagara and the St. Lawrence.

Both the latter regiments had an interesting connection with the study of Swiss military history. Jost von Dürler was married to the daughter of Baron Zurlauben, Colonel in the Swiss Guards and author of the definitive early work on Swiss troops in French service, while Emmanuel von Rodt, author of important early works on the origins of the Swiss military system, was a lieutenant in the Regiment von Wattenwyl.

In November, 1798, Joubert defeated the King of Sardinia at Turin and incorporated the remnants of the five Swiss regiments in Sardinian service(2) as demibrigades in the French army with the title of the Legions Helvetiques d'Italie. The intention was to raise a further six demibrigades to join them but in January, 1800, this plan was scaled back to three demibrigades because of the difficulty of finding recruits.(3)

The First Demibrigade Helvetique under Colonel Perrier of Fribourg spent four years garrisoned in France without seeing any action, other than one company that became marines, serving on French vessels in the West Indies and at the Battle of Trafalgar (where it is claimed that it was a shot from a Swiss musket that killed Nelson). At the end of 1805, the First Demibrigade became the 3rd Battalion of the First Swiss Regiment.

The Second Demibrigade under Colonel Wattenwyl of Berne served without distinction in Italy before being dissolved in May, 1805. The Third under Colonel Raguettly of the Grey Leagues served on Corsica and Elba. In 1803 one battalion was completely wiped out by yellow fever in Santo Domingo, only 11 men surviving out of 840. This Demibrigade was also absorbed into the First Swiss Regiment.

In August, 1802, the widespread opposition to the French within the Confederation boiled over into a general insurrection. Napoleon, by this time First Consul, deciding that the Swiss would be less trouble as allies than as subjects, withdrew the French troops and in February, 1803, signed the Acte de Médiation. This measure reinstated the old Confederation, but with the addition of six new cantons — Ticino, the Grey Leagues, Thurgau, St. Gallen, Vaud and Aargau. The governing body of the Confederation was the Diet, presided over by a Landamman rotated between the main cantons. Louis d'Affry of Fribourg, son of the commander of the Swiss Guards in 1792, was the first holder of this position.

In September, 1803, a new defensive alliance, referring back to the perpetual peace of 1516, was signed between France and the Confederation. This alliance required the Swiss to provide 8000 men for the defence of France, and a new capitulation signed at the same time gave the French the right to recruit a further 16,000 men. Four regiments of 4000 men each were stipulated, each commanded by a colonel. Each regiment had four battalions commanded by a Chef de Batallion. In turn, each battalion consisted of nine companies commanded by captains, eight fusilier companies of 112 men each and a grenadier company of 92 men. Each regiment also formed one company of artillery. Recruits should be aged 18-40, have a minimum height of five feet six inches,(4) sign on for four years and receive the same pay as the French regiments, one franc 20 centimes per day with the grenadiers earning an additional sou. The troops retained the rights to freedom of religion and to be subject to Swiss justice. The regiments could be recruited throughout the Confederation and had no cantonal ties. The uniform was the traditional Swiss red with facings of yellow for the first regiment, royal blue for the second, black for the third and sky blue for the fourth. Otherwise uniforms and equipment were the same as for the French line infantry.

As with the earlier demibrigades, service in these regiments was not popular and recruitment proceeded extremely slowly, not helped by the clearly ambivalent attitude of the Swiss authorities. Napoleon was becoming increasingly impatient: "Write to the Landamman, write to the colonels, use M. Maillardoz [the representative of the Confederation in Paris]. There is no lack of money. I absolutely count on these regiments for the defence of the borders of France."(5) The first regiment was finally organized from the remains of the demibrigades in July, 1806. 2200 men served under Colonel Raguetly as part of the French army of occupation in Italy. One battalion saw action at Santa Eufemia against the English invasion force under General Stuart,(6) but basically the regiment was employed in the unpopular task of suppressing the widespread resistance to the French occupation in southern Italy. The first Swiss regiment remained in Italy carrying out policework until the end of 1811. The only formal action it saw was in the battles with the English for Capri and Ischia, losing nearly 800 men to malaria; and standing by to participate in Murat's eventually aborted invasion of Sicily.(7)

The creation of the other three regiments envisaged in the capitulation of 1803 proceeded at a snail's pace. Despite the appearances of the alliance, the Swiss still regarded the French with covert hostility. The Swiss attitude threw Napoleon periodically into fits of rage. At one point he declared: "You throw the gauntlet down to me. I will send 50,000 men. I wiped out the Russians and I've just about had enough of the Swiss. One of these days at midnight I'll swallow your country into France."(8)

Finally in 1807 the three remaining regiments were enrolled, the Second

Swiss Regiment under Colonel Castella of Fribourg, the Third under Colonel May of Berne, and the Fourth under Colonel Perrier of Estavayer in Vaud. To speed up recruitment the companies of the three regiments were each allocated to individual cantons, who could recruit throughout the Confederation but took over the responsibility of administering the recruiting process. Nevertheless the three regiments were still not up to full strength when they were mustered, the second totalling 3600 men, the third 2700 and the fourth 3800, all far short of their desired complement of 4182 each.

Napoleon recruited two other units from territories that are part of today's Switzerland, the Battalions of Valais and Neufchatel. In 1802 he had declared the Valais an independent republic allied to the Swiss Confederation but under the protection of France. This move was intended to safeguard plans to construct a new military highway across the Alps through the Simplon Pass. In October, 1805, a separate capitulation was signed with the Valais to raise one battalion of 960 men with recruits from either the Valais or the Confederation. Recruitment was again very slow, not just because of the ill will to France but also as 1500 Valaisans were already serving for Spain in the Regiment de Preux and for France in the four Swiss regiments. At the end of 1807 a battalion of 600 men under Colonel de Bons was finally recruited and sent to Spain. The uniform was a dark red coat with white facings. In 1810 the Valais became the French department of the Simplon and the Valaisan Battalion was incorporated in the French 11th Light Infantry Regiment.

In 1805 the Principality of Neufchatel was ceded by Frederick-William of Prussia to France and Marshal Berthier, future Prince of Wagram, became Prince of Neufchatel. In May, 1807, Napoleon signed a decree raising one battalion under essentially the same terms as the Swiss regiments. Recruitment was again difficult and the battalion was finally organized in 1809 under Captain Bosset with a strength of 875 men. The uniform was yellow with red facings which gained the battalion the nickname of Berthier's canaries. The Neufchatel Battalion was incorporated in the Imperial Guard where Berthier treated it as his own household unit. Having served with distinction at Wagram the battalion was transferred to Spain in 1810.

In 1807 while the First Swiss Regiment was still stationed in Italy elements of the other three Swiss Regiments were transferred to the Iberian Peninsula. For the first time individual Swiss battalions were separated from their regiments. The Segesser Battalion of the Second Regiment, the Felber Battalion of the Fourth and half the Bleuler Battalion of the Third, nearly 3000 men in total, formed part of Junot's Corps d'Observation de la Gironde for the first thrust into Spain and Portugal. The Von Flue Battalion of the Second Regiment, the D'Affry Battalion of the Third and the Christen Battalion of the Fourth were part of Dupont's second army of invasion, while

Duhesme's third army included the Graffenried and Castelberg Battalions. Nearly three full Swiss regiments took part in the French invasion.

On the other side, there were also six Swiss regiments in the Spanish army — Wimpfen of Solothurn, Young- and Old-Reding and Betschardt of Schwyz, Trachsler of Unterwalden and Preux of Valais — a total of 12,000 men. According to their capitulation of 1804 only one-third needed to be Swiss and these regiments were not of the highest quality. From their pale blue uniforms they were known as the Suizos Azurros. Napoleon tried to win these troops over to the French side, but many of the Swiss troops had actually been born and raised in Spain. All remained loyal to the Spanish cause except the Regiments Young-Reding and Preux which were surrounded by French troops in Madrid and forced to declare for the French.

In July, 1808, after sacking Cordoba, Dupont's army of 23,000 men was cut off at Baylen by a Spanish army under the command of General Castanos and Marechal de Camp Théodor von Reding.(9) During the battle the impressed Young-Reding and Preux Regiments changed back to the Spanish side. At one point in the battle the Swiss of the Spanish Old-Reding Regiment came face to face with the Swiss Christen battalion on the French side. Both units decided to follow their predecessors at Ivry rather than Malplaquet and downed arms. After Reding succeeded in driving a wedge between the French forces, Dupont was forced to surrender, the first time an entire Napoleonic army was defeated in open battle. The surviving Swiss troops from Dupont's army were among the captives that spent the next five years in the most appalling conditions on the hulks of Cadiz and on the uninhabited island of Cabrera south of Majorca. A number of the captured Swiss accepted the offer to join the Regiment de Meuron in the service of Spain's English allies.

At the end of 1808 when Napoleon arrived to take personal command of affairs in the Peninsula, the French army in Spain contained four Swiss battalions. These took part in the actions at Coruna and Oporto before being used for the unpopular duty of suppressing the Spanish partisan movement.

By the end of the Peninsular War 22,000 men had served in the Swiss units involved in this theatre. They were enrolled in the eleven battalions that served in the French army, the six regiments in the Spanish army and the Regiments von Roll and Wattenwyl in Wellington's army.

In March, 1812, under the terms of a modified capitulation signed that same month, Napoleon's four Swiss regiments gathered at Magdeburg to prepare for the invasion of Russia.(10) Their total strength of 7265 men was well below the 12,000 required by the Capitulation. The continued Swiss disenchantment with the French had only been exacerbated by the reports reaching home from the Peninsular War. In particular, the use of the Swiss troops for suppressing the Spanish resistance was most unpopular in the

Confederation where there was much sympathy for the partisans in their struggle against French oppression.

Although under strength, all four Swiss regiments were included in the Division Merle as part of Marshal Oudinot's Second Army Corps. Oudinot's Corps took up position on the left or northern flank of the invasion force. The Seventh Army Corps, consisting mainly of Saxons, was commanded by Marshal Reynier of Lausanne, while Jomini, Amey, Richter, Jacquet, Gressot, Remonde and du Mont were all Swiss officers of General rank serving on the staff of the various Corps. The Battalion Neufchatel formed part of the Imperial Guard. In June the Grande Armée crossed the Niemen and began its ill-fated venture. At the end of July, the Second Corps entered Polotsk, the original 44,000 men already reduced to 21,000 by casualties, sickness and desertions. St. Cyr's Sixth Corps, similarly reduced in strength, joined the Second and St. Cyr took over the joint command when Oudinot was injured. On 18 August St. Cyr attacked the Russian forces under Wittgenstein outside Polotsk. The Third and Fourth Swiss regiments formed part of the French left flank, while the First and Second were held in reserve protecting the bridges across the River Dvina. When asked why he had not placed all the Swiss in the front line as usual, St. Cyr replied prophetically: "I know the Swiss. One of their battalions was under my command at Castel-Franco. The French are more impetuous in attack, but if it comes to a retreat, we can certainly count on the coolness and bravery of the Swiss. That is why today I have kept them in reserve."(11)

The French claimed the victory at Polotsk but each side lost 5000 casualties and the Russians withdrew only a few miles. During the next two months, as the cold set in, the two sides skirmished constantly. By the middle of October the strength of the combined Second and Sixth Corps was down to 21,000 men, including 4000 Swiss but 1200 of them sick or injured. On 17 October the Russians opened a general advance on Polotsk. Exposed on the extreme right of the army, the Third Swiss Regiment retreated under heavy fire. Similarly on the left the grenadier company of the First Swiss held up the attack.(12) The main Russian attack followed on the 18th. The First and Second Swiss Regiments formed the centre of the French line and surprised both St. Cyr and the Russians by counterattacking before eventually retreating in good order. Etting reports how the Swiss "closed up like a red wall behind an incessant perfectly controlled blaze of musketry, literally shooting their way clear."(13)

The next day, as Wittgenstein was reinforced with 15,000 fresh troops, St. Cyr decided to retreat across the Dvina under cover of night. The Division Merle was left to cover the retreat and the Fourth Swiss Regiment under Colonel d'Affry was ordered to hold the town until the rest of the army had crossed the river. The lone Swiss regiment held the whole Russian army from eight in the evening until three in the morning in a house-by-house retreat. The Swiss lost four hundred men but the whole French army reached safety for the loss of one cannon. The last company across, Landolt of Zurich, destroyed the bridge behind it and the company commander, Captain Bleuler, had his horse shot from under him as he swam the river as last man across.

In November St. Cyr's Corps met up with the retreating Grande Armée. On the night of the 27th, as heavy snow fell, the 1500 remaining Swiss learned that they would again be called on to cover the army's retreat, this time across the Beresina. From nine the following morning until nine at night the Swiss held the Russian army at bay with eight desperate bayonet charges as their ammunition ran out. At roll call that night 1200 men were missing, and of the 300 present 100 men were wounded. Only 2 officers and 12 men were present from the whole Second Regiment. In his subsequent report Colonel d'Affry compared the action with the retreat from Meaux. The next morning the remaining Swiss crossed the Beresina and formed part of the rearguard of the retreating army for the long march back. 4000 Swiss finally returned to safety of the 14,000 that had left for Russia. While there may have been a question mark on the quality of the Swiss troops that served in Spain, those in Russia certainly performed their traditional indomitable role.

During 1813 Napoleon rebuilt his army and 4000 fresh Swiss troops were recruited for the four Swiss regiments. They served in France until Napoleon capitulated and went into exile. During this period General Jomini went over to the allied side. Jomini had already followed a glittering career. Adjutant to Marshal Ney with the rank of colonel at the age of 26, his first work of military scholarship, *Traites des Grandes Operations Militaires* attracted the attention of Napoleon who transferred Jomini to his personal staff. There, however, he became victim of Berthier's jealousy. After the Battle of Bautzen in 1813 Berthier converted Ney's recommendation that Jomini be promoted for an adventurous and successful change of plan into a censure for insubordination. In August, 1813, Jomini left for Prague where he was welcomed with open arms by Tsar Alexander. Initially furious, Napoleon later recognized that: "General Jomini did not betray our operational plans to the allies....He did not dishonour his flags. He had reason to be blinded by a great injustice and by honourable sentiments. He was not a Frenchman and patriotism did not retain him".(14) Jomini served the Russians until he retired and eventually died in Paris in 1869 aged 90.

In April, 1814, following the exile of Napoleon, the Diet instructed the Swiss regiments to serve the King. Colonel d'Affry was ordered to Paris to form the guard at the Palace of Vincennes and 100 men were selected to form the *Cent-Suisses* who accompanied the King on his entry to Paris.

The Swiss regiments were again faced with the difficult question of their allegiance when Napoleon returned from Elba for the 100 Days. When d'Affry encountered a French division acclaiming the Emperor and demanding the support of the Swiss, he replied: "I have served the Emperor as long as my duty bound me to him. Now I have sworn my loyalty to the King."(15) The regiments requested urgent direction from the Diet and were ordered to return home. In response to French efforts to retain them with offers of double pay and rapid advancement, Captain Boesselet explained: "I have 27 years service, 20 campaigns, many wounds, five children, and today as always I want to do my duty and follow my conscience. I am returning to my homeland."(16) Napoleon ordered the Swiss officers home but retained the troops to offer them further temptations to remain in French service. After 14 days without success, he released all the Swiss troops and the NCOs led the men without harm back to Solothurn.

No official troops served at Waterloo, although several Swiss officers served on the allied side and a 300-man free company under Colonel Stoffel of the Thurgau served with the French. The survivors of this company were severely punished by the Swiss authorities.

XX

The Foreign Legion and the Papal Guard

King: 'Where are my Switzers? Let them guard the door.'
William Shakespeare − *Hamlet* Act IV Scene V

During the first half of the nineteenth century the numbers of Swiss mercenaries serving in the various armies of Europe reduced sharply. Looking firstly at France, historically the largest employer of Swiss troops, the military relationship was briefly reestablished after the final defeat of Napoleon. In January, 1815, Louis XVIII was escorted back to Paris by the Cent-Suisses and the same year a capitulation was signed to raise 14,000 troops in six regiments. The first and second regiments under Colonels Hogger and d'Affry were brigaded under General Mallet of Geneva as part of the Royal Guard, while the line regiments Bleuler, Freuler, Steiger and Salis-Zisers were garrisoned in the provinces. Two Battalions of the Guard took part in the war with Spain in 1823.

During the last years of the Bourbon monarchy, the Swiss troops again became the hated representatives of an oppressive regime. In 1827 and 1828 there were serious confrontations with Parisian workers, and in November, 1828, a pitched battle took place at Versailles with the Second French Grenadiers Regiment.

By 1830 the Swiss troops were again caught up in a French Revolution and events followed a similar course to those of forty years earlier. On 28 July the First Guard Regiment under Colonel Salis-Zisers suffered 130 casualties when ordered to take down dozens of barricades in the centre of Paris at the point of their bayonets. The following day the French regiments deserted to join the uprising and the Swiss troops were again left alone defending the Tuileries, once more the symbol of repression in the eyes of the people. The regiment lost a further 300 men fighting its way through the crowd to reassemble at St. Cloud. On 2 August Charles X abdicated and the six Swiss regiments stood down for the last time. With the Treaty of Lucerne in April, 1831, France renounced the last of the capitulations with the Confederation. The Prince de Joinville wrote about the Day of Barricades in his memoirs: 'What can one say about these superb Swiss battalions, by age old tradition the most solid infantry in the world?'(1)

The Swiss regiments in Spain were left to fade quietly away. No further recruits were hired after the end of the Peninsular War and most of the remaining troops married and settled in Spain. Their military activities could be considered more those of partisans than mercenaries. In 1820 the Cortes officially pronounced the dissolution of the Swiss Regiments although this measure was not finally enacted until 1835 when only 300 elderly soldiers remained.

Elsewhere, Holland raised four Swiss regiments of 10,000 men in 1814 which remained in service until 1829. Small detachments continued to be recruited for service in the Dutch colonies throughout most of the nineteenth century. Prussia retained a small battalion from Neufchatel until 1848, and one company of guards remained with Savoy until 1832. The British secretly recruited 3300 troops for service in the Crimea. The British Swiss Legion as it was known underwent training in Dover before being shipped to Smyrna at the end of 1855. The war ended before the legion reached the Crimea and it was discharged without seeing action.(2)

Around 4000 Swiss served in the American Civil War, mainly for the North where most of the Swiss settlements had taken place. Most enlisted as individuals and only one unit larger than a company could be described as Swiss. This was the Fifteenth Missouri Regiment, also known as the Swiss Regiment or Swiss Rifles. The Ninth New York Militia, the Thirty-ninth New York and the Eighty-second Illinois Volunteers each had a Swiss company. One of the captains in the last regiment was Emil Frey, who went on to become President of the Swiss Confederation and to write a popular history of Swiss mercenaries.(3)

The main employer of Swiss mercenaries in the nineteenth century, however, was the Kingdom of Naples. Swiss had served the Bourbons of the Two Sicilies since 1731, twenty-five reaching the rank of General.(4) In the nineteenth century the four Swiss regiments formed the core of the Neapolitan army. They were uniformed in the traditional red coats, the first regiment with white collars, the second with yellow, the third with blue and the fourth with black.(5) In 1848 the Swiss troops were caught up in the revolution that swept through Italy. They lost 200 men in the street fighting to retain control of Naples, and a further 400 retaking the citadel of Messina.

It was increasingly apparent by this time that the day of the mercenary had passed. Conscription, voluntary or not, had become sufficiently widespread for nations to meet their own needs for soldiers. Mercenaries were increasingly used as police rather than soldiers and in that role found themselves defending unpopular monarchs against attacks by their subjects. The Confederation received vociferous complaints that the mercenary soldiers of the respected Swiss republic were being employed to suppress the democratic aspirations of others. Within the Confederation the longstanding opposition to mercenary service led by the church gained much popular support following the French Revolution, and even more so after the second French Revolution of 1830. The feeling that Swiss troops were being used to prop up corrupt and despotic regimes became yet more widespread as a result of their repressive role during the 1848 revolution in Naples.

The new Swiss Constitution of 1848 took the first step in formally prohibiting the supply of mercenaries. Article XI clearly stated that no new military capitulations may be agreed. The cantons argued that they could not break their commitments under existing capitulations and this first measure in 1848 was therefore limited to a ban on further recruitment. Mercenary service in its entirety was finally forbidden in 1859.

The only Swiss troops left in foreign service by mid-century were those in Naples, and their employment was no easy matter. Fresh troops could now only be obtained by secret recruiting and in 1849 the regiments mutinied at the Confederation's insistence that the Swiss cross be removed from their flags in deference to Swiss public opinion. In view of these difficulties the Swiss regiments were disbanded in 1850, the King retaining only 1800 men in three battalions for his personal protection. The last action of these troops was in 1860, defending King Francis II in the citadel of Gaeta against Garibaldi and Victor Emmanuel's Piedmontese army. After holding out for 100 days the King went into exile, Gaeta was surrendered with honour, and the final Swiss battalions in mercenary service were disbanded.

Following the rapid demise of the mercenary business two anachronisms remained — the Papal Guard, and the French Foreign Legion. The latter for the first time gave the Swiss the opportunity to engage openly in foreign service as individual volunteers, without the support of the Confederation but also without its opposition.

The Foreign Legion was formed in March, 1831, by an ordinance of Louis Philippe. Marshal Soult is generally believed to have been behind the idea, which had two objectives. Firstly, political refugees and deserters from the disbanded and unpopular foreign regiments were taken off the streets and, secondly, experienced troops were made available for the expected war in Algeria. The regiment had seven battalions, the first consisting mainly of the old Hohenlohe Regiment, which had been formed in 1815 from the German troops in French service discharged after the fall of Napoleon. The second and third battalions contained Swiss and Germans. The Swiss Colonel Stoffel(6) was appointed the first commander of the Legion. Recruiting started immediately and the first troops left for Algeria before the end of the year. Other than a brief period on loan to Spain from 1835 to 1838, the Legion remained in Algeria until 1854 when it was transferred to the Crimea. At this time, a second Foreign Legion was formed which was known as the Legion Suisse on account of the Swiss origin of most of the troops. The Legion Suisse was commanded by General Ochsenbein and enjoyed the same privileges as the old regiments hired under capitulations, including the right to Swiss justice. The following year, 1856, the Legion Suisse became the first regiment of the Foreign Legion, while the troops returning from the Crimea became the second regiment.

Studies in the 1950s indicated that about 250,000 Swiss served in the Foreign Legion during its existence. Because of the Legion's guarantee of anonymity the origins of recruits cannot be determined with complete accuracy, but this estimate would indicate that Swiss formed about 5 per cent of the total strength.(7)

The Papal Guard was founded in 1506 when Pope Julius II requested the cleric Peter von Hertenstein to recruit men for a bodyguard. On 22 January, 1506, Hertenstein arrived in Rome with 150 men commanded by Kaspar von Silenen of Uri. According to tradition the original uniform of the Guard was designed by Rafael, a billowing tunic in the Medici colours of bright blue, yellow and red. Through its many changes during the following centuries the costume retained its striking and colourful appearance. The weapons carried by the Guard have remained unchanged from the beginning, each soldier armed with a halberd and sword.

In 1527 an army of 22,000 *landsknechts* and Spaniards under Constable Bourbon and Georg von Frundsberg marched on Rome. After a furious and costly assault in which Bourbon was killed, the *landsknechts* ran amok and sacked the city with unimaginable ferocity and obscenity. 147 of the Swiss Guard were killed defending Saint Peter against the invaders. The remaining 42 guards escorted the Pontiff to the Castel San Angelo which they defended for a month until terms for a surrender were negotiated. The terms included the supercession of the Swiss Guard by a troop of *landsknechts*. Not until 1548 was the Swiss Guard restored and the strength increased to 225 men under a captain, a lieutenant and four sergeants. In 1557 they were supplemented by 6000 men raised by Melchior Lussy under a capitulation to defend the Papal states against the Spaniards. This army was decisively beaten by Colonna, however, at the battle of Paliano.

From 1566 until 1878 all the commanders of the Guard were citizens of Lucerne. The first, Jost Segesser of Baldegg, captain from 1566 to 1592, was as much diplomat as soldier acting as the Confederation's ambassador to the Holy See as well as captain of the Guard. The Pfyffer family of Altishofen, descendants of Ludwig Pfyffer 'Le Roi des Suisses', then made the captaincy a hereditary possession. Nine Pfyffers held the position for all but 15 years of the period from 1652 until 1847.

Today the Guard performs mainly ceremonial duties. The effective strength was established at 200 men in 1824 and new recruits swear their oath on 6 May each year, the anniversary of the Sack of Rome. These few soldiers in their quaint uniforms are a far cry from their feared and respected predecessors who fought and died from Marignano to the Beresina.

CONCLUSION

"These in the day when heaven was falling,
The hour when earth's foundation fled,
Followed their mercenary calling,
And took their wages and are dead."

A. E. Housman, *Last Poems*, 1922

There is an important business concept called the Product Life Cycle. This recognizes that products have a limited life during which they pass through different phases. The concept is shown below in diagram form.

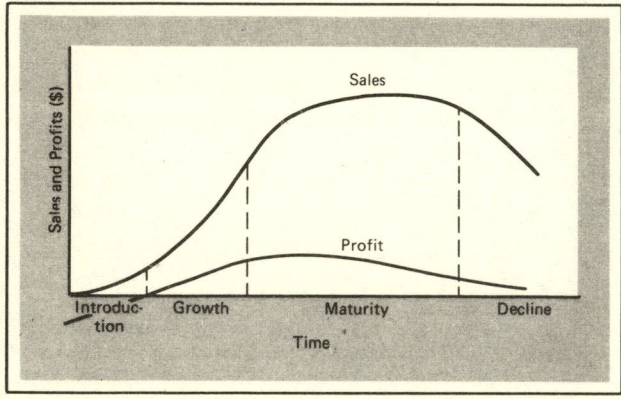

It is interesting to consider the Swiss Mercenary as a product that follows this concept. The introduction phase occurred during the fourteenth and fifteenth centuries. The long pike as a weapon and the pike square as a tactical formation were developed by the Swiss during the struggle to secure the political independence of the Confederation. The rulers of the Great Powers, anxious to introduce the new heavy infantry into their own armies, provided a ready and growing market for this new military product.

The growth phase took place during the sixteenth century, when armies grew significantly in size, the proportion of infantry to cavalry increased dramatically, and large numbers of mercenaries were hired to meet the demand. The Swiss and the *landsknechts* were the two groups of mercenaries most readily available, the former tied exclusively to France after the Treaty of 1521. The provision of troops was regulated through contracts or capitulations that laid out financial and administrative arrangements in detail.

During the mature phase in the seventeenth century, the business was largely in the hands of bold entrepreneurs, the Military Enterprisers, who took considerable risks in the hope of making enormous profits. Gradually, as standing armies became the norm, States themselves took over the role of the general enterprisers. During this period 40-60,000 Swiss were in foreign service at any one time.

The declining phase of the Swiss mercenary business took place in the eighteenth century. Firstly the demand for expensive Swiss troops reduced as local recruits supplemented by low-grade cannon fodder met the needs of eighteenth-century warfare. Secondly the supply of men started to dry up as mercenary service became less attractive and less well paid in relation to other employment opportunities. Originally the Swiss mercenaries had provided special expertise in a new weapons system, the pike-carrying heavy infantry. Even as pikes became subordinated to firearms and eventually replaced by muskets with bayonets, Swiss mercenaries were still prized for their discipline and steadiness. By the end of the eighteenth century, however, the Swiss regiments were more Swiss in name than composition, and the battlefield need was for larger numbers of moderately trained troops rather than an expensive elite. In business terms, the Swiss product advantage had largely disappeared.

Looking at the Swiss Mercenary as a business proposition in this way(1) goes some way to answering two questions — why was the small country of Switzerland at the forefront in the supply of mercenaries? and why did one million Swiss choose such a dangerous profession?

There can be no doubt that the pike square was developed a) by the Swiss and b) during the second half of the fifteenth century. The young Confederation required military support for the political objective of independence from both the Habsburgs and the other great powers jockeying for position in Central Europe. A social structure had emerged in which all citizens had the duty to bear arms and defend their territory. Large numbers of men were therefore available. Because of the mountainous terrain and the absence of the feudal infrastructure that produced the medieval cavalry, the army consisted of foot-soldiers. This infantry discovered in the halberd, and then the long pike, weapons that determined men working together could use to defend themselves against cavalry. The violent and bellicose attitudes of a herder society then led to the development of the pike square as an offensive as well as a defensive weapons system. This is a much simplified description of the thousands of separate actions and causes that combined to put the Swiss on the battlefields of Morat, Dornach and Novara in their pike squares. But certainly, for this brief period around the year 1500, the Swiss deployed a new and unique way of war.

The uniqueness disappeared as other armies, most notably the landsknechts, copied the pike square. Furthermore, by 1515 Swiss supremacy had already been overtaken by combined arms tactics. Nevertheless, although not capable of beating a well-commanded force of infantry, cavalry and artillery, the infantry remained an integral part of the battle line, and the Swiss were still generally regarded as the best infantry in Europe. These military developments coincided with political changes in the Confederation. Having effectively secured their independence, the Swiss lacked the will or the political structures to pursue an expansionary policy. The highly regarded Swiss infantry therefore became redundant to the political needs of their country, and Swiss soldiers were available to become Swiss mercenaries in the service of other powers.

Even though the uniqueness of Swiss weapons and tactics disappeared, the Swiss troops retained a highly regarded discipline and esprit de corps. Companies and regiments maintained close ties with their home cantons. The troops were members of their society serving abroad, and identified themselves with the standards and expectations of relations and friends at home. They preserved a separateness from the domestic troops of the army in which they served with their jealously preserved system of justice, religious freedom, and different language (at least the largely German-speaking troops in French service). A hereditary officer caste guaranteed regimental standards and pride, using the draconian punishments of the justice system as required. The Swiss were throughout the period the most sought-after and highest paid of the mercenaries available for hire.

Considering the Swiss mercenaries as professional soldiers with valuable skills for sale provides a more convincing explanation of why one million Swiss became mercenaries than the simplistic phrase overpopulation suggests. Each individual had his own personal, complicated and half-understood reasons for enlisting. Many were escaping a difficult domestic situation, or staying one step ahead of the law. Many were stirred by a desire for adventure and a lust for glory. This was particularly important in the first part of the period when the deeds of the heroes of Morat and Marignano were still fresh in the popular consciousness, when individual feats could still stand out and be remarked, and when recruitment was for one campaign and therefore a matter of an outing for a few months. As time went on, individual prowess was subordinated to drilled conformity, and the signing-on period really did entail a lifetime commitment. Nevertheless, the red-coated veteran returning home remained a glamorous figure in the local community. The opportunity for travel and adventure must have remained a strong motivation for many a restless soul.

The word overpopulation has regularly been used to explain the mercenary phenomenon. Certainly there existed in the Confederation, as in the rest of Europe, a stratum of urban and rural poor living on the edge of starvation. Correlations between recruitment and failed harvests have been identified. It would nevertheless be an exaggeration to picture a society breeding large numbers of surplus children, the boys being pushed into the army to get rid of them. Over time societies adopt mechanisms to adjust the birthrate to the level that economic possibilities can support. It is reasonable to suppose that families and communities would have considered, consciously or not, that mercenary service offered an attractive employment opportunity and a valuable economic resource. The soldiers not only earned their pay; they also brought income in the form of pensions and trade benefits. As the financial attractiveness to the individual reduced in the eighteenth century, the business went into decline. Until then, mercenary service provided a welcome alternative way of earning a living.

It must also be remembered that to be a mercenary was generally accepted in Switzerland as to follow a respectable occupation. Although there had been a vociferous minority against mercenary service since the days of Zwingli, the profession was thoroughly integrated into the Swiss way of life. A large proportion of the influential politicians and rich businessmen not only owed their positions to their association with foreign service, but eventually came to form a hereditary aristocracy, the Patriciate, that dominated Swiss society. For three hundred years the "Swiss Mercenary" was not a term of vilification but the description of an accepted professional occupation.

During the nineteenth century foreign service came into disrepute, and then in the twentieth century historians have tended to overcorrect the view of the "vile mercenary" by stressing concepts of loyalty and honour. Gos states that "Foreign service was never regarded by the cantons as a commercial or financial institution. The Swiss made war for love of arms not for money."(2) This seems as simplistic as the opposite explanation of overpopulation. A picture of men honourably selling their skills as soldiers to meet other powers' demand for troops during the period between the rise of the infantry as a military force in the fifteenth century and the spread of conscription in the nineteenth century presents a more balanced view of the Swiss Mercenary.

NOTES

INTRODUCTION

A technical difficulty arises with place names where English, German and French language versions may exist. I have used any generally accepted English version (for example, the Grey Leagues rather than French Grisons or the German Graubunden) and spelling (for example Berne and Basle). Where there is no generally accepted English equivalent, I have followed the name used by the inhabitants (for example, Solothurn and not Soleure, and Vaud not Waadt). The site of one of the most famous names in Swiss military history has the dual names of Morat and Mürten. I have selected Morat as being more familiar through the writings of Oman.

1. There have been several attempts by Swiss economic historians to quantify the number of Swiss who served as mercenaries. The first estimate was made by J. H. Waser in 1780 in his *Swiss blood and French gold*. Most recently, Wyler, Bickel, Peyer and Mattmüller have all tackled the question.

All use as a starting point May de Romainmotier's researches into the known capitulations in order to arrive at totals of the number of men required by the contracts. These totals are understated by not including the unofficial troops and the free companies, but are overstated to the extent that the regiments were not up to full strength or were partially filled by the employment of non-Swiss.

The estimates then attempt to calculate a replacement rate, ie. the men not returning each year due to death in action, death from disease, desertion or retirement. Each of these men needed to be replaced by a new soldier to keep the regiment up to the number required in the capitulation. The total of these replacements is then the total number of new mercenaries.

The most recent calculations can be summarized as follows:

Losses in foreign service (thousands)

Century	Wyler	Bickel	Peyer	Mattmüller
15	-	50-100	30-60	-
16	500	250-300	270	-
17	400	250-300	300	150-200

| 18 | 500 | 300-350 | 220-340 | - |
| Total | 1400 | 850-1050 | 820-970 | - |

A round figure of one million somewhere in the middle of the various estimates is probably close enough to give a realistic guide to the number of Swiss who served as mercenaries.

2. Hale — *War and Society* P.71
3. McNeil — *Pursuit of Power* P.126
4. Addington — *Patterns of War* P.78
5. Ropp — *War in the Modern World* P.8
6. Duffy — *Fortress in the Age of Vauban* Preface XIV

CHAPTER I

1. Well-known religious institutions included the monasteries of Einsiedeln, Engelberg and Disentis.
2. Known as a *Markgenossenschaft*.
3. The actual date has been the subject of much discussion among Swiss historians, with 1215 as the most likely.
4. Interestingly, this Charter followed the participation of troops from Schwyz in the army of the Emperor Frederick, possibly the first political advantage gained by the use of Swiss mercenaries.
5. The story of William Tell describes dramatically the relationship between the proud mountaineers and the Habsburg's bailiffs at the end of the thirteenth century. The story did not appear until 1471 in the *White Book of Sarnen* and is therefore more folklore than historical fact. Bergier's *Guillaume Tell* fully discusses the legend and its origins.

CHAPTER II

1. Called *Letzi* — Delbrück quotes evidence that this defensive work was 5 kilometres long and 4 metres high. (*Medieval Warfare* P.553).
2. The leader of the Swiss is not named in the chronicles, but Stauffacher is identified as the leader of the attack on Einsiedeln the previous year, and, as Landamman, must have been in charge at Morgarten also.
3. In German, the *eidgenossenschaft*.
4. Other than a slight slope that forced the opposing cavalry to attack uphill.
5. Fortescue has pointed out that in an attempt to imitate the English tactics used successfully at Crecy, "the Austrian commander at Sempach, who by dismounting his knights deliberately gave away every advantage to the Swiss and thus helped forward that nation on the way to make its infantry the model of Europe; a very significant matter in the history of the art of war".

6. A further extension of the central authority initiated with the Pfaffenbrief some twenty years earlier.

CHAPTER III

1. Description of the Zapoleten in Sir Thomas More's *Utopia* which are assumed to be the Swiss. Reference in Schauffelberger — *Charakterologie* P.52.
2. *Reiserödel*.
3. This band was called a *Freieharst*.
4. *Heimsuchung*.
5. *Dachabdeckung*.
6. *Blutrache*.
7. The young men were called *knaben*, equivalent to the *knecht* of Southern Germany. Their associations were called *Knabenschaften*.
8. The *morgenstern* was not introduced until much later, in the seventeenth century.
9. Only rarely will a horse gallop straight at an object which it cannot see how to jump or pass through.
10. The *schutzenhauptmann*.
11. The bull of Uri was lost on the battlefield of Marignano.
12. Machiavelli — the *Art of War*, Book Seven.
13. Häne — *Zum Wehr und Kriegswesen* P.29.
14. For example, the Bernese authorities were anxious not to delay the start of the battle of Morat, even though the last troops had not arrived, as they had been unable to make adequate provisioning arrangements for such a large army.
15. Described in Häne — *Alten Zürichkrieg*.
16. The *ordnungsmacher*.
17. These were the *verlorene haufen* in German or *enfants perdus* in French.
18. In contradiction to the value placed on the speed of their attack was the Swiss habit of kneeling with arms spread to pray once they reached the battlefield — much to the derision of their opponents.
19. The most extreme example of this were the 1500 *knaben* who attacked 30,000 French Armagnacs at St. Jakob an der Birs in 1444. Although wiped out, this small force caused so many enemy casualties that the advance of the Armagnacs was directed away from Swiss territory and the ferocity of the attackers made an indelible impression on the watching dauphin, who later as Louis XI was most keen to seek an alliance with these redoubtable warriors.
20. Not to be confused with the older wedge formation of Sempach and earlier.

21. It is interesting to follow Keegan's approach and consider how *The Face of Battle* would have looked in the front ranks. Contemporary illustrations show the two sides separated by the length of their pikes, presumably stabbing at each other searching for an advantage. If "push of pike" really meant pressure from the ranks behind, however, the room to manoeuvre the long pikes must have been squeezed out until eventually the front ranks would have been forced against each other spitting and gouging. Yet at Marignano, for example, the push lasted for hours and covered several hundred yards. It is inconceivable that the front ranks forced tight against each other could have held upright for so long. I have not come across an adequate account of what actually happened at the point of contact between two squares of heavy infantry.

22. The main exception to this point was Morat, where Swiss tactics were carefully planned to cut off the Burgundian retreat so that the enemy could be driven into the lake and annihilated.

23. For example, Hans Waldmann took part in more than twenty pillaging expeditions, was captain of the main *schlachthaufen* at Morat, and then became Mayor of Zurich. In this position, however, his dictatorial style created such animosity that he was eventually overthrown and executed.

24. Again using Morat as the example, the *vorhut* was under the command of Hans von Hallwyl, the *schlachthaufen* under Hans Waldmann and the *nachhut* under Kaspar von Hertenstein. The names of the captains in charge of main formations and individual companies are generally recorded in the chronicles that describe all the Swiss battles.

25. It was for a long time speculated that Wilhelm Herter was the commander in chief at Morat, but it is now accepted that he was the *ordnungsmacher*.

26. The works of Schaufelberger have been at the forefront of this new approach.

27. Häne – *Blütezeit* Pp.38-9.

CHAPTER IV

1. The Bernese policy had the inherent weakness that all the alliances were with Berne itself and the other Cantons tended to view any dispute with Burgundy as a purely Bernese affair.

2. The same month, the Confederation joined the League of Constance, a defensive alliance with the so called Lower Union, that included Strasbourg, Basle, Colmar and Schettstatt.

3. The number of troops was originally left open and only quantified the following January in a secret addendum. As this had been negotiated by Nicholas von Diesbach who was a major beneficiary of French pensions, there was much questioning of Diesbach's probity. Rich in his own right

Diesbach probably acted in good faith. A statesman of European stature he was unfortunately killed by a kick from a horse the following year.

4. The Fruhjahrfeldzug, the Blamonterzug and then in October the Herbstfeldzug when Morat, Grandson and Yverdon were occupied and Estavayer was sacked.

5. Later identified by Parker as the Spanish Road.

6. This proposal was apparently made by a Captain Hassfurter of Lucerne.

7. This is known as the *Burgunderbeute*, and Deuchler has taken a whole book to describe it. One huge diamond later known as the Sancy, was casually picked up by one unknown Swiss soldier who sold it for a few sous. Guillaume de Diesbach bought it a few days later for 5000 florins and in turn sold it on to the Fuggers for 47,000 florins.

8. Bubenberg had retired from public life rather than support Berne's pro-French policy but answered the call when needed to lead the defence of Morat.

9. The numbers involved in these early battles are always open to challenge, as contemporary chroniclers were either not possessed of the facts or deliberately over- or under-estimated to support their particular bias.

10. The *Gemeinpfennig*.

CHAPTER V

1. Mallet — *Mercenaries and their Masters* P.13.

2. Contamine — *War in the Middle Ages* P.99.

3. Kiernan — *Foreign Mercenaries* P.66.

4. Mülinen — *Schweizer-Söldner* P.19.

5. Redlich — *Military Enterpriser* P.118.

6. A typical example of this in the 1490's was Hans Etterlin of Berne, who led 600 men into the service of Maximilian of Austria, who sent them to assist Duke Francis of Brittany, and were eventually paid off by the French king Charles VIII.

7. This was the generation that had been brought up on their fathers' stories of the loot at Grandson and the glory at Morat.

8. Quoted by Vallière — *Honneur et Fidelité* P.111.

9. The Swiss method was supposedly more effective in the push of pike, but the issue is not well documented.

CHAPTER VI

1. To be imprisoned in France where he died ten years later.

2. Howard — *War in European History* P.27.

3. Monluc — *Commentaires* P.38.

4. Arrears by this time had reached a total of 300,000 livres.

5. Guerrilla or *kleinkrieg*.

6. Quoted by Parker – *Spanish Road* P.12.

7. Chiefly from St. Gallen, Baden, and the Valais.

8. There had been no less than 32 expeditions between 1331 and 1503 aiming at conquering this key access town.

9. The absence of this successful military leader from the battle of Marignano due to ill health has been advanced as one of the reasons for the Swiss defeat.

10. The first under Hans von Hertenstein of Lucerne, the second under Jakob Stopfer of Zurich and the third under Rudolf von Salis of the Grey Leagues.

11. As at Dornach. The 2000 *enfants perdus* were under the command of Albrecht vom Stein of Berne, later to play a leading role at Marignano and Bicocca.

12. Commanded by Wilhem Herter, son of the hero of Morat.

13. Under constant harassment by the cavalry of the French vanguard under the famous chevallier Bayard.

14. This action has been strongly criticized over the years, especially by comparison with the behaviour of Adrian von Bubenberg at Morat forty years earlier, who had subordinated his personal views for the common cause.

15. The Bull of Uri that was lost on the battlefield and the Cow of Unterwalden.

16. Taylor – *Art of War in Italy* P.124.

17. Vallière – *Honneur et Fidelité* P.148.

CHAPTER VII

1. Peter Falk of Fribourg and Hans Schwarzmaurer of Zug.

2. Maximilian, and after his succession in 1519, Charles Quint.

3. Including the Duchy of Milan.

4. Rott – *Representation Diplomatique* P.307.

5. Which was then known as a *compagnie avouée*.

6. Burin des Roziers – *Capitulations Militaires* P.78.

7. Guicciardini – *History of Italy* Book XIV.

CHAPTER VIII

1. Parker – *Military Revolution* P.12.

2. So called because each parish was required to provide one bowman, who would be exempted (franc) from taxes as an incentive to join up.

3. After training by the Swiss at Pont-de-l'Arche.

4. Susane – *Infanterie Francaise*, Volume I. P.75.

5. Kiernan — *Foreign Mercenaries* P.68.
6. Guicciardini — *History of Italy* Book I.
7. Quoted by Orliac — *Suisses et Grisons* P.80.
8. May de Romainmotier — *Histoire Militaire* Book 6 P.59.
9. Peyer — *Wirtschaftliche Bedeutung* P.703.
10. Text in Zurlauben—*Histoire des Suisses* IV Pp 531-4.
11. Roughly equivalent to four and a half guilders of the Rhine or nine livres tournois. (Allemann — *Söldnerwerbungen* P.98).
12. The Constitutio Criminalis Carolina or Caroline Code was published in 1532 by Charles Quint with the intention of regulating the practice of war. Although no longer part of the Empire, the Cantons adopted this code. An edition of the Code as followed by the Swiss along with a collection of documents referring to the privileges of the Swiss was published in the 1730's by Franz Adam Vogel, Grand Juge of the Swiss Guards — see bibliography.
13. Quoted in Bickel — *Bevölkerungsgeschichte* P.94.
14. Viazzo — *Upland Communities* P.294.
15. Viazzo — *Upland Communities* P.295.
16. Schelbert — *Einführung* P.154. Schelbert goes further and suggests that mercenary service was not a response to over-population but an economic resource that allowed the population to increase.
17. Such as the Zollikofer of St. Gallen.
18. Peyer — *Wirtschaftliche Bedeutung* P.711.
19. Burnand — *Colonel Henri Bouquet* P.6.
20. Quoted by Dubler — *Kampf um den Soldienst* P.20.
21. Quoted by Dubler — *Kampf um den Soldienst* P.23.

CHAPTER IX

1. Quoted in Bodin — *Les Suisses au Service de la France* P.114.
2. Delbrück — *History of the Art of War* Book IV P.53.
3. Including the oldest captain, Jost Ab Yberg.
4. Some of which are still displayed in the National Museum in Zurich.
5. Curiously the leaders of both sides, Condé and Montmorency, had been captured.
6. Parker's book *The Army of Flanders and the Spanish Road* (see bibliography) has explained the logistical importance of this route for the transfer of troops between the widely spread territories of the Spanish Empire.
7. Zurlauben — *Histoire des Suisses* Vol.IV Pp 540-3.
8. Quoted in Feller — *Service Militaire* P.33.
9. Bodin — *Les Suisses en Service de la France* P.113.

CHAPTER X

1. The six Protestant cantons were Zurich, Berne, Glarus, Basle, Schaffhausen and Appenzell, and the seven Catholic cantons were Lucerne, Schwyz, Uri, Unterwalden, Zug, Fribourg and Solothurn.
2. Vallière — *Honneur et Fidelité* P.268. After the battle the King presented Colonel Aregger with his own armour.
3. Although the two countries were not at this time direct neighbours.
4. Including the diamond lost by Charles the Bold at Grandson — see Chapter IV note 7.
5. Quoted by Vallière — *Honneur et Fidelité* P.274.
6. The Captains-Colonels of the *Cent Suisses* are listed in Appendix VII.
7. The command of all the Swiss regiments including the *Cent Suisses* was always in German language.
8. It was widely believed that this new campaign was to pursue Henry's infatuation with the young and beautiful Charlotte de Montmorency, whose husband had fled with her to Brussels to avoid the King's attentions.

CHAPTER XI

1. A manoeuvre known as the caracole.
2. Black — *Military Revolution* P.94.
3. Taylor — *Italian Wars* Pp 31-2.
4. Lynn — *Tactical Evolution in the French Army* P.179.
5. Quoted by Corvisier — *Histoire Militaire* P.350.
6. Godet — *L de Marvel* P.49.
7. The colonels of the Swiss Guards are listed in Appendix V.
8. Redlich — *Military Enterpriser* P.210.
9. By Steffen in *Die Kompanien Kaspar Jodok Stockalpers*.
10. The first European army to introduce uniforms with regulation colours was Cromwell's New Model Army in 1645.
11. Steffen — *Stockalper* P.228.
12. Steffen — *Stockalper* Pp.258-9.
13. Grimmelshausen's *Simplicissimus* was published in 1668.
14. 9000 Spaniards used this route to play a decisive role at the battle of Nordlingen in 1634.
15. Tearing the head and entrails from his body in front of his daughter.
16. At which the Confederation had been ably represented by Rudolf Wettstein, Mayor of Basle.
17. Quoted by Vallière — *Honneur et Fidelité* P.310.
18. Quoted by Vallière — *Honneur et Fidelité* P.314.

CHAPTER XII

1. Machiavelli — *The Prince* Book XII.
2. Kiernan — *Foreign Mercenaries* P.71.
3. Parker — *Spanish Road* P.185.
4. Cruickshank — *Elizabeth's Army* P.108.
5. Corvisier — *Histoire Militaire* P.350.
6. Quoted in Vallière — *Honneur et Fidelité* P.348.
7. Although not for Spain, somewhat surprisingly but for unknown reasons.

CHAPTER XIII

1. Though collection of the taxes was another matter.
2. For example, Howard in *War in European History* P.66: "the French army was the most remarkable instrument of state power that Europe had yet seen".
3. Possibly by the fortifications expert Vauban.
4. Susane — *L'Infanterie Francaise*, Book I P.203.
5. White for the French, orange for the Dutch, red for the Spanish, and so on.
6. The red Swiss coats occasionally led to confusion with the English, and with Irish regiments in the French army.
7. Quoted by Stüssi — *Schweizer Militärwesen* P.128.
8. The tapestry by Gobelin celebrating this event hangs in the Palace of Versailles.
9. His wife was a cousin of Colbert.
10. Especially the Vaud, Aargau, St. Gallen and Mulhouse.
11. The most expensive item being the coat at 26 livres.
12. Around the year 1700 no less than 13 of the Cent Suisses ran inns in the districts where the Swiss troops were quartered.
13. Allemann — *Söldnerwerbungen* P.155.
14. Such as the *Ranz des Vaches*.
15. He was called the *tapissier de Notre Dame*, the paper hanger of Notre Dame.
16. Susane — *L'Infanterie Francaise* Book IV P.338.

CHAPTER XIV

1. Where it fought with honour for the next twenty-four years.
2. Zurich, Berne, Glarus, Schaffhausen and Appenzell.
3. The Duc d'Albemarle was at this time appointed Colonel-General des Suisses et Grisons as well as Colonel of the first regiment.

4. Hirzel — *Aus der Zeit Marlboroughs* P.28.

CHAPTER XV

1. Jomini called the musket with bayonet "the most complete arm ever known".
2. Approximately two rounds a minute.
3. See Quimby, Ross and Nosworthy for discussion of the theories of Folard, Puysegur, Saxe and Guibert.
4. Such methods reached their extreme in the Prussian army of Frederick the Great, but were more or less common to all eighteenth century armies.
5. Keegan quotes Marshall in *The Face of Battle* P.71.
6. See bibliography — Baron BFA de Zur-Lauben — *Histoire Militaire des Suisses au Service de la France*. Paris 1751-3.
7. Quoted by Vallière — *Honneur et Fidelité* P.484.
8. Quoted by Vallière — *Honneur et Fidelité* P.530.

CHAPTER XVI

1. As usual the estimates need to be treated with caution. While the information on the regiments is more detailed than for previous centuries, the number of non-Swiss was higher.
2. Only privileged personnel such as NCOs and grenadiers slept two in a bed, the ordinary soldiers sleeping three or four together — Mention *L'Armée de l'Ancien Regime* P.272.
3. Bräcker — *Pauvre Homme* P.123. The soldiers organized themselves into cookgroups of 7 to 15 men, who pooled rations, purchased cooking equipment together and shared chores. They bought provisions mainly from the captain, who employed a specialist quartermaster to ensure his one remaining profitable sideline was properly administered.
4. Phillips — *Roots of Strategy* P.196.
5. On average every three years.
6. Normal routine in garrison was seven hours' sleep, two hours' rest, one hour eating, four hours training, and ten hours for free time which was the time an industrious soldier could use for a side job.
7. Figures from Dubler — *Der Kampf um den Soldienst* P.73, but challenged by Bührer in *Der Zürcher Soldienst* Pp.11-13.
8. Quoted by Schelbert — *Einführung* P.168.
9. Suter — *Innerschweiz* P.132.
10. Quoted by Dubler — *Kampf um den Soldienst* P.25.
11. Quoted by Dubler — *Kampf um den Soldienst* P.55.
12. Quoted by Dubler — *Kampf um den Soldienst* P.53.

13. Quoted by Zurlauben – *Histoire des Suisses* Book VII. P.278.

14. Including epileptics and those with problems of sight or hearing.

15. The number of criminals and vagabonds has been questioned by recent researchers (see Scott page 19), who believe that while the communes were happy to rid themselves of their problem children, the soldiers generally formed a fairly representative cross section of the lower strata of society.

16. Quoted by Corvisier – *L'Armée Francaise* P.267.

17. Schaffroth – *Fremdendienst* P.12. The higher pay of the guards allowed them to attract a higher percentage of native Swiss.

18. Quoted by Suter – *Innerschweiz* P.44.

19. Figures from Schaffroth – *Fremdendienst* P.19.

20. Bräcker – *Pauvre Homme*.

21. Pfister – *Aargauer* Pp.55-72.

22. From 1727 in France.

23. Quoted by Dubler – *Kampf um den Soldienst* P.31.

24. Erismann – *Organisation* P.140 quotes the case of a captain Burkhardt who retired as a captain in 1715, with an agreement that his company would be passed on to his son. He was not actually married at the time and this son was born only two years later, to become eventually captain at the age of 18, twenty years after the agreement was made.

25. Many Swiss would also maintain that their influence continues unabated in the fabric of modern Swiss society. Service as an officer in the Swiss army is generally considered to go hand-in-hand with a senior position in a bank or insurance company.

CHAPTER XVII

1. The numbers are taken from Bickel – *Bevölkerungsgeschichte* P.90. The 1787 numbers are from May de Romainmotier.

2. Alt-Sturler, Constant, Planta, Hirzel, Graffenried, Jung-Sturler, Chambrier, and Bude.

3. Masons were also numerous in the French regiments, including Louis d'Affry, commander of the Swiss Guards.

4. The Goumoens family still enjoys the freedom of the cities of Glasgow and Stirling.

5. Suter – *Innerschweiz* P.8.

6. Bürkli, Erlach, Leodogar von Wiederöst, Anton von Wiederöst, Buol, Schmid and Sprecher.

7. Kilchenmann – *English-ostindischen Kompanie* P.7.

8. Lätt – *Eroberung Indiens* Pp.19 and 23 quotes Cuttru and Fortescue – The Swiss officer "Paradis showed us the secret of how to conquer India".

9. Fort Pitt was commanded by another Swiss, Simeon Ecuyer of Neufchatel.

CHAPTER XVIII

1. Quoted by Vallière – *Honneur et Fidelité* P.567.
2. Quoted by Bodin – *Les Suisses au Service de la France* P.247.
3. Quoted by Bodin – *Les Suisses au Service de la France* P.251.
4. The Club Helvetique de Paris made the Swiss troops its particular target.
5. Quoted by Vallière – *Honneur et Fidelité* P.602.
6. Quoted by Vallière – *Honneur et Fidelité* P.605.
7. Quoted by Vallière – *Honneur et Fidelité* P.614.
8. Just Lieutenant Diesbach and 25 men were left at the Port-Tournant as an advance guard.
9. Both sides later insisted emphatically that the other side fired first.
10. The accounts all record that his head was sawn off slowly.
11. Bodin – *Les Suisses au Service de la France* P.268. Both quotations from *Mémorial de Sainte-Hélène*.

CHAPTER XIX

1. Scott *Royal Army* P.166.
2. Bellemont, Ernst, Peyer-Imhof, Bachmann and Zimmermann.
3. The demibrigade was equivalent to a battalion in the army of the Ancien Régime.
4. 5 pieds 2 pouces. Less than 12% of the Swiss were below this minimum height compared with 20% in the French line regiments (Scott op cit P.11).
5. Quoted by Vallière – *Honneur et Fidelité* P.666.
6. Which included the Regiment von Wattenwyl as described above.
7. Where the Regiment de Meuron formed part of the English defences.
8. Schaller – *Troupes Suisses* P.113.
9. Whose brothers were the Alois von Reding who had led the Swiss resistance to the French invasion of the Confederation, Rudolf who was killed with the Swiss Guard at the Tuileries, and Nazar who was Governor of Malaga. Théodor von Reding was killed in 1809 at the battle of Valls.
10. By this time the French nation had grown weary of war. Between 1800 and 1812, 4.3 million Frenchmen reached military age and Napoleon drafted 1.4 million of these. He was forced to turn again to foreign troops, especially from his occupied territories. As Elting has pointed out: "The French being a thrifty and practical people have always been eager to let any available foreigners assist them in the necessary bleeding and dying for La Patrie". Two thirds of the 1812 invading force were foreigners, but it is a moot point whether they could properly be called mercenaries.
11. Quoted by Schaller – *Troupes Suisses* P.136.

12. Using a graveyard for protection as had their ancestors at St. Jakob an der Birs in 1444.
13. Elting — *Napoleon's Army* P.376.
14. Quoted by Bodin — *Les Suisses au Service de la France* P.288.
15. Quoted by Schaller — *Troupes Suisses* P.198.
16. Quoted by Schaller — *Troupes Suisses* P.202.

CHAPTER XX

1. Quoted by Vallière — *Honneur et Fidelité* P.719.
2. Their history is told in Bayley — *Mercenaries for the Crimea*.
3. The book was published around 1900 and called *Les Suisses sous les Drapeaux*.
4. One Swiss military engineer, Karl von Weber, directed the first excavations at Pompeii.
5. In 1829, the colonel of the third regiment was a Stockalper and descendant of the military enterpriser Kaspar-Jadok Stockalper we have met in Chapter XI, and the colonel of the fourth regiment was a Gingins-le-Sarraz in the grounds of whose chateau much of this book was written.
6. Baron Christophe Antoine Jacques Stoffel who had fought at Waterloo in the only Swiss company taking part in the battle.
7. Maradan — *Légion Etrangère* P.72.

CONCLUSION

1. Sablonier uses the phrase "industry of war" P.444.
2. Gos — *Généraux Suisses* P.17.

APPENDIX I

EUROPEAN WARS IN WHICH SWISS TROOPS PARTICIPATED

Wars	Battles with important Swiss involvement	Dates
Battles for independence	Morgarten	1315
	Laupen	1339
	Sempach	1386
	Näfels	1388
	Arbedo	1422
	St Jakob an der Birs	1444
War with Burgundy 1475-7	Grandson	1476
	Morat	1476
	Nancy	1477
Naples Expedition 1494-5	Fornovo	1495
Swabian War 1499	Schwaderloh	1499
	Frastanz	1499
	Calven	1499
	Dornach	1499
Italian Wars 1499-1509	Novara	1500
	Cerignola	1503
	Genoa	1507
1510-1515	Chiasso expedition	1510
	Pavia expedition	1512
	Novara	1513
	Marignano	1515
1516-1544	Bicocca	1522
	Pavia	1525
	Cerisoles	1544
French Wars of Religion 1559-1598	Dreux	1562
	Retreat from Meaux	1567
	St. Denis	1567
	Jarnac	1569

	Moncontour	1569
	Arques	1589
	Ivry	1590
Thirty Years War 1618-48	Rocroy	1643
	Lens	1648
War with Holland 1672-8	Seneffe	1674
War of the League of Augsburg 1688-1697	Fleurus	1690
	Steenkerque	1692
	Neerwinden	1693
War of the Spanish Succession 1701-1713	Blenheim	1704
	Ramillies	1706
	Oudenarde	1708
	Malplaquet	1709
War of the Austrian Succession 1741-8	Fontenoy	1745
	Laufeld	1746
Seven Years War 1755-63	Rossbach	1757
Napoleonic Wars 1796-1815	Bailen	1808
	Polotsk — First	1812
	Polotsk — Second	1812
	Beresina	1812

APPENDIX II

IMPORTANT DATES IN SWISS SERVICE FOR FRANCE

French King	Dates of reign	Important events relating to Swiss Troops	Date
Louis XI	1461-1483	Alliance with France	1474
		Training Camp Pont de l'Arche	1480
Charles VIII	1483-1498	Formation of Cent Suisses	1497
Louis XII	1498-1515	Pensionenbrief	1503
Francis I	1515-1547	Perpetual Peace	1516
		Treaty of Alliance	1521
Henry II	1547-1559	Renewal of Alliance	1549
		First Regiments Formed	1549
		Capitulation Generale of Baden	1553
Francis II	1559-1560		
Charles IX	1560-1574	Renewal of Alliance	1564
Henry III	1574-1589	First Colonel General des Suisses et Grisons	1571
		Renewal of Alliance	1582
Henry IV	1589-1610	Renewal of Alliance	1602
Louis XIII	1610-1643	Formation of Swiss Guards	1616
Louis XIV	1643-1715	Renewal of Alliance	1663
		First Permanent Swiss Line Regiments	1672
		Introduction of Bayonets	1703
		Introduction of Uniforms	1703

Louis XV	1715-1774	New Capitulation Generale	1764
		Renewal of Alliance	1777
Louis XVI	1774-1793	Massacre of the Tuileries	1792
Napoleon I	1798-1815	Invasion of the Confederation	1798
		Acte de Mediation	1803
Louis XVIII	1815-1824		
Charles X	1824-1830	Day of the Barricades	1830

APPENDIX III

ENTRY DATES OF CANTONS TO THE SWISS CONFEDERATION

Canton	Date of entry
Confederation of VIII Cantons	
1. Uri	1291
2. Schwyz	1291
3. Unterwalden	1291
4. Lucerne	1332
5. Zürich	1351
6. Glarus	1352
7. Zug	1352
8. Berne	1353
Confederation of XIII Cantons	
9. Fribourg	1481
10. Solothurn	1481
11. Basle	1501
12. Schaffhausen	1501
13. Appenzell	1513
Act of Mediation	
14. St. Gallen	1803
15. Grey Leagues	1803
16. Aargau	1803
17. Thurgau	1803
18. Ticino	1803
19. Vaud	1803
Conference of Vienna	
20. Valais	1815
21. Neufchatel	1815
22. Geneva	1815
Twentieth Century	
23. Jura	1979

APPENDIX IV

COLONELS-GENERAUX DES SUISSES ET GRISONS 1571-1830

Reign	Dates of appointment	Colonel-General
Charles IX	1531-1596	Charles de Monmorency-Méru, Duc de Damville
Henri IV	1596-1605	Nicolas de Harlay, Seigneur de Sancy
Louis XIII	1605-1614	Henry, Duc de Rohan
	1614-1635	Francois de Bassompierre, Marquis d'Harouel
	1635-1642	César de Cambout, Marquis de Coislin
	1643	Edme de la Chatre, Comte de Nancay
	1643-1646	Francois de Bassompierre, Marquis d'Harouel
Louis XIV	1647-1656	Charles de Schomberg, Duc d'Halluin
	1657-1673	Eugène-Maurice de Savoye, Comte de Soissons
	1674-1719	Louis-Auguste de Bourbon, Duc de Maine
Louis XV	1721-1736	Louis-Auguste de Bourbon, Duc du Maine
	1736-1755	Louis-Auguste de Bourbon, Prince des Dombes
	1755-1762	Louis-Charles de Bourbon, Duc d'Aumale
	1762-1770	Etienne-Francois, Duc de Choiseul
Louis XVI	1770-1792	Charles-Philippe de Bourbon, Comte d'Artois
Napoleon I	1807-1809	Jean Lannes, Duc de Montebello
	1809-1815	Alexandre Berthier, Prince de Wagram
Louis XVIII	1815-1824	Charles-Philippe de Bourbon, Comte d'Artois

Charles X	1824-1830	Henri-Charles-Ferdinand de Bourbon, Duc de Bordeaux

SWISS WHO ADMINISTERED THE POSITION

1674-1688	Peter Stuppa	During the minority of the Duc du Maine
1719-1721	Francois de Reynold	During the disgrace of the Duc du Maine
1789-1792	Louis-Auguste d'Affry	During the exile of the Comte d'Artois
1824-1830	Jean-Antoine de Gady	During the minority of the Duc de Bordeaux

APPENDIX V

THE COMMANDERS OF THE SWISS GUARDS

Commandment	Colonel	Canton of origin
1616-1619	Kaspar Gallati	Glarus
1619-1626	Fridolin Hessi	Glarus
1628-1633	Hans-Ulrich Greder	Solothurn
1635-1651	Kaspar Freuler	Glarus
1651-1654	Hans-Melchior Hessi	Glarus
1655-1685	Laurent d'Estavayer	Fribourg
1685-1701	Peter Stuppa	Grey Leagues
1701-1702	Maritz Wagner	Solothurn
1702-1722	Francois de Reynold	Fribourg
1722-1736	Hans-Vicktor von Besenval	Solothurn
1736-1742	Jean-Jacques d'Erlach	Fribourg
1742-1743	Rodolphe de Castella	Fribourg
1743-1767	Beat-Franz-Placid de Zurlauben	Zug
1767-1792	Louis-Auguste-Augustin d'Affry	Fribourg

APPENDIX VI

COLONELS COMMANDING THE SWISS LINE REGIMENTS OF THE FRENCH ARMY

63
1672 Erlach
1694 Manuel
1701 Villars-Chandieu
1728 May
1739 De Bettens
1751 Jenner
1762 Erlach
1782 Ernst
1792 Watteville

64
1672 Stuppa
1701 Brendlé
1738 Seedorf
1752 Boccard
1782 Salis-Samade

65
1672 Salis-Zisers
1690 Porlier
1692 Reynold
1702 Castella
1722 De Bettens
1739 Monnin
1756 Reding
1763 Pfyffer
1768 Sonneberg

66
1672 Pfyffer
1689 Hessy
1729 Burky
1737 Tschudy
1740 Vigier

1756 Castella

69
1673 Greder
1691 Greder
1703 Greder
1714 D'Affry
1734 Wittmer

1757 Waldner
1781 Vigier

76
1677 Stuppa
1692 Surbeck
1714 Hemel
1720 Besenval
1738 La Cour-au Chantre
1748 Grand-Villars
1749 Balthazar
1754 Planta
1760 Arbonnier
1763 Jenner
1774 D'Aulbonne
1783 Lullin de Chateauvieux

85
1690 Salis
1702 May
1715 Buisson
1721 Diesbach
1764 Diesbach
1785 Diesbach

86
1690 Courten
1723 Courten
1724 Courten
1744 Courten
1766 Courten
1790 Courten

95
1734 Travers
1744 Salis-Soglio
1744 Salis-Mayenfeld
1762 Salis-Marschlins

	97		100
1752	Lochmann	1758	Eptingen
1777	Muralt	1783	Schonau
1782	Steiner	1786	Rheinach

NB: The numbers refer to the order of Regiments d'Infanterie applicable in 1792.

APPENDIX VII

CAPITAINES-COLONELS OF THE COMPAGNIE DES CENT SUISSES

Dates of Command		Capitaines-Colonels
1.	1497-1500	Louis de Menton, Seigneur de Lornay
2.	1502-1516	Guillaume de la Marck, Seigneur de Montbazon
3.	1516-1536	Robert de la Marck, Seigneur de Fleuranges
4.	1536-1554	Robert de la Marck, Duc de Bouillon
5.	1554-1556	Henri-Robert de la Marck
6.	1556-1608	Charles-Robert de la Marck
7.	1608-1652	Henri-Robert de la Marck, Duc de Bouillon
8.	1653-1655	Jean de Souillac, Seigneur de Montmege
9.	1655-1678	Francois-René du Bec, Marquis de Vardes
10.	1678-1686	Jean-Baptiste de Cassagnet, Marquis de Tilladet
11.	1686-1722	Michel-Francois Le Tellier de Louvois
12.	1722-1734	Louis-Cesar d'Estree Le Tellier
13.	1734-1754	Cesar-Francois Le Tellier, Marquis de Montmirail a)
14.	1754-1764	Cesar-Francois Le Tellier, Marquis de Montmirail b)
15.	1764-1781	Louis-Cesar d'Estree Le Tellier c)
16.	1781-1791	Louis-Hercule-Timoleon de Cossé, Duc de Brissac

a) Nephew of Louis-Cesar No. 12
b) Son of Cesar-Francois No. 13
c) Same Louis-Cesar as No. 12

APPENDIX VIII

COMMANDERS OF THE SWISS PAPAL GUARD

	Date of Command	Commander	Canton
1.	1505-1517	Kaspar von Silenen	Uri
2.	1518-1524	Marcus Roeist	Zurich
3.	1524-1527	Kaspar Roeist	Zurich
	1527-1548	Vacant	
4.	1548-1558	Jost von Meggen	Lucerne
5.	1558-1564	Kaspar von Silenen	Uri
6.	1566-1592	Jost Segesser	Lucerne
7.	1592-1629	Stephan Alexander Segesser	Lucerne
8.	1629-1640	Nicolaus Fleckenstein	Lucerne
9.	1640-1652	Jost Fleckenstein	Lucerne
10.	1652-1657	Johann-Rudolf Pfyffer von Altishofen	Lucerne
11.	1658-1686	Ludwig Pfyffer von Altishofen	Lucerne
12.	1686-1698	Franz Pfyffer von Altishofen	Lucerne
13.	1699-1704	Johann-Kaspar Mayr von Baldegg	Lucerne
	1705-1712	Vacant	
14.	1712-1727	Johann-Konrad Pfyffer von Altishofen	Lucerne
15.	1727-1753	Franz Ludwig Pfyffer von Altishofen	Lucerne
16.	1754-1792	Jost-Ignaz Pfyffer von Altishofen	Lucerne
17.	1792-1798	Franz Ludwig Pfyffer von Altishofen	Lucerne
	1799-1801	Vacant	
18.	1801-1834	Karl-Leodegar Pfyffer von Altishofen	Lucerne
19.	1835-1847	Martin Pfyffer von Altishofen	Lucerne
20.	1848-1860	Franz-Leopold Meyer von Schauensee	Lucerne
21.	1861-1878	Alfred von Sonnenberg	Lucerne
22.	1878-1900	Louis-Martin de Courten	Valais
23.	1901-1910	Leopold Meyer von Schauensee	Lucerne
24.	1910-1921	Jules Repond	Fribourg
25.	1921-1935	Aloys Hirschbuehl	Grey Leagues

26.	1935-1942	Georg von Sury d'Aspremont	Solothurn
27.	1942-1957	Heinrich Pfyffer von Altishofen	Lucerne
28.	1957-	Robert Nunlist	

BIBLIOGRAPHY

ÄLLIG, J.J.   *Die Aufhebung der Schweizerischen Soldnerdienste*. Basel. 1954

ADDINGTON, L.H.   *The Patterns of War Through the Eighteenth Century*. Indiana. 1990

ALLEMAN, G.   *Söldnerwerbungen im Kanton Solothurn von 1600-1723*. Solothurn. 1946

ANDERSON, M.S.   *War and Society in Europe of The Old Regime 1618-1789*. London. 1988

ANDRE, L.   *Michel le Tellier et l'Organisation de l'Armée Monarchique*. Paris. 1906

ASCHMANN, R.   *Memoirs of a Swiss Officer in the American Civil War*. Bern. 1972

BABEAU, A.   *La Vie Militaire sous l'Ancien Regime Volume 1. Les Soldats*. Paris. 1889

BARRAZ, F.   *Peter Stoppa 1621-1701*. Cully. 1990

BAXTER, D.C.   *Servants of the Sword French Intendants of the Army 1630-70*. Urbana Illinois. 1976

BAYLEY, C.C.   *Mercenaries for the Crimea*. Montreal. 1977

BERENGER, J.   *Turenne*. Paris. 1987

BERGER, H.   *Der Alte Zürichkrieg im Rahmen der Europäischen Politik*. Zurich. 1978

BERGIER, J-F.   *Histoire Economique de La Suisse*. Lausanne. 1983

BERGIER, J-F.   *Guillaume Tell*. Paris. 1988

BICKEL, W.   *Bevölkerungsgeschichte und Bevölkerungspolitik der Schweiz seit dem Ausgang des Mittelalters*. Zurich. 1947

BLACK, J.(ED)   *The Origins of War in Early Modern Europe*. Edinburgh. 1987

BLACK, J.   *A Military Revolution? Military Change and European Society 1550-1800*. London. 1991

BLICKLE, P.   *Friede und Verfassung in Innerschweiz und Frühe Eidgenossenschaft*. Olten. 1990

BODIN, J.   *Les Suisses au Service de la France*. Paris. 1988

BORY, J-R.   *Regiments Suisses au Service de France (1800-1814)*. Sion. 1975

BORY, J-R.   *La Suisse à la Rencontre de l'Europe.* Lausanne. 1978

BOUTARIC, E.   *Institutions militaires de la France avant les Armées permanentes.* Paris. 1863

BRADY, T.A.   *Turning Swiss Cities and Empire 1450-1550.* Cambridge. 1985

BRAECKER, U.   *Vie et Aventures d'un Pauvre Homme du Toggenbourg.* Soldats Suisses au Service Etranger. Geneva. 1912

BÜHRER, W.   *Der Zürcher Solddienst des 18 Jahrhunderts.* Berne. 1977

BUNDI, M.   *Bündner Kriegsdienste in Holland um 1700.* Chur. 1972

BURIN DES ROZIERS, M.   *Les Capitulations Militaires entre la Suisse et la France.* Paris. 1902

BÜRKLI, A.   *Das Schweizerregiment von Roll in Englischem Dienste.* NFG. 1893

BÜRKLI, A.   *Das Schweizerregiment von Wattenwyl in Englischem Dienste.* NFG. 1894

BURNAND, A.   *Le Colonel Henry Bouquet — Vainquer des Peaux-Rouges de l'Ohio.* Soldats Suisses au Service Etranger. Geneva. 1909

BUSINGER, L.   *Das Kriegsrecht der Schweizer in Fremden Diensten.* Stans. 1916

CADUFF, G.   *Die Knabenschaften Graubündens.* Chur. 1932

CASTELLA, G.   *La Garde Fidèle du Saint-Père.* Paris. 1935

CASTELLA, R. DE.   *Le Régiment des Gardes-Suisses au Service de France.* Fribourg. 1964

CASTELLA, R. DE.   *Le 76e Régiment d'Infanterie.* Fribourg. 1970

CHABOCHE, R.   *Les Soldats Francais de la Guerre de Trente Ans, Une Tentative d'Approche.* Revue d'Histoire Moderne et Contemporaine. 1973

CHANDLER, D.G.   *Marlborough as Military Commander.* Tunbridge Wells. 1973

CHANDLER, D.G.   *The Art of War in the Age of Marlborough.* London. 1976

CHILDS, J.   *Armies and Warfare in Europe 1648-1789.* Manchester. 1982

CLARK, Sir George — *War and Society in the Seventeenth Century.* Cambridge. 1958

CONTAMINE, P. — *Guerre, Etat et Société à la Fin du Moyen Age.* Paris. 1972

CONTAMINE, P. — *La Guerre au Moyen Age.* Paris. 1980 English translation as *War in the Middle Ages.* Oxford. 1984

COPE, C. — *Phoenix Frustrated — The Lost Kingdom of Burgundy.* London. 1986

CORVISIER, A. — *L'Armée francaise de la Fin du XVIIe Siècle au Ministère de Choiseul. Le Soldat.* Paris. 1964

CORVISIER, A. — *Armées et Sociétés en Europe de 1494 à 1789.* Paris. 1976

CORVISIER, A. — *Louvois.* Paris. 1983

CORVISIER, A. — *Une Armée dans l'Armée: Les Suisses au Service de France.* In *Cinq Siècles de Relations Franco Suisses.* Neuchatel. 1984

CORVISIER, A. (Ed) — *Histoire Militaire de la France.* Paris. 1992

CRUICKSHANK, C.G. — *Elizabeth's Army.* Oxford. 1946

DELBRÜCK, H. — *Geschichte der Kriegskunst im Rahmen der Politischen Geschichte.* Berlin. 1907. New Translation Westport CT. Vol. III 1982. Vol. IV 1985

DEUCHLER, F. — *Die Burgunderbeute.* Berne. 1963

DICKINSON, G. — *Introduction to Fourquevaux's Instructions Sur le Faict de la Guerre.* London. 1954

DIERAUER, J. — *Geschichte der Schweizerischen Eidgenossenschaft.* Gotha. 1919-22

DIESBACH, L. DE — *Chronique et Mémoires.* Paris. 1901

DIESBACH, G. DE — *Service de France.* Paris. 1972

DUBLER, H. — *Der Kampf um den Solddienst der Schweizer im 18. Jahrhundert.* Frauenfeld. 1939

DUFFY, C. — *The Army of Frederick the Great.* Newton Abbot. 1974

DUFFY, C. — *Siege Warfare. The Fortress in the Early Modern World 1494-1660.* London. 1979

DUFFY, C. — *The Fortress in the Age of Vauban and Frederick the Great, 1660-1789.* London. 1985

DUFFY, C. — *The Military Experience in the Age of Reason.* London. 1987

DUPUY, T.N. — *The Evolution of Weapons and Warfare.* Fairfax. VA. 1984

DÜRR, E. — *Die Politik der Eidgenossen im 14. Jahrhundert und 15. Jahrhundert.* SKG.4. 1933

DURRER, R. — *Die Ersten Freiheitskämpfe der Urschweiz.* SKG.1. 1915

DURRER, R. — *Die Schweizergarde in Rom und die Schweizer in Päpstlichen Diensten.* Lucerne. 1927

ELGGER, C. von — *Kriegswesen und Kriegskunst der Schweizerischen Eidgenossen im XIV., XV. und XVI. Jahrhundert.* Lucerne. 1873

ELTING, J.R. — *Swords Around a Throne — Napoleon's Grande Armée.* New York. 1988

ERISMANN, O. — *Peter Stuppa — Freifähnlein und Ständige Linienregimenter der Schweizer in Französischem Dienst.* Blätter für Bernische Geschichte. 1913

ERISMANN, O. — *Organisation und Innerer Haushalt der Schweizer Regimenter in Frankreich.* Berne. 1915

ESCHER, H. — *Das Schweizerische Fussvolk im 15. und Anfang 16. Jahrhundert.* NFG. 1905/6

ESDAILE, C.J. — *The Spanish Army in the Peninsula War.* Manchester. 1988

FELLER, R. — *Bündnisse und Söldnerdienst.* SKG.6. 1916

FIEFFE, E. — *Histoire des Troupes Etrangères au Service de France.* Paris. 1854

FISCHER, R. von — *Die Feldzüge der Eidgenossen Diesseits der Alpen vom Laupenstreit bis zum Schwabenkrieg.* SKG.2. 1936

FORTESCUE, J.W. — *A History of the British Army.* London. 1899

FRAUENHOLZ, E. von — *Das Heerwesen in der Zeit des Freien Söldnertums.* Bd 2 i *Das Heerwesen der Schweizer Eidgenossenschaft.* Bd 2 ii *Das Heerwesen des Reiches in der Landsknechtszeit.* Munich. 1936

GANTER, H. — *Histoire des Regiments Suisses au Service de l'Angleterre, de Naples et de Rome.* Geneva. 1901

GASSER, A.   *Ewige Richtung und Burgunderkriege*. RSH. 1973

GIDDEY, E.   *James Francis Erskine et Son Regiment Suisse (1779-1786)*. RSH. 1954

GINGINS LA SARRAZ, F. de   *Dépèches des Ambassadeurs Milanais sur les Campagnes de Charles-Le-Hardi*. Geneva. 1858

GIONO, J.   *Le Désastre de Pavie*. Paris. 1963

GODET, M.   *L De Marval. Un Officier Neuchatelois au Service de France (1641-1654)*. Soldats Suisses au Service Etranger. Geneva. 1915

GONZENBACH, A. von   *Der General Hans Ludwig von Erlach*. Berne. 1880-2

GOS, C.   *Généraux Suisses Commandants en Chef de l'Armée Suisse de Marignan à 1939*. Lausanne. 1932

GYSIN, N.   *Les Troupes Suisses dans le Royaume de Sardaigne*. Revue Militaire. 1914

HALE, J.R.   *War and Society in Renaissance Europe, 1450-1620*. London. 1985

HÄNE, J.   *Mailändische Gesandtschaftberichte und ihre Mitteilungen über Züricherische und Luzernische truppen (1490)*. Anzeiger für Schweizerische Geschichte. 1899

HÄNE, J.   *Zum Wehr — und Kriegswesen in der Blütezeit der Alten Eidgenossenschaft*. Zurich. 1900

HÄNE, J.   *Die Kriegsbereitschaft der Alten Eidgenossen*. SKG. 3. 1915

HÄNE, J.   *Militärisches aus dem Alten Zürichkrieg*. Zurich. 1928

HESS, G.   *Schon Damals. Lebensbild Einer Schweizer-Söldnerfamilie in Briefen*. Stans. 1947

HESS, O.   *Die Fremden Büchsenmeister und Söldner in den Diensten der Eidgen. Orte bis 1516*. Zurich. 1918

HIRZEL, W.   *Aus Der Zeit Marlboroughs und seinen Zürcher Regimentern in Holländischen Diensten*. Coppet. 1972

HIRZEL, W.   *Tanta est Fiducia Gentis. Les Regiments Suisses au service des Pays-Bas.* Coppet. 1972

HIRZEL, W.   *The Swiss in Foreign Services.* Coppet. 1979

HOFFMANN, G.   *Die Grossbritannische Schweizer-Legion im Krimkrieg.* RSH-1942

HOWARD, M.   *War in European History.* Oxford. 1976

HÜBSCHER, B.   *Die Entwicklung und Struktur des Luzernischen Heerwesens von 1291-1500.* Lucerne. 1943

HUGHES, B.P.   *Firepower Weapons Effectiveness on the Battlefield, 1630-1850.* London. 1974

JACQUART, J.   *Bayard.* Paris. 1987

JONES, A.   *The Art of War in the Western World.* Illinois. 1987

JONES, C.   *The Military Revolution and the Professionalisation of the French Army under the Ancien Régime* in *The Military Revolution and the State 1500-1800.* Ed. M. Duffy. Exeter. 1980

KEEGAN, J.   *The Face of Battle.* London. 1976

KELLER, CH. Félix   *Iconographie du Costume Militaire Suisse et Suisse au Service étranger.* Paris. 1938

KELLER, W.   *Theodor von Reding 1755-1809 Lebensbild Eines Schweizeroffiziers in Fremden Diensten.* Mitteilungen des Historischen Vereins des Kantons Schwyz. 1961

KENDALL, P.M.   *Louis XI.* London. 1971

KENNETT, L.   *The French Armies in the Seven Years' War.* Durham. N.C. 1967

KIERNAN, V.G.   *Foreign Mercenaries and Absolute Monarchy.* Past and Present 1957 No.11 Pp.66-86

KILCHENMANN, F.   *Die Mission des Englischen Gesandten Thomas Coxe in Der Schweiz 1689-1692.* Zurich. 1914

KILCHENMANN, J.E.   *Schweizersöldner im Dienste der Englisch-Ostindischen Kompanie.* Bern. 1911

KNECHT, R.J.   *Francis I.* Cambridge. 1982

KRIEG, P.M.   *Die Schweizergarde in Rom.* Lucerne. 1960

KURZ, H.F.   *Schweizerschlachten.* Berne. 1962

KURZ, H.R.   *Das Schweizer Heer*. Zurich. 1969

LÄTT, A.   *Der Anteil der Schweizer an der Eroberung Indiens*. NFG. 1934

LEONARD, E.G.   *L'Armée et ses Problèmes au XVIIIe Siècle*. Paris. 1958

LOT, F.   *L'Art Militaire et les Armées au Moyen Age*. Paris. 1946. Tomes I et II.

LOT, F.   *Recherches sur les Effectifs des Armées Francaises des Guerres d'Italie aux Guerres de Religion 1494-1562*. Paris. 1962

LOT, F.   *Les Armées en Présence à la Bataille de Dreux*. RHA. 1983-3

LUGINBÜHL, R.   *Gab es in Der Schlacht bei Murten auf Seite der Schweizer und ihrer Verbündeten Einen Oberanführer?* Jahrbuch für Schweizerische Geschichte. 1906

LYNN, J.A.   *Tactical Evolution in the French Army, 1560-1660*. French Historial Studies. 1985

MAAG, A.   *Geschichte der Schweizer Truppen in Französischen Dienst während der Restauration und Juli Revolution (1816-1830)*. Biel. 1899

MAAG, A.   *Geschichte der Schweizertruppen in Neapolitanischen Diensten 1825-1861*. Zurich. 1909

MAAG, A.   *Der Schweizer Soldat in der Kriegsgeschichte*. Berne. 1931

MALLETT, M.   *Mercenaries and their Masters — Warfare in Renaissance Italy*. London. 1974

MARADAN, E.   *Les Suisses et la Légion Etrangère de 1831 à 1861*. Marsens. 1987

MARCHAL, G.P.   *Les Racines de l'Indépendance—* In *Nouvelle Histoire de la Suisse et des Suisses*. 1982

MARTIN, W.   *Histoire de la Suisse*. Lausanne. 1980. English translation as *Switzerland*. London. 1971

MATTMÜLLER, M.   *Bevölkerungsgeschichte der Schweiz*. Basel. 1987

MAY DE ROMAINMOTIER, E.   *Histoire Militaire de la Suisse et des Suisses dans les Différens Services de l'Europe*. Lausanne. 1788

McNEIL, W.H.   *The Pursuit of Power*. Oxford. 1983

MENTION, L.	*L'Armée de l'Ancien Régime de Louis XIV à la Révolution*. Paris. 1880
MEURON, G. DE	*Le Régiment Meuron 1781-1816*. Lausanne. 1982
MEYER, B.	*Die Schlacht am Morgarten*. RSH. 1966
MEYER, K.	*Aufsätze und Reden*. Zurich. 1952
MEYER, W.	*Kriegstaten von Zürich in Ausländischen Dienst*. NFG. 1874-6
MICHAUD, H.	*Les Institutions Militaires des Guerres d'Italie aux Guerres de Religion*. Revue Historique. 1977
MIQUEL, P.	*Les Guerres de Religion*. Paris. 1980
MOCKLER, A.	*The Mercenaries*. London. 1970
MOCKLER, A.	*The New Mercenaries*. New York. 1985
MÖLLER, H-M	*Das Regiment der Landsknechte*. Wiesbaden. 1976
MONLUC, BLAISE DE	*Commentaries*. Edited by I. Roy. London. 1971
MORARD, N.	*L'Heure de la Puissance*. In *Nouvelle Histoire de la Suisse et des Suisse*. 1982
MÜHLEMANN, L.	*Wappen und Fahnen der Schweiz*. Lucerne. 1977
MÜLINEN, W.F. von	*Geschichte der Schweizer-Söldner bis zur Errichtung der Ersten Stehenden Garde 1497*. Berne. 1887
MÜLINEN, W.F. von	*Das Französische Schweizer Garderegiment am 10 August 1792*. Lucerne. 1892
NABHOLZ, H.	*La Suisse sous la Tutelle Etrangère 1798-1813*. SKG 8. 1921
NEUHAUS, L.	*Die Schweizerregimenter im Spanischen Dienst 1734-1835*. Mitteilungen des Historischen Vereins des Kanton Schwyz. 1959
NOSWORTHY, B.	*The Anatomy of Victory. Battle Tactics 1689-1763*. New York. 1990
OMAN, C.	*The Art of War in the Middle Ages, AD 378-1485*. London. 1924
OMAN, C.	*A History of the Art of War in the Sixteenth Century*. London. 1937
ORLIAC, J.d'	*Suisses et Grisons*. Tours. 1936
PADRUTT, C.	*Staat und Krieg im Alten Bünden*. Zurich. 1965

PAGES, G.	*La Guerre de Trente Ans*. Paris. 1939
PARKER, G.	*The Army of Flanders and the Spanish Road 1567-1659*. Cambridge. 1972
PARKER, G.	*The "Military Revolution", 1560-1660 — A Myth?* In *Spain and the Netherlands, 1559-1659*. London. 1979
PARKER, G.	*The Thirty Years War*. London. 1984
PARKER, G.	*The Military Revolution*. Cambridge. 1988
PEDRAZZINI, D.M.	*Le Régiment Bernois de Tscharner au Service de Piémont Sardaigne (1760-1786)*. Fribourg 1979
PEYER, H.C.	*Frühes und Hohes Mittelalter die Entstehung der Eidgenossenschaft*. In *Handbuch der Schweizer Geschichte*. 1970
PEYER, H.C.	*Die Wirtschaftliche Bedeutung der Fremden Dienste für die Schweiz vom 15. bis 18. Jahrhundert*. Beiträge zur Wirtschafts-geschichte. 5. 1978
PEYER, H.C.	*Verfassungsgeschichte der Alten Schweiz.* Zurich. 1978
PFISTER, W.	*Aargauer in Fremden Kriegsdiensten*. Aarau. 1980 and 1984
PFISTER, W.	*Die Bernischen Soldregimenter im 18. Jahrhundert*. Berner Zeitschrift für Geschichte und Heimatkunde. 1983
PHILLIPS, T.R.	*Roots of Strategy*. Harrisburgh. Pa. 1940
PORCH, D.	*The French Foreign Legion*. New York. 1991
QUIMBY, R.S.	*The Background of Napoleonic Warfare — The Theory of Military Tactics in Eighteenth-Century France*. New York. 1957
REDLICH, F.	*De Praeda Militari. Looting and Booty 1500-1815*. Wiesbaden. 1956
REDLICH, F.	*The German Military Enterpriser and his Workforce*. Wiesbaden. 1965
REICHEL, D.	*Grandson — 1476 Essai D'Approche Pluri-disciplinaire d'une Action Militaire du XVe Siécle*. Lausanne. 1976
REPOND, J.	*Les Suisses au Service d'Espagne*. Annales Fribourgeoises. 1923

ROBERTS, M.	*The Military Revolution, 1560-1660.* In Roberts. M. *Essays in Swedish History.* London. 1967
RODT, E. von	*Geschichte des Bernischen Kriegswesens.* Bern. 1831
RODT, E. von	*Die Feldzüge Karls des Kühnen.* Schaffhausen. 1843
ROGERS, H.C.B.	*Napoleon's Army.* London. 1974
ROPP, T.	*War in the Modern World.* London. 1959
ROSS, S.	*From Flintlock to Rifle. Infantry Tactics, 1740-1866.* London. 1979
ROTT, E.	*Histoire de la Représentation Diplomatique de la France auprès des Cantons Suisses.* Berne. 1900-13
ROY, J.	*Turenne sa Vie et les Institutions Militaires de son Temps.* Paris. 1884
RUMPEL, R.	*Der Krieg als Lebenselement in der Alten und Spätmittelalterlichen Eidgenossenschaft.* RSH. 1983
SABLONIER, R.	*Etat et Structures Militaires dans la Conféderation autour des Années 1480.* In *Cinq-Centième anniversaire de la Bataille de Nancy.* Nancy. 1977
SCHAFFROTH, M.F.	*Fremdendienst von Innen Betrachtet.* Schweizerischen Monatschrift für Offiziere aller Waffen. 1939
SCHAFFROTH, M.F.	*Der Fremdendienst.* RSH. 1973
SCHALLER, H. DE	*Histoire des Troupes Suisses au Service de France sous le Règne de Napoleon 1er.* Lausanne. 1883
SCHALLER, H. DE	*Souvenirs d'un Officier Fribourgeois.* Fribourg. 1890
SCHAUFELBERGER, W.	*Der Alte Schweizer und sein Krieg.* Zurich. 1952
SCHAUFELBERGER, W.	*Zu Einer Charakterologie des Altschweizerischen Kriegertums.* Schweizerisches Archiv für Volkskunde 56. (1960)
SCHAUFELBERGER, W.	*Guerre et Guerriers Suisses à la Fin du Moyen Age.* Revue Militaire Suisse 1970

SCHAUFELBERGER, W.	*Zum Problem der Militärischen Integration in der Spätmittelalterlichen Eidgenossenschaft.* Allgemeine Schweizerische Militärschrift. No. 136 1970.
SCHAUFELBERGER, W.	*Spätmittelalter.* In Handbuch der Schweizer Geschichte. 1970
SCHAUFELBERGER, W.	*Der Wettkampf in der Alten Eidgenossenschaft.* Berne. 1972
SCHELBERT, L.	*Einführung in die Schweizerische Auswanderungsgeschichte der Neuzeit.* Zurich. 1976
SCHMITTHENNER, P.	*Das Freie Söldnertum im Abendländischen Imperium des Mittelalters.* Munich. 1934
SCHNITZER, M.	*Die Morgartenschlacht im Werdenden Schweizerischen Nationalbewusstsein.* Berne. 1969
SCOTT, S.F.	*The Response of the Royal Army to the French Revolution.* Oxford. 1978
SEGESSER, A.	*Ludwig Pfyffer und Seine Zeit.* Berne. 1880-2
SENNHAUSER, A.	*Hauptmann und Führung im Schweizerkrieg des Mittelalters.* Zurich. 1965
SOURNIA, J-C.	*Blaise de Monluc.* Paris. 1981
STEFFEN, H.	*Die Kompanien Kaspar Jodok Stockalpers.* Brig. 1975
STEIGER, R. DE	*Coup-D'Oeil Général sur L'Histoire Militaire des Suisses au Service Etranger.* Archiv für Schweizerische Geschichte. 1871
STETTLER, B.	*Habsburg und die Eidgenossenschaft um die Mitte des 14. Jahrhunderts.* RSH. 1973
STÜSSI, J.	*Das Schweizer Militärwesen des 17. Jahrhunderts in Ausländischer Sicht.* Zurich. 1982
SUSANE, L.	*Histoire de l'Infanterie Francaise.* Paris. 1875
SUTER, H.	*Innerschweizerisches Militär-Unternehmertum im 18. Jahrhundert.* Zurich. 1971
TAYLOR, F.L.	*The Art of War in Italy 1494-1529.* Cambridge. 1921

VALLIERE, P. DE	*Le Régiment des Gardes-Suisses de France.* Lausanne. 1912
VALLIERE, P. DE	*Honneur et Fidélité.* Neufchatel 1913. New Edition Lausanne. 1940
VALLIERE, P. DE	*Morat.* Lausanne. 1926
VALLIERE, P. DE	*Le 10 Aout 1792.* Lausanne. 1930
VALLIERE, P. DE	*Education du Soldat, Formation des Chefs et Traditions Nationales dans les Troupes Suisses à l'Etranger.* In *Bürger und Soldat.* Zurich. 1944
VALLOTTON, G.	*Les Suisses à la Bérézina.* Neufchatel. 1942
VAUGHAN, R.	*Charles the Bold.* London. 1973
VERBRUGGEN, J.F.	*The Art of Warfare in Western Europe during the Middle Ages.* Amsterdam. 1977
VIAZZO, P.P.	*Upland Communities.* Cambridge. 1989
WACKERNAGEL, W.G.	*Kriegsbrauche in der Mittelalterlichen Eidgenossenschaft.* Basel. 1934
WACKERNAGEL, W.G.	*Altes Volkstum der Schweiz.* Basel. 1956
WATTENWYL, M. von	*Die Schweizer in Fremden Kriegsdiensten.* Bern. w/o date
WEDGWOOD, C.V.	*The Thirty Years War.* London. 1938
WEIGLEY, R.F.	*The Age of Battles.* Bloomington. Ind. 1991
WEYGAND, H.	*Histoire de l'Armée Francaise.* Paris. 1938
WILD, E.	*Die Eidgenössischen Handelsprivilegien in Frankreich 1444-1635.* St. Gallen. 1909
ZUR-LAUBEN, B.F.A.	*Histoire Militaire des Suisses au Service de la France.* Paris. 1751-1753
R.H.A.	Revue Historique des Armées
R.S.H.	Revue Suisse d'Histoire
SKG	Schweizer Kriegsgeschichte
NFG	Neujahrssblatt der Feuerwerker Gesellschaft in Zurich

INDEX